INTERNET GUIDE TO

CyberHound's THE COOLEST STUFF OUT THERE

VISIBLE INK PRESS

Detroit • New York • Toronto • Washington, D.C.

contents

V

the coolest
of the cool

**A special listing
of four-coffee mug
entries**

CyberHound's Internet Guide to the Coolest Stuff Out There helps you plot your web adventure, selecting and rating more than 800 sites that are fairly nifty, particularly appealing, digitally hip, or highly individual. They range from sites like *Alternative X,* created by "dissident post-punk literati" to personal resume pages like *Crossing the Line* to hobbyist pages like *Hang Gliding* to entertainment sites like the *Mammoth Music Meta-List.* Art, angels, architecture, babies, bugs, bikes, books, business, music, movies, money, and more are covered.

Since the book is arranged alphabetically by site name, we've added a 400-term category index to help you browse by subject, with terms ranging from **SexNet** to **Sci-Fi** to **Shameless Self-Promotion** to **Sports**, and from **Walt Disney** to **Virtual Cities** to **Deep Thoughts**. In addition, *Cyber-Hound* includes sidebars containing excerpts taken from World Wide Web home pages and from Internet-related magazines, offering a broad range of information from the goofy and absurd to the informative and insightful.

The sites were chosen after scanning various "cool site" lists, eyeballing the Web at length, consulting professionally with "people in the know," and receiving strong vibes from certain URLs. Each of these 800 sites inevitably link to other sites, which then link to yet more sites and so on. The 800 sites selected here, therefore, represent connections to more than 1.6 million web sites (by our conservative count) making this book a considerable bargain. Of course, this is many times larger than the known Web, a discrepancy we choose to ignore for now. It is our expressed hope that *CyberHound* will save you connect time (and, of course, money) as you drive, fly, or jog through cyberspace, the place where your every 'Net fantasy can come true. *CyberHound* is a starting point; where you end up is your business.

Each web profile begins with the rating, based on a sliding scale of one to four piping hot mugs of joe. As you are probably well aware, caffeine is often a prerequisite for effective 'Net surfing. As you wile away the hours in an online daze, coffee can become your friend and constant companion.

The hours go by like minutes, as, hopped on java, you stroll solitaire through the vast cold vacuum of cyberspace. And there's nothing like a good case of jitters to help propel you from web page to web page. Can't stop to chat, gotta go.

A four-mug rating is a very, very good thing, while one mug indicates a certain substandard standing in the small world of cool web sites. Not that you should avoid one-mug sites, since the building process at many web sites is ongoing. A two-mug rating indicates potential perhaps not yet realized, while three mugs suggests a visit is well worth your while, or for that matter, the while of friends and family members. The rating is followed by the site name, the electronic address, the review, and in many cases, a short excerpt from the home page. Screen graphics are included for sites carrying the esteemed ranking of four mugs of piping hot joe.

A last note: *CyberHound* is sibling to *VideoHound's Golden Movie Retriever*, the most comprehensive annual guide to movies on video. We expect that *CyberHound*, as it grows, will do the elder *VideoHound* proud. The Internet poses problems not encountered in the world of video: while a movie is a static piece of work, the Web is ever evolving. And the number of sites on the Web is growing at an exponential rate. But in keeping with the *VideoHound* philosophy, expect *CyberHound* to become a definitive guide to the Internet. *CyberHound's Internet Guide to the Coolest Stuff Out There* is a step in that direction.

EarthLink Network's TotalAccess Service

EarthLink now services over 110 U.S. cities and is growing daily. All the necessary software is enclosed in one easy to launch package. Your FREE Total-Access software includes the latest version of Netscape (the world's most popular web browser), Eudora (the world's most popular E-Mail program), automatic dialer, auto registration, and all the regular Internet access capabilities. Look for the software on the inside of the back cover of *CyberHound*.

Internet access costs $19.95 per month for 15 hours. Each additional hour is only $1.95. EarthLink's one-time registration fee of $25.00 per hour will be waived as part of the *CyberHound* package.

Your access service includes unlimited tech support on EarthLink's toll-free 800 line.

With this software you could be "surfing" the net in five minutes. Just install, and launch, and we'll see you on the 'Net!

Acknowledgments

Thanks to Joe Tardiff, Brandon Trenz, Julia Furtaw, and Terri Schell for their help in putting *CyberHound* together, Brad Morgan, Dean Dauphinais, Kelly Cross, and Jim Lower for incidentals, Tracey Rowens for her design work, Sue Stefani for copy, Evi Seoud for production assistance, Andy Malonis and Gary Oudersluys for research, and Marco Di Vita for his usual inspired typesetting.

Aaron A. Aardvark's Aardvark Abstract

http://www.cts.com/~aardvark/abstract.html

If you like whimsical digital art, this site's for you. So why is an art gallery called the "Aardvark Abstract?" Well, because it features, among other things, a comic strip starring an aardvark and a nerdy turtle. Take a peek at the art and computer graphics video galleries, and don't forget to suggest a word or two beginning with the letter "A" to help Aaron expand his vocabulary, then zip over to other computer graphics sites via links.

Abigail's Home Page

http://www.teleport.com/~mabs/

Abigail Larsen is a Bryn Mawr graduate with a love of fine art, a love she feels compelled to share with everybody on the World Wide Web. Her web site features lots of gorgeous reproductions from pre-Raphaelite painters like William Holman Hunt and Dante Gabriel Rossetti, as well as sketches by Albrecht Durer and Aubrey Beardsley. Not the most useful web site, but visually pleasing just the same.

About US

http://www.starwave.com:80/people/luisp/

About US is a collection of images that suggests many different stories,

Cisler suggested that banning children from the Internet because of its occasional graphic content is "the equivalent of finding one objectionable book and closing the whole library."

Steve Cisler of Apple Computers,
American Libraries, **July/August, 1995.**

depending on the visitor's path through them. Each image is a clickable map; clicking different points leads the visitor to one of nine different images, each of which is also a clickable map with links to nine different images....

EXCERPT:

Think of a book where the order of the chapters is decided by you in an arbitrary way.

Academy of Motion Picture Arts and Sciences

http://www.oscars.org/ampas/

Also known as the home of Oscar, the sought-after golden boy handed out by the members of the Academy every year. This site provides access to a number of Academy publications and posts schedules of lectures by prominent people in the motion picture industry. Expect more activity at the beginning of the year as the nominations are announced and the March ceremony approaches.

The Ada Project

http://www.cs.yale.edu/HTML/YALE/CS/HyPlans/tap/tap.htm

A collection of resources for women in computing, TAP's goal is to provide a central location through which these resources can be "tapped." This site includes information on conferences, projects, discussion groups and organizations, fellowships and grants, notable women in computer science, and other electronically accessible information sites. TAP also maintains a substantive bibliography of references. Serves primarily as a collection of links to other online resources, rather than as an archive. TAP is an official project of the ACM Committee on the Status of Women in Computing.

Adam's Fox Box

http://tavi.acomp.usf.edu/foxbox/

This British site reflects Adam Moss' obsession with the fox. There are lavish photos of the furry creatures (they take a long time to download), news articles decrying fox hunting—even a list of taverns that have the word "fox" in their names. Too many broken links mar a generally amusing site.

EXCERPT:

Foxes are my favourite animals by a long way. I sympathise and empathise with foxes, and they're just so darn clever and attractive too.

ada'web

http://adaweb.com/

An experiment in interactive digital avant garde art (that's art with a lower case "A"). Lots of images, lots of truisms (add your own or vote for your favorite); very little navigational help or explanation. Not for the traditionalist or the timid.

AEon Flux

http://www.expanse.com/aflux/index.html

This web site is the home of AEon Flux, the sensuous and dangerous animated action heroine of MTV's Liquid Television series. This fan home page features several neat graphic images of AEon Flux, as well as articles and news stories about this emerging animated sensation.

Please don't think I spend all my time eavesdropping, but I do have another bizarre conversation to report. It's just that some people talk so loudly and I happen to be observant. Anyway, I heard a man telling his 3 (rather bored) dinner companions at some length just what he IS and IS NOT willing to do in order to get to a bathroom....He says: "I'll go down the hall if I have to in the morning to get a shower, but to go all the way down the hall in the middle of the night just to take a leak—that's outrageous. I don't care." I was tempted to walk over and pin my "victim of the day" badge on him, but alas, I didn't have the energy.

Buzznet:www.hooked.net/buzznet/

EXCERPT:

One of the most engaging heroines of our age flows from the brain and pen of Peter Chung. Her name, AEon Flux.

AIDS Walk San Francisco

http://buckaroo.bonsai.com:80/sfaids/

The home page for the AIDS Walk in SF was surely a good idea prior to the event, held Sunday, July 16, 1995. There's a registration form, list of benefactors, and celebrity endorsements for the 10k fund-raising walkathon. But, alas, the page is no longer active and there's no e-mail means to contact AIDS Walk. It appears that the organization plans to sponsor future events, but this news is not apparent on the home page.

EXCERPT:

The fight against AIDS is a fight we must all fight together.

Alchemy of Africa, Shopping and Entertainment Web

http://aztec.co.za/biz/africa/

It may take you a while to figure out how Alchemy of Africa qualifies as a shopping and entertainment web. You'll hear some African background music and see some art work that seems to originate in Capetown, South Africa, but the rest is perplexing. Still it's cool, and though the graphics are VERY slow, diversity-minded shoppers/surfers can visit the top ten Africa sites and a see a rainbow of Africa's flora, fauna, and people.

EXCERPT:

Welcome to the magical African website....In order to spare you hours of frustration, we decided to devote much of our time scouring "extra cool sites" for you.

Alex: A Catalogue of Electronic Texts on the Internet

http://nearnet.gnn.com/gnn/wic/lit.44.html

Alex allows users to find and retrieve the full text of documents on the Internet. It currently indexes over 700 books and shorter texts by author and title, incorporating texts from Project Gutenberg, Wiretap, the Online Book Initiative, the Eris system at Virginia Tech, the English Server at Carnegie Mellon University, and the online portion of the Oxford Text Archive. For now it includes no serials. Alex does include an entry for itself.

Alex Bennett's World

http://www.hooked.net/alex/index.html

Fans of Alex Bennett's radio programs should enjoy this site's mix of Bennett's broadcast schedules, comedy and music events listings for northern California, Bennett's journals and interviews, photos, columns, the "Live 105" countdown list, and other tantalizing tributes to American culture in the '90s. If you've never heard of Alex Bennett, if tastelessness offends you, and/or if your idea of American culture extends beyond the latest *National Enquirer* headline, you may want to surf somewhere else.

EXCERPT:

As always, if you have any suggestions.....keep them to yourself, we know what we're doing.

Alian Nation

http://www.alias.com/

Featuring SIGGRAPH 95 and the events surrounding Alias Wavefront's ride into the new era of high-end computer graphics, this site includes a gallery of animations and images created by various groups using Alias|Wavefront software (including tips for maximizing MPEG performance), as well as information about Project Maya (new digital media content creation software). This site just plain looks cool—as long as your browser understands image maps.

EXCERPT:

Life will never be the same.

Alias Update From CES

http://www.alias.com:80/Product/tradeshows/CES/Alias_at_CES.html

If you're still blue because you missed this year's Winter Consumer Electronics Show, get happy. With daily reports, lots of photos, and juicy gossip courtesy of the fine folks at Alias, you'll feel as though you were there. (But be patient—all those images take a long time to download.)

EXCERPT:

There was no shortage of hair at the Alias booth! Alias staffers, wearing wild florescent wigs, invited gamers to join the Alias Hair Club for Animators and put an end to digital baldness forever.

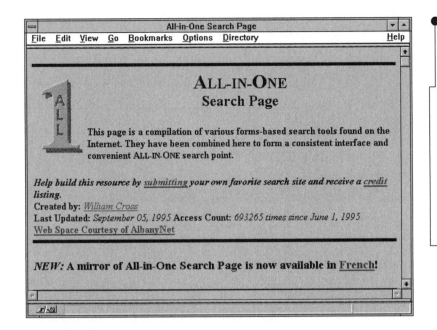

All-in-One Internet Search

http://www.albany.net/~wcross/all1srch.html

A compilation of various forms-based search tools found on the Internet, combined here to form a consistent interface and convenient ALL-IN-ONE search point. Extremely useful; however, you do need a forms-capable browser to use it.

Alternative Music

http://uenics.evansville.edu/~da

Dustin Anders' Alternative Music page is a wealth of information and links to hundreds of supplementary pages featuring almost any cool, so-called brand of alternative music. There's so much to wade through...Quicktime movies, digital recordings, JPEG & GIF images, text files, and a huge chat area. Users can add their own links to the page, and many have added newsy bits or retouched concert photos ("I am here" marks). This is a very cool hangout, but be prepared to wait while the massive record file loads up.

Mosh Pit DONT's and Dos. DON'T ELBOW, KICK, PUNCH, THRASH, SMASH, SKANK, or do any other dance that can only be performed at the expense of others. Respect all peoples, not just yourself!

DO HELP PEOPLE WHEN THEY SCREAM "HELP!" OR FALL DOWN! Don't just stand there grinning like an idiot! Take charge of a bad situation, tell people to mellow out and help the disadvantaged party to their feet. Be Pro-Active — and not just in the pit! Don't let hassles happen anywhere on the premises. If you want hassles, take it to the Marines.

Beastie Boys: http://www.nando.net/Beastie Boys: moshpit.htm

Alternative-X

http://marketplace.com/alt.x/

The best way to describe this site is to quote what others are saying about it: "Brush shoulders with dissident post-punk literati while perusing new work from all corners of the belletristic, counterculture world...free form essays on literature vis-a-vis computers, rock, and 'avant-pop' culture keep the energy high (closer to a poetry slam than a classroom) and intellectually provocative."—*Wired*. "The new literary MTV!" *Kreuzer Magazine*.

E X C E R P T :

This month's BUZZWORDS: ...Waiting Bones, Food Politics, Killer Beef, Mythological Workers...Counter-Culture Cave Men, Musical Self-Defense...New Media Consumers and Market Behavior.

The Amazing Fish Cam

http://www.mcom.com/fishcam/fishcam.html

You say you don't have the time or room for your own aquarium? Don't despair; Fish Cam is here! Live images of real fish in a real fish tank are updated every 30 to 60 seconds. Learn about the fish in the tank, the filtration system under the tank, the camera that is taking the pictures in front of the tank, and how to set up your own live Net camera. Use Netscape 1.1 or later to see a continuously updated fish movie!

EXCERPT:

The Economist recently had a feature on the Internet. This is what they had to say about the fishcam...In its audacious uselessness—and that of thousands of ego trips like it—lie the seeds of the Internet revolution.

Amberyl's Almost-Complete List of MUSHes

http://www.cis.upenn.edu/~lwl/muds.html

Everything you ever wanted to know about MUSHes and MUDs. Includes addresses, commentary, links to home pages, and, if available, MudWHO queries, organized in alphabetical order; an automated MUSH list that's updated every two hours (with address, server type, last successful connect time, and the number of players logged in over the past 24 hours); and links to MUD resources such as FAQs, FTP archives, Web interfaces, and newsgroups.

EXCERPT:

The information here is a mixture between fact and opinion. The "reviews"...are based both upon my personal assessment, which can vary from an hour's look (for new and empty places) to a few days or more of play, and comments which come to me from players of that MUSH....

American Memory of the Library of Congress

http://rs6.loc.gov/amhome.html

No-frills, but very informative and useful page from the Library of Congress. Provides web access to American cultural and historical materials. American Memory receives bonus points for fully explaining its purpose and its service on the home page and for loading up very quickly. Some available materials are four extant Walt Whitman notebooks, early motion pictures, and Civil War photographs.

EXCERPT:

American Memory consists of collections of primary source and archival material [from] the Library of Congress' key contribution to the national digital library. Most of these offerings are from the unparalleled special collections of the Library of Congress.

American Stock Exchange

http://www.amex.com

It's no surprise that the American Stock Exchange has its own web page. It might be surprising that it won the stock market race to the web and that the page is designed for Netscape. (If you load with Mosaic, you'll get an error message). The page offers news, market summaries, a list of all American Stock Exchange companies, and more. There's not a lot on the home page, but the links provide a wealth of information for financially minded surfers.

EXCERPT:

The American Stock Exchange provides extraordinary visibility for over 800 innovative, growing companies....We are proud to be the first U.S. stock market on the World Wide Web....

American Wine on the Web

http://www.2way.com:80/food/wine/

American Wine, the Internet wine magazine, documents the renaissance of American wine. Features include columns and articles on wines, wine festivals and auctions, and foods; reports from wine country; an art gallery; a book club; book, CD, and video reviews; a hypertext wine glossary; and links to food and beverages resources around the Net.

EXCERPT:

We believe that wine is an everyday drink with everyday food for everyday people, and that American wines are among the best in the world.

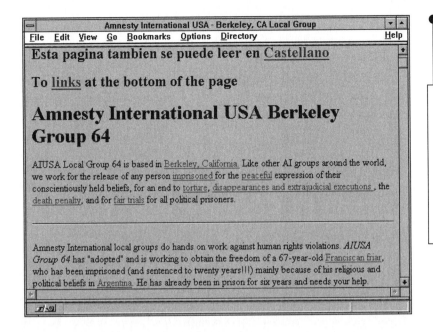

Amnesty International USA - Berkeley, CA Local Group

File   Edit   View   Go   Bookmarks   Options   Directory   Help

Esta pagina tambien se puede leer en Castellano

To links at the bottom of the page

Amnesty International USA Berkeley Group 64

AIUSA Local Group 64 is based in Berkeley, California. Like other AI groups around the world, we work for the release of any person imprisoned for the peaceful expression of their conscientiously held beliefs, for an end to torture, disappearances and extrajudicial executions, the death penalty, and for fair trials for all political prisoners.

Amnesty International local groups do hands on work against human rights violations. *AIUSA Group 64* has "adopted" and is working to obtain the freedom of a 67-year-old Franciscan friar, who has been imprisoned (and sentenced to twenty years!!!) mainly because of his religious and political beliefs in Argentina. He has already been in prison for six years and needs your help.

America's Cup On-Line

http://www.ac95.org/

Lots of information about the America's Cup regatta, including race results, news, photos, discussion groups, FAQs, on-line shopping for race- and sailing-related items, and links to other sailing resources. Includes today's San Diego weather forecast.

Amnesty International USA, Berkeley, CA Local Group

http://www.best.com/~mlacabe/grp64.html

Margarita Lacabe runs this excellent site that offers complete and in-depth information on Amnesty International's activities in the USA and abroad. This is a wonderful site not just for the politically conscious cool-types but for everyone who cares about human beings. There's a jump to the main Amnesty International page and a directory to local Amnesty International chapters. A page like this is the reason there is a worldwide web.

EXCERPT:

Amnesty International Group 64 is based in Berkeley, California....We work for the release of any person imprisoned for the peaceful expression of their conscientiously held beliefs, for an end to torture, disappearances and extra-judicial executions, the death penalty, and for fair trials for all political prisoners.

The Tori Amos Homepage

http:www.mit.edu:8001/people/nocturne/tori.html

Photos, lyrics, news clippings, and links to other sites from a Massachusetts Institute of Technology student who is absolutely nuts about singer Tori Amos. Says she learned about Tori from her roommate and is hooked on the emotion-packed music.

EXCERPT:

I first learned about Tori from my first roommate here at MIT...[and] I eventually started to listen to all of Little Earthquakes...

Anand's Home Page

http://seraphim.csee.usf.edu:123

Mr. Gupta provides an intricate series of images, informative links, tutorial pages, resources, and amusements in a personalized home page that is at once personable and edifying. The site lacks clear organization or thematic precision, but is cleverly constructed and fun. Browse the links to Stocks and Mutual Funds; Art Crimes; Christmas; Art Gallery; Software Tools; Amnesty International; Lion King; and more.

EXCERPT:

Hi, this is experimental. I am just trying to make my life easier.... Here is more information on HTML [or]...on furthering your career.... You could go to Boston or India or take a course in C++...

We live in the age of information, as Nicholas Negroponte, director of M.I.T.'s Media Lab, is fond of pointing out, in which the fundamental particle is not the atom but the bit—the binary digit, a unit of data usually represented as a 0 or 1. Information may still be delivered in magazines and newspapers (atoms), but the real value is in the contents (bits). We pay for our goods and services with cash (atoms), but the ebb and flow of capital around the world is carried out—to the tune of several trillion dollars a day—in electronic funds transfers (bits).

Philip Elmer-DeWitt, in *Time*

Angelnet

http://alive.mcn.org:80/angelnet.html/

Angels, yoga, dolphins, images, and music; a labyrinth to explore; meditation guides and angel water for sale; stories of angelic encounters; a guitar raffle (your chance to win costs only a buck); massage; phobias; even an interactive poem. What more could your inner flower-child want? Obviously commercial (most of what's here are ads for products), but a peaceful rest stop on the Info Highway. Groove with it, man.

EXCERPT:

Fly back & visit or hover, there will be MORE to come. Angelnet will send your spirit soaring!!

Animations

http://bakmes.colorado.edu/~bicanic/

Only Netscape viewers can see this one. There's not much here anyway. Someone named Nick—no last name—has developed what he claims is a way to do animation on a web page, but you can only do it and/or see it with Netscape. He calls it the most "cutting-edgest animationest page on the web," so you know he's not a scholar of English grammar. Even with Netscape, this site is lame at best.

Ankiewicz Galleries (Kristen's Evil Web Empire)

http://deeptht.armory.com:80/~kristen/

Kristen Ankiewicz is one of those very active, renaissance artist types. Though her work is vaguely reminiscent of her influences—Man Ray, Pollock, Van Gogh, and Warhol—it breathes with its own language and stands on its own merits. Kristen has a lot of work to show: paintings, photos, poems, fractals, fonts, and more. It's well worth a stop.

EXCERPT:

During the evening, Kristen is a painter, photographer, poet, and hacker. During the day, she looks for bugs at PrePress Solutions. Kristen's goal in life is to tie all these threads together.

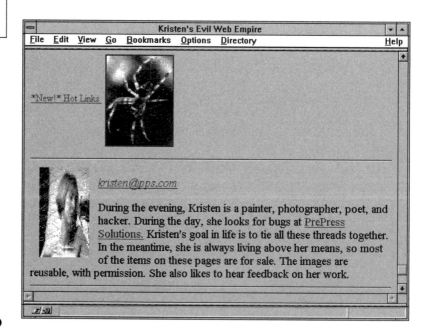

Antics

http://www.ionet.net/~rdavis/antics.shtml

Need a chuckle? Come test your wits against this "ant-eractive ant-thology" of ant cartoons. Click an ant (yes, a graphic browser is required) to display a cartoon and then try to guess the "ant" word it represents. Cute, but not much here if you're not into ant-related picture games. Corresponds to the print *Antics—An Ant Thology*.

E X C E R P T :

...My sister-in-law was doing one of her craft projects and asked me to draw an ant...I asked her specifically what kind. She said, "What do you mean, there's only one kind of ant." I grinned mischievously...

Apple Computer

http://www.apple.com/default.html

Apple's home page goes right for the jugular: "Why Macintosh is superior to Windows." For Mac users, the answer comes as no surprise. PC users may not want to explore further. Apple has a reasonably dense home page, offering a variety of pathways and good information, though the rivalry with that other company may seem like a waste of time to some users.

Arc, The Interactive Media Festival

http://www.arc.org/

The Interactive Media Festival is a collection of computerized, digital, hypertextual, and hypervisual experiences that explore the potential of interactive expression in a gallery of internationally diverse offerings. Though the home page is somewhat mystifying in its simplicity and cryptic quality, the links are clear and fascinating.

J udged purely as a place to do business, the Internet stinks. As Bill Towler, founder of a computer services company in Oklahoma City and a believer in cyberspace, aptly puts it, "The Internet is a solution looking for a problem."

Peter Nulty, *Fortune,* June 26, 1995.

EXCERPT:

Arc, the Interactive Media Festival, makes a pilgrimage once a year to Los Angeles....How, why, and where we did it are all posted here as well.

Ari's Today Page

http://www.uta.fi/~blarku/today.html

What happened on this day in 1925? Find out at the Today Page site. It's a record of this date in history, complete with a listing of birthdays of famous people and links to daily news reports, horoscopes, numerology and other pages dealing with....today.

EXCERPT:

Fast and reliable link to some miscellaneous daily information. Taken daily in deadly doses.

Walter S. Arnold, Sculptor/Stone Carver

http://www.mcs.net/~sculptor/home.html

An advertising page, but an interesting one, this site has samples of gargoyles and grotesques; custom fireplaces; signage and entry panels; public sculpture; architectural ornaments; and portraiture created by a Chicago limestone and marble cutter. Check it out and dream about having some of this stuff in your house. The site also includes some very interesting background on a stonecutter's union, which may be the country's oldest labor union.

Around the World and Home Again, Week

http://www.unitedmedia.com/comics/peanuts/archive.html

Billed as an archive of Peanuts cartoons, this site is a poorly constructed, bad idea of a guessing game. There's no evidence of the Peanuts gang except a monstrous in-line graphic that loads slowly if at all. Even Peanuts fans will find this site a frustration.

Around-the-World Journal

http://www.city.net/travel/atwj/

One traveler's journal of his nine-month honeymoon through 26 countries. Features 260K of text and more than 120 color pictures, expense break-downs by country, reader comments, PostScript and plain-text versions of the journal, and links to detailed country and city information (provided through links to City.Net) and other travel-related resources.

EXCERPT:

Ever think about quitting your job and hitting the road? Well that's exactly what we did, and this is the journal I kept along the way.

Art Comics

http://www.cais.com/artcomic/home.html/

Art Comics is a page for nonsuperhero oriented, alternative comic lovers. It's a well-designed page of wacky comic work by various artists from around the country. There's work of all kinds and scads of information, such as the Xeric Grant program that awards money to aspiring cartoonists and comics creators to produce a so-called independent comic book, often self-published. And there's lots of greats comics here.

EXCERPT:

Art Comics is constantly bombarded with e-mail broadcasts from the Living Cartoon Characters Employment Agency of Hollywood.

Art Crimes

http://www.gatech.edu/desoto/graf/Index.Art_Crimes.html

Much more than a gallery of graffiti art from around the world, Art Crimes includes a graffiti FAQ, glossary, and bibliography; graffiti-related maga-zines and videos; tips for photographing graffiti, scanning images for use on the Web, and transferring images using FTP; critical reviews of graffiti liter-ature; essays; and calendars of graffiti art shows and events.

EXCERPT:

Our goals are to provide cultural information and scholarly resources [and] to help preserve and document the constantly d isappearing works of the graffiti art movement...

@art Gallery

http://gertrude.art.uiuc.edu/@art/gallery.html

@art is an electronic art gallery where form truly follows function. The

"**N**ot being on the Internet will soon be like not having a mailing address or phone number. You will simply be unable to do business in the 21st century without it," Ryan says.

Steve Ryan, associate with the law offices of Howard L. Nations

site's design is spare and clean, with lots of white space to draw the visitor's attention to the works, rather than to the walls on which they "hang." Notes on the artists and their featured pieces accompany each work. Some interesting ideas here, but watch out—unless you're using a Macintosh and the Monaco typeface, the page layouts look a little garbled.

EXCERPT:

Exhibits are curated by the founding members, with the intention of providing an electronic viewing space for talented and mature artists of outstanding merit.

Art Gallery of H.R. Giger

http://heiwww.unige.ch/art/Giger/

Fans of the "Alien" movie, the ELP "Brain Salad Surgery," and other things created by H.R. Giger will be compelled to visit this site. The page offers a seemingly endless array of Giger imagery. Each in-line graphic links to a larger, higher resolution image. The only problem is that there are so many in-line graphics on the home page that it can take up to an hour to load. Still it's a worthwhile visit if you're a very patient Giger fan.

(Art) Laboratory

http://www.artn.nwu.edu/

(Art) Laboratory is a gallery of virtual 3-D photographic art for those of you who surf the Net for a little eye candy. The web site also features informational and technical articles, a glossary, instructions for creating and submitting files for making virtual 3-D images, a bibliography, artists' and critics' statements, essays, and a calendar of exhibitions.

EXCERPT:

They copied all they could follow / but they couldn't copy my mind / I left them sweating and stealing / a year and a half behind.— Rudyard Kipling

Art on the Net

http://www.art.net/

Art on the Net provides studios and gallery rooms for visual and performing artists, musicians, poets, sculptors, and animators and helps them place their art on the Internet. Includes news of art happenings on the Net (with links to related sites), links to other arts-related resources, and artists' comments.

EXCERPT:

Welcome to Art on the Net! Join fellow artists in sharing works together on the Internet. Enjoy visiting artists studios and roaming the gallery.

aRt_sLab

http://www-apparitions.ucsd.edu:80/~webmngr/

A gallery of student art, with links to other arts-related resources. Graduate and undergrad artists display their works and explore various issues concerning art and contemporary culture. Visually interesting.

EXCERPT:

This is a view of the undergraduate and graduate artists at work here, exploring a variety of issues in art and contemporary culture.

ArtAIDS LINK Gallery

http://artaids.dcs.qmw.ac.uk:8001/entrance/

Not just another art gallery on the Net, the ArtAIDS LINK is an Internet art

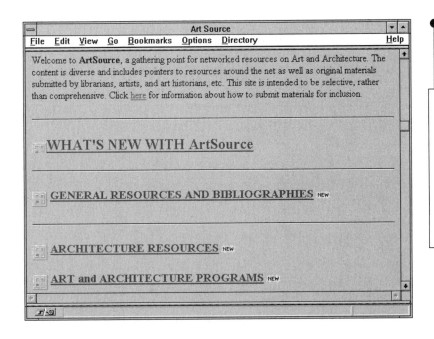

project for digital artists to commemorate and celebrate the fight against AIDS. Includes technical help, guidelines for contributors, and links to other arts-related sites.

Artful Things Gallery

http://emporium.turnpike.net/Z/zen/Artful.html

A gallery of intriguing digital art by Max Fellwalker divided into categories like Chiaroscuro; Dramatis Personae; Vampyre; Vault of Heaven; and Zephyr.

The ArtMetal Project

http://wuarchive.wustl.edu/edu/arts/metal/ArtMetal.html

A visit to a gallery that showcases the works of blacksmiths, whitesmiths, jewelers, sculptors, and bladesmiths. ArtMetal also features metalworking news from around the world; stories, graphics, movies, and sounds illustrat-

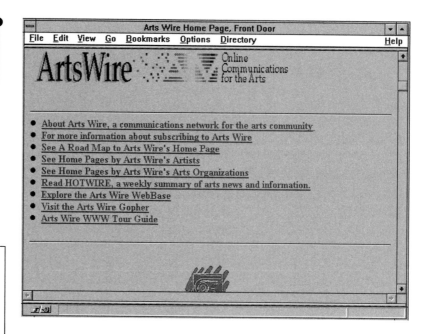

ing aspects of this ancient craft; and a resource list with information on materials, processes, finishes, and design.

Arts Network for Integrated Media Applications

http://www.anima.wis.net/

An online supermarket for the integrated media art world, ANIMA offers an art gallery, guides to arts-related resources and events, online publications, research, and more. Plenty of cool links, including NEXUS, a gallery of artworks exploring the use of telecommunications as both content and medium; ATLAS, an information map of ideas, tools, organizations, people, and sources; and Persona, featuring community discussion and individual exploration on the evolving world media network.

EXCERPT:

Explore the images, ideas, sounds and experiences of the digital art spaces on the net worldwide.

Arts Wire

http://www.tmn.com/0h/Artswire/www/awfront.html

Arts Wire publishes HOTWIRE, a weekly summary of arts-related news and information, and provides discussion areas, commissioned texts, and a searchable database of grant deadlines and other opportunities for artists and organizations. Arts Wire has cool links to other home pages for artists and organizations and e-mail as well as Internet access for its members.

EXCERPT:

In collaboration with others, Arts Wire works to ensure a place for the arts in the development of the national communications infrastructure...

ArtSource

http://www.uky.edu/Artsource/artsourcehome.html

A collection of networked resources on art and architecture, with pointers to resources around the net as well as original materials submitted by librarians, artists, and art historians. Try the links to Architecture Resources; Art/Architecture Gopher Sites; Art Journals On-Line; Artist's Projects; Electronic Exhibitions; and Museum Information.

ArtsUSA

http://www.artsusa.org/

ArtsUSA was rated as one of the top web sites by Point Survey, and when you log on, you will see why. This is one of the best home pages you will ever find. It is a comprehensive and very detailed look at arts-related subjects. ArtsUSA marries so-called high art with popular culture. There's a chat area, an online bibliography, updates on public policy, and a culturally diverse catalog of work dealing with arts careers, art education, etc. Worthwhile and loads quickly.

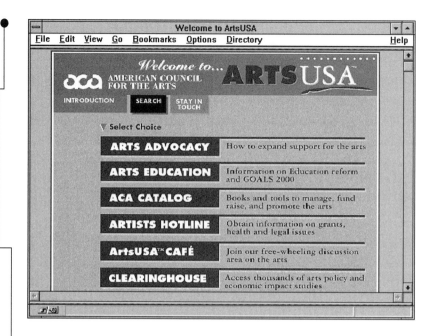

As the WWWeb Turns...

http://www.rubyslippers.com/sadtuna/asturns.html

Not much heavyweight content, but a mildly amusing virtual soap opera played out entirely in e-mail. The best part about As the WWWeb Turns... is following the links in the characters' messages as they travel through a web (ha-ha) of scandal, enlightenment, and mischief.

EXCERPT:

Join us, now, as we eavesdrop into the real-life e-mailings of Lulu and Durango, occasional friends and your virtual companions to Scandal, Enlightenment and Mischief on the World Wide Web!

Asia Inc. Online

http://www.asia-inc.com

Asia, Inc., the online version of the monthly business magazine of the same

. . . the Internet is on the brink of hosting real cyber-casinos through which users can bet real money...Warren Eugene, Internet Casinos president, has been developing the concept for a few years. The company conducted research before launching the casino and posted a questionnaire on its server....One of the questions asked, "If we publish our algorithms, and have verification conducted by a well-known accounting firm, will this assist you in making a decision to gamble here?"....A question not asked on the server is, Will you believe the computer when it deals itself 21 in blackjack and you lose real money?

Dave Zgodzinski, *Internet World*

name, features discussion forums, Asian financial information, Asia Inc.'s radio show, and the Asia Inc. Report. Catch up on Today's Financial News; This Week's Special Items; About Asia, Inc. Online; Conference Rooms; Feature Stories; Departments; The Asia, Inc. Report; and Worldwide Business Headlines from Knight-Ridder Financial News.

EXCERPT:

Asia, Inc.'s editorial mission is to tell the extraordinary story of Asia's executives and their enterprises (in their own words and images), and to serve in this manner as the voice of business in Asia.

Asian Arts

http://www.webart.com/asianart/index.html

Asian Arts is a forum for scholars, museums, and commercial galleries to display and study materials related to Asian art. Scholarly articles discussing various aspects of Asian art supplement the exhibitions and gallery shows.

Asian Astrology

http://www.deltanet.com/users/wcassidy/astroindex.html

Think Asian astrology is just the I Ching? Wrong. Explore this site and you'll find out more than you ever wanted to know about Asian, Chinese, Tibetan, and Vietnamese astrology. Includes bibliographies; calendar conversion and calculation utilities; Chinese, Tibetan, and Vietnamese studies; paths for further study; and, of course, the I Ching, Sidpaho, Feng Shui, and other methods of divination.

EXCERPT:

What we find deplorable is "pop" astrology. At last count, we have received over 380 queries regarding the O.J. Simpson affair....

Ask Ken!

http://www.efn.org/~andrec/ask_ken.html

Ask Ken! is the online world's answer to Dear Abby. Ken's advice covers a wide range of human experience, from the baseball strike of 1994 ("True, it is too bad about the World Series, but think about all the little kids that wanted to grow up to be Major League Baseball Players and now will want to grow up to be great Union Negotiators.") to being addicted to advice columns.

EXCERPT:

Need advice? Have a problem that seemingly has no solution? Ask Ken!

Ask Mr. Puddy

http://www.sils.umich.edu/~nscherer/AskPuddy.html

Ann Landers he ain't, but some might consider this advice columnist the cat's meow. Yes, Mr. Puddy is a cat, and he answers your questions about life, liberty, and the pursuit of happiness. There are also the expected photos, and just to show you he takes his advice giving seriously, there's Mr.

Puddy's Reference Desk where you'll find an index of Internet resources including phone books, government documents, and weather around the world.

EXCERPT:

Mr. Puddy's advice on life, business, medicine, affairs of the heart. Wondering what to do? Ask Mr. Puddy.

AskERIC

http:// ericir.syr.edu

Educating educators is ERIC's job, and AskERIC provides online help for specific problems. You can browse through the vast resources of this Department of Education information system for lesson plans, teaching aids, and resources to help you use PBS, Discovery Channel, and Learning Channel programs in your classroom. You can read the Digest file for the latest education news or check the calendar of conferences for educators.

EXCERPT:

Catch up on the hot topics in the field of education with ERIC.

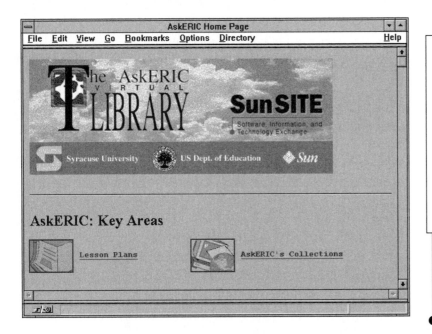

T echnology already makes it feasible to link living rooms —and bank accounts — with lotteries, racetracks, sports betting parlors and casinos, on-line gaming supporters note. And the rapid growth of legalized gambling across the country means the climate is right.

Detroit Free Press

Associated Press Wire Service

http://www1.trib.com/NEWS/APwire.html

Unfortunately, this potentially useful site may still be under construction. Features such as searching the newswire may or may not be available. What should be accessible are recently transmitted stories in such areas as general news, foreign, finance, sports, and weather. Keep checking back, though, because AP should have a great site upon completion.

EXCERPT:

This service is under construction—not all items may work at all times.

Astro-2 Live

http://astro-2.msfc.nasa.gov

Three, two, one, liftoff. As part of their public awareness program, NASA is allowing the public to participate in shuttle missions via the Web. Astro-2, the first such open mission is archived here, along with links to other shuttle sites.

The Asylum

http://www.galcit.caltech.edu/~ta/cgi-bin/asylhome-ta

The Asylum's interactive playground isn't for the faint of heart. Visitors will find a gallery of peg-light art, a "scratch pad" they can draw on, an interactive "fiction therapy" salon, a cuckoo clock (sound required), a mascot they can feed or smush, a "core dump" of useless stuff, and last but not least, a chance to immortalize themselves among the ranks of The Asylum's inmates.

EXCERPT:

I see the Rev. Door and I want to paint it black.

AT&T Home Page

http://www.att.com

Talk about "reach out and touch someone," this home page has complete information about AT&T and then some. The index goes on and on, highlighting what seems like every division of this vast enterprise. There are quarterly reports, AT&T magazines and journals, communications services including Internet access, multimedia products, affiliates, conferences and forums, and community services. One-stop shopping for all your AT&T needs.

atom

http://www.atom.co.jp/

Read MACLIFE, the online version of a monthly Macintosh magazine published in Japan; view a gallery of contemporary art, photos, and illustrations by Japanese artists; check the Japanese Independent Music Archives; and listen to UNSOUND, a collection of music clips by pop and "unpop" artists.

AudioWeb

http://www.audioweb.com/index.html

Hi-fi enthusiasts will want to tune into the AudioWeb for audio component and music reviews; a library of hi-fi audio information with a company and organization directory, links to other audio-related sites, and a selection of articles from top audio magazines; free classified ads; vendor information; interaction with other audio clubs and societies around the world; and even a product raffle.

EXCERPT:

We are dedicated to becoming a major resource to people to whom the emotionally satisfying reproduction of The Musical Experience matters.

The Aurelliac

http://www.galcit.caltech.edu/~aure/aure.html

A doctoral student at Cal Tech, Aurelius could be called the Christopher Columbus of the Web. He has sailed to nearly every site on the Internet, and the purpose of his home page is to tell you all about it. Very useful resources ranging from California sites to computer, music, graphics, entertainment and more sites from around the globe.

EXCERPT:

Being on the web is me being social.

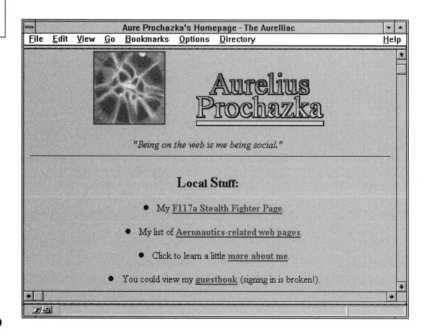

Cincinnati's Aurora Casket Co. "is bringing the funeral business to life," according to a release announcing an interactive kiosk Aurora has developed for funeral directors. You can browse the "Value Line" of caskets or drag-and-drop images of bronze, pewter, steel and wooden cremation urns into a display case to view various arrangements. Best of all, funeral directors can download the program to a floppy disc and take it into customer's homes.

Scott Donaton, *Advertising Age*, June 26, 1995.

Austin City Limits

http://www.quadralay.com/www/Austin/Austin.html

Everything you ever wanted to know about Austin, Texas, and then some, including landmarks, armadillos (what do armadillos have to do with Austin?), businesses and organizations, city and state government, community events, restaurants, education, media, recreation, services, and photos of the city and environs. Includes links to other city-related sites on the Web.

EXCERPT:

Austin is by far the greatest town in Texas and one of the greatest in the country. We have a mix of college students (the University of Texas and St. Edward's University are here), politicians,...and computer people...

Automatic Talking Machine

http://www.inference.com/~hansen/talk.html

The message you type in the Automatic Talking Machine form box will be spoken out loud in an office in Los Angeles. Depending on your particular frame of mind, this site is either a massive time waster or an ingenious example of applied technology. What do you think?

EXCERPT:

If I'm around, I'll hear what you say. And so will anyone else who happens to be within earshot. So be creative—not insulting!

AutoPages of Internet

http://www.clark.net/pub/networx/autopage/autopage.html

AutoPages of Internet is a service for dealers and individual sellers of exotic and classic automobiles and motorcycles. AutoPages features full-color photographs and descriptions of automobiles for sale around the United States. Future issues will contain information from manufacturers, restorers, and parts suppliers, as well as announcements of auctions, trade shows, and other important events for automotive enthusiasts.

AUX500DIABLES

http://dufy.aquarel.fr:80/500diables/500txt1.html

A collection of huge art posters by various European artists. Very little context, but a whole lot of bytes and self-expression by artists who want to escape the fetters of time, space, and place.

EXCERPT:

Rooted in the plastic arts but open to other forms, AUX500DIABLES functions as artists do, in total self-freedom, irregularly, unbounded by the limits of time and space or place.

Available Information on MUDs

http://www.cis.upenn.edu/~lwl/mudinfo.html

This web site has compiled an extensive listing of reference sources and information about multiuser dimensions (MUDs), object-oriented MUDs (MOOs), social MUDs (MUCKs and MUSEs), and multiuser shared hallucinations (MUSHes). If you have no idea what this means, check the site and try the links to MUDlists and MUDWho.

Avalon

http://reality.sgi.com/employees/chris_manchester/arthur.html

If you're searching for the Holy Grail or a lover of the Arthurian legends, you'll want to visit the mystical island to which King Arthur was taken after he was wounded by his son. Avalon sports a new age or symbolic outlook to the legends and has information on books and articles, movies, geography, and societies.

EXCERPT:

Avalon: the mystical isle to which King Arthur was taken after being mortally wounded by his son Mordred.

Avenger's Front Page

http://tklab1.cs.uit.no/%7Epaalde/Revenge/

If putting salt in the sugar shaker isn't quite the revenge you had in mind, check out Avenger's Front Page, where you'll find revenge strategies that range from lively pranks to how to properly say good-bye to your old job. You'll also find HTML, PostScript, and plain-text versions of the Avenger's Handbook as well as links to other revenge-related resources, including how to pick a lock and the ultimate list of practical jokes.

EXCERPT:

Need to get even? This is probably the place for you to look for a neat revenge scheme. But before you start, you should be aware of that I do not take responsibility for actions performed as in the scripts on this page.

B

B-EYE: The world through the eyes of a bee.

http://anu.edu.au/andy/beye/beyehome.html

A bee's eye view of the world. How's that for an interesting perspective? This site is the work of a scientist who studies the habits of honey bees. Moderately interesting for honey lovers, but a must-visit destination for apiarists. Calling Winnie-the-Pooh.

EXCERPT:

...Have you ever wondered how other creatures see the world?...Find out what we THINK the world looks like to a bee....

Babes on the Web II

http://ucsub.colorado.edu/~kritzber/new/babes.html

With the idea that what's good for the gander is certainly good for the goose, we have Babes on the Web II. Born out of the controversy of Babes on the Web, a home page that provides an index to women's personal home pages, at least the ones with pictures, Babes on the Web II gives you an index to men's personal home pages. Rather than providing a scale rating though, Babes II places the men in categories chosen by the Mistress herself: Dangerous; Cuddly; and Steamy.

EXCERPT:

Diotima is the spirit lurking in the mesodermis of your desktop; she conducts an untiring search for masculine babeliness.

Computer enthusiasts predict that in five years people will either buy custom-cut CDs with songs plucked from the Internet or skip the store altogether and copy songs onto discs at home right off the Net.

Marc Peyser, in *Newsweek*

Banana Slug Home Page

http://www.slugs.com/slugweb/slug_home_page.html

Most mascots tend to be something you can make into a cuddly stuffed animal. Not at Santa Cruz. Here they chose the banana slug, a very large bright yellow shell-less mollusk found slithering around the vegetation. Learn why such an illustrious mascot, what it is, and even purchase a tee shirt while you're there.

EXCERPT:

OK, so enough of these slug references, just what the heck is a Banana Slug anyway?

The Barney Fun Page

http://ugweb.cs.ualberta.ca/~gerald/barney

I love you, you love me, blow him up with an Uzi. Yes, all you surfers who have been subjected to the big purple dinosaur once too often—take your revenge on the Barney Fun Page. You'll be supplied with a picture of Barney and a list of weapons; the rest is up to you. Or if you're not in a particularly destructive mood, just view some of the corpses made by your compadres (for inspiration perhaps).

EXCERPT:

What do you get when you cross a picture of Barney with a list of weapons? I bet you'd like to find out.

The Bastard Operator from Hell

http://www.fn.net/~thrasher/BOFH

You've probably had to deal with one of these yourself. Ask for more disk space on the main frame and s/he deletes what you already have. Peeks into other peoples files, etc. Here, you can read all 15 episodes, as well as 2 more from the British Isles. Maybe it's a franchise.

Batman Forever

http://batmanforever.com/welcome/welcome.html

Riddle me this. Suppose you're a great big movie company giant and you want to promote your cool new film. What are you going to do to promote your film? Create a web page, of course. So, here's the latest on the caped crusader and *Batman Forever*, including bios on the stars, artwork and photographs, movie trailers, riddles, and the soundtrack.

EXCERPT:

In this thriving metropolis, you can find out all you'd ever want to know about the Warner Bros. movie *Batman Forever*.

The BBC Home Page

http://www.bbcnc.org.uk

The BBC has been a voice in the wilderness to many, and its top-notch programming has graced many a television set in both Britain and abroad. The BBC page has TV and radio schedules; Education Online, which has programs and resources for teachers; World Service Radio frequencies; and even BBC job listings. Jolly good.

W orld Wide Web, whose name in Chinese means: "Ten thousand dimensional web in heaven and net on Earth."

Steven Mufson, in *The Washington Post*

Tim Berners-Lee

http://www.w3.org/hypertext/WWW/People/Berners-Lee-Bio.html

Learn a little WWW history. This site serves as a biography for the guy who created the World Wide Web in 1989 and lists his recent studies and publications. Tim works in the Laboratory for Computer Science (LCS) at MIT where he directs the W3 Consortium, which coordinates W3 development.

Betty Boop Archive

http://www.phantom.com/~voidmstr/BettyBoopArchive.html

Betty Boop is having a revival, so here's some help in the promotional arena. You can see images, watch clips from some of her famous cartoons, even hear her sing "boopboopedoop." There's also news of the "Betty Boop Confidential" national screen tour & the address for her fan club. Well 23 skidoo.

Bianca Troll Productions

http://bianca.com/btp/

Bianca Troll Productions provides access to a wide range of Internet information on foods, cooking, flowers and herbs, music and theater. There are even opportunities for online chat sessions and links to Bianca's Smut Shack and Bianca's Underground Movie Palace.

EXCERPT:

Bianca Troll productions is dedicated to uniting the "alternative" and "underground" of the Net and keeping the Net anarchic, liberated, free, and open...

Bibliotheque Bajazzo

http://www.xs4all.nl/~arthur/

Bibliotheque Bajazzo is an online art museum. You'll find only graphic images in the so-called first sector, with each image guiding the user through the exhibits. The art creations display best in Netscape 1.1 (or newer) or Mosaic 2.0 (or other browsers that support tables and background colors), but there is access to a nontable and nonbackground-colors version. The first sector is located on the server of XS4ALL.NL in Amsterdam, the Netherlands.

Big Black Hole of Pain

http://offworld.wwa.com/bighole.html

The provider calls it "a new concept in the therapeutic use of the WWW for healing the human race." If you need a place to vent or to get your jollies reading other people's purges, stop here and enjoy.

EXCERPT:

We suggest that you take three deep breaths and begin writing in the box below all of the crap you would like to get off your chest.

Big Time Television

http://crow.acns.nwu.edu:8082/

Big Time Television provides access to various counter-culture sites. Read the EFF Alert and Kultur, your guide to living in a fallen world (where you'll find the unofficial Pogues home page). Check out Film at Eleven; HyperNews for HyperHeads; Poeticus; the Page o' Literature, The Walking Man Project; and the World's Most Dangerous Writing Game. Take Big Time's eL train to the best of the Web.

EXCERPT:
Between the Networks and the Web's Edge lurks... Big Time Television, twenty minutes ahead of where we should be.

Bike'alog Complete Bike Specs

http://www.bikealog.com/

A brilliant idea, botched. Bicycling enthusiasts could profit from this potentially informative site, which is supposed to feature exact specifications for bikes made by leading companies from around the world. However, the homepage contains so many bad links that much of the information is inaccessible. What a pity—with a little work, this site could be top-notch.

EXCERPT:
Complete bike specs from the folks that know!

Black Holes and Neutron Stars

http://cossc.gsfc.nasa.gov/htmltest/rjn_bht.html

A dry, academic paper that explores the physics of black holes and describes both a neutron star with a relatively weak surface gravity add an ultra compact neutron star with an extremely high surface gravity. Avoid it, unless college physics really interested you. Online movies on are also available to those with the adequate viewing software. See the site for details.

Bobaworld

http://gagme.wwa.com/~boba/

Bobaworld contains links to a plethora of exciting and interesting sites and has been selected as one of the top 5% of web sites by Point Survey. Definitely worth a visit, but you may find the organization of the multiple pages to be difficult to navigate.

EXCERPT:
Welcome To BOBAWORLD. You will find many links here, both to sub-

Almost seventy years ago, Belgian chocolatier Joseph Draps created his widely acclaimed bonbons and named them after the legendary Lady Godiva of Coventry. Godiva chocolates soon became as famous as the Lady herself. Today, Godiva is made from the same recipes used in 1926....Packaged in wonderfully creative presentations, each collection reveals a decorative array of chocolates to tempt your palate and please the eye.

Godiva Online Home Page: http://www.godiva.com/

pages of this page, and to other sites on the Web. I hope you like these pages, as others have.

BOB(c)WEB

http://www4.ncsu.edu/unity/users/a/asdamick/www/

BOB(c)WEB is a conglomeration of "stuff," primarily the archives of those newsgroups with the name Bob, e.g., alt.fan.the-bob, and other miscellaneous newsgroup writings of a humorous nature. One desirable feature is the information on how to create a news group. Other fun-sounding links to The Spiffo Links; The Most Spiffo Links on the World Wide Web; Kibological Archive; The Unauthorized Archive of James "Kibo" Parry; and He Who Greps.

EXCERPT:

The BOB, Warrior Poet, Emperor of the Usenet.

The Body Electric

http://www.surgery.com/body/topics/body.html

Pick the part of you that you want to change and then check the Body Electric to get an idea of how you would look after cosmetic surgery. Information includes before and after pictures, an approximation of the costs, and even a listing of doctors in your area that perform this type of surgery.

EXCERPT:

Pick the area you would like to improve.

bOING bOING Online

http://www.zeitgeist.net/public/bOING-bOING

Unfortunately, bOING bOING Online does not BOING BOING off the web page. Derived from a magazine that began in 1989, bOING bOING sprouted up in cyberspace in 1992 on The Well. But its web home page is hardly as intriguing as its name or its magazine. The home page lists a series of mysterious links for 'zine reviews, a bazaar, and an art gallery, but offers no explanation of itself or the links. Though the graphics are cute, counterculture, retrostyle imagery, the presentation is lame.

EXCERPT:

A blueprint for the flipside of serious culture.

Book Stacks Unlimited, Inc.

http://www.books.com

Books Stacks Unlimited is a multipurpose web page for book lovers. The home page explains the provider's services and is a delightful resource for the book lover who's hungry for information and conversation about books new and old. It includes a chat area, news and gossip from the publishing world, and an author locator. But the Book Stacks' main and best feature is its online bookstore with 320,000 titles, as opposed to the 50,000 maintained by most earthbound emporiums.

EXCERPT:

...The Book Stacks Web Bookstore is finally open! With over 320,000 titles, you can search by author, title, subject, ISBN, and order online.

BookWeb

http://www.ambook.org

"Hot off the Press: Borders loses $4.9 million before charges." If headlines like this are what you're after, here's the place to go. BookWeb has the news of the book industry, as well as bookstore directories and links to bookstore pages, discussion groups, and information on specialty genres like Science Fiction. You can even enter a monthly contest.

EXCERPT:

I'm Charlotte, your guide to the BookWeb, a complete resource for news and information about books, bookstores, authors, the First Amendment, and much, much more!

Bordeaux and Prague

http://www.winternet.com/~carl/bp/bp.html

Bordeaux and Prague is a hypertext of creative experiments launched on the precepts of hyperintelligence. There are children's stories and art projects in a variety of styles for a range of audiences though the core reasons for the intellectual lingo is no more apparent in the work than it is in the blurbs on the home page. The work is pretty good and the concepts and vocabulary (abecedarian roller coaster) might make good chat fodder for psuedointel-lectual parties.

EXCERPT:

...Kid A in Alphabet Land is an abecedarian roller coaster ride through the phallocentric obscurantism of Jacques Lacan.

The Borderline

http://www.cts.com/~borderln/

The Borderline is a web page maintained by teen-age Gabe Martin. The young San Diego cartoonist offers a new one-panel comic strip every day as well as archives to his previous work. Clever in-line graphics delineate

> **W**hat the Internet offers that is unprecedented is an egalitarian community where anyone can talk to everyone. We haven't had this since the world ended at the edge of our village, and even then each person had a place in the hierarchy that determined when he or she could speak and who would listen.
>
> Carolyn Caywood, in *School Library Journal*

each month's collection. Martin's cartoons are clever, well-drawn, and consistently amusing.

EXCERPT:

The second daily, Internet cartoon in the known world.

James K. Boyer's Home Page

http://141.217.10.195:8080/

This site is a personal home page chosen as Cool Site of the Day on July 22, 1995. The page has nice graphics and an autobiography of a well-read and well-traveled employee of Wayne State University in Detroit, Michigan with links to Mr. Boyer's personal interests—Albert Einstein, Nelson Mandela, Tai Chi, exotic foods, and travel (check out the links to the ruins of Tulum). A nicely presented and fun to explore web site!

Branson Net Home Page

http://www.digimark.net/branson

Want to visit one of the country's top vacation destinations? Branson, Missouri, is your spot. Nestled in the foothills of the Ozarks, the Branson area is home to entertainment parks, resorts, music, and shopping, as well as natural scenic beauty. Visit the Branson site, then start packing. You'll get a wealth of information on Resorts; Music Shows; Lodging; Restaurants; Ozark Shopping Mall; Tour Packages; Entertainment Parks.

EXCERPT:

Even before there was a Branson, our area was known as one of the nicest places in the country to visit.

Bravo

http://www.uaep.co.uk/bravo.html

It's not just TV, it's interactive medium. The people at Bravo, the UK cable and satellite TV channel, want you not only to learn about them but also to find out more about interactive media on the Net. Look for the usual promotional information: programs, schedules, episode guides, etc., and check links to The Bravo Bulletin; Treasure Chest; Seamail; Follow the Fish; and Findex.

EXCERPT:

These are the pages for Bravo, the UK-based cable and satellite television channel, where we show such weird and wonderful programs as "Twin Peaks," "The Adventures of Robin Hood," and "UFO."

Michael Breen's Personal Music Page

http://orpheus.ucsd.edu/webmaster/music.html

Mr. Breen has more than 1,000 links to music-related resources. The main database is the Harmony Music List and some of the links go to San Diego Area Music; Official Studio Releases; Downloadable Music; Songs in Progress and Status; Biographies of Studio Musicians; Biographies of Studio Bands; Archive of Completed Recordings; Studio and Equipment Lists; Song Lyrics.

EXCERPT:

I'm using a new tool to generate a new version of the Harmony Music list. The count is well over a thousand links, and growing!

BRETTnews

http://www.timeinc.com/vibe/vibeart/brettnews/index.html

Hipsters unite! Brett Leveridge, an artist-in-residence at *Vibe Magazine*, established his own web page in 1992. Mods and retro-beatniks will find familiar pabulum here. Brett's writing, self-described as "pithy fluff," is just that and tongue-in-cheekedly self-indulgent besides. The most decent feature is the Skyvue Cable Drive-In that lists quirky B-movies on cable networks, though half of them are available in New York City only.

EXCERPT:

Welcome to the world of BRETTnews, a sporadic zine of pithy fluff. You'll find...a day-by-day (complete with photos!) account of our four-month, 48-state, 23,000 mile journey across the good ol' U. S. of A....

Brian

http://streams.com/brian/

Though it sounds simple enough, Brian is an odd little web page that is for surfers 18-years and older only. The enigmatic Brian exists in cyberspace and leaves personal messages for friends and family on his home page. The main feature is a game and series of contests for experimenting with body piercing on a variety of graphic images. The host supplies real prizes, like Sea Monkeys to the winners. There's not much in here, but the game may prove to be an interesting, momentary diversion.

EXCERPT:

You made it just in time to catch Piercing Mildred—The Interactive Body Modification Game....

Britannica Online

http://www.eb.com kgi-bin/bio.pl

Britannica's Lives, the introductory page to Britannica Online, might be a fun place to visit on your birthday to discover what famous people were

Most historians believe that Roman soldiers were the first people to use condoms. While fraternizing with local women on long marches away from Rome, the soldiers used dried sheep intestines as sheaths for protecting themselves against disease, the most notorious of which was the "Mount Vesuvius Rash."

The protection that proper use of latex condoms provides against HIV transmission is most evident from studies of couples in which one member is infected with HIV and the other is not, i.e., "discordant couples." In a study of discordant couples in Europe, among 123 couples who reported consistent condom use, none of the uninfected partners became infected. In contrast, among the 122 couples who used condoms inconsistently, 12 of the uninfected partners became infected.

Welcome to Condom Country: http://www.ag.com/Condom/Country/

born on the same day as you. Otherwise there are impediments to further enjoyment of Britannica services. The typical boolean logic database search service is only available to subscribers of Britannica's Online encyclopedia service. The demo of the service is lame and uninspired.

Broadway World-Wide

http://webcom.com/~broadway/

The news is somewhat worldwide, but most of the listings are for the good ol' U.S.A. It's a good service for theater lovers seeking ticket prices and locations for shows in the Big Apple and other parts of the country. The information is up-to-date and far more extensive than newspapers provide. Also, the national tour information is useful when you want to know what shows will be playing near you and when.

Buena Vista Movie Plex

http://bvp.wdp.com/bvpm/

The Buena Vista Movie Plex opens into a virtual cinema house with six to eight almost-new releases (none more than a few months old) and the Magnificent Movie Brain, a not-too-easy movie trivia area. To get the full effect, users need a browser with JPEG support and a Quicktime movie player. This is a cool site if you're so equipped; otherwise it's an experience in frustration and disappointment. It's a page whose time has not yet come.

Build-A-Card

http://infopages.com/card

Build-A-Card is a point-and-click card-making experience, and 7,000 webbers have actually created cards. Now that e-users can send virtual cards, they can totally avoid the post office and the Hallmark shop in the mall. The graphics are cute, though at times a little too cute, but you'll love the great clip art, including the Hirschfield Star Trek caricatures. Build-A-Card is a popular site, especially on holidays, so do your card building early. (Only 20 people can work at a time.)

Burlingame On-Line

http://www.spectrumnet.com/~spectrum/burlingame.html

With some very nice in-line graphics and peppy text, Burlingame, California, puts its municipality on the online map. The Pez exhibit alone makes a visit to this site worthwhile. You get a detailed view of the community—its government, calendar of events, town history, and a visitor's guide. The home page loads quickly, and Burlingame looks like a great place to visit in real reality as well as web reality.

E X C E R P T :

Burlingame On-Line...was created for Burlingame residents, people living in surrounding communities, and guests to Burlingame and to the San Francisco Bay Area....

Burtz Virtual Atelier

http://www.ping.ch/burtz/home.html

An atelier is an artist's studio or workshop. Here in Burtz Virtual Atelier, you'll find works such as Science Class, one of 20 artworks selected for the Russian Mir Space Station, or Tojek/Digital Media Man. You can link to International Graffiti; ARt crimes Index; The Weblouvre Museum; and A Proposal for a 13-month Year.

E X C E R P T :

Information connection: I'm your pusher.

BU's Interactive Games

http://www.bu.edu/Games.html

Here's a cool web page of interactive games, especially Hunt the Wumpus, which is a simple but obsessively distracting foray into the wilds of interconnecting cybercaves. You are welcomed to the "Wumpus Caves" and receive simple clues like "I see a light" and "I smell a wumpus." You must shoot arrows and kill the Wumpus before it eats you or you're carried off by bats. Outside of Wumpus, there are many other fun games, and way cool site picks by weird and wacky game master Glenn.

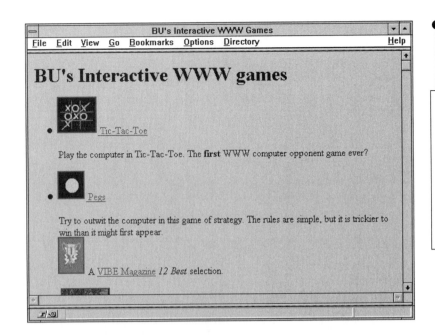

BU's Interactive WWW games

- Tic-Tac-Toe

  Play the computer in Tic-Tac-Toe. The **first** WWW computer opponent game ever?

- Pegs

  Try to outwit the computer in this game of strategy. The rules are simple, but it is trickier to win than it might first appear.

  A VIBE Magazine *12 Best* selection.

Buzz Online

http://www.buzzmag.com/

Buzz Online is all links. It's self-consciously punsterish, coining its own lingo and self-referential nonsense, like Buzzuniverse, Buzz Bets, Buzz Words, and Buzz 100. The chat area hops and bops, especially the Buzz Salon allegedly frequented by Buzz writers and editors. Try the links to fiction and Buzz archives that load quick enough, but there's nothing to look at while you wait.

EXCERPT:

Welcome to Buzz Online. Born and bred in Los Angeles, Buzz Online aims to reflect the singular blend of creativity, sophistication, edginess, and diversity that defines LA today.

Buzz the Fly

http://www.portal.com/~corsa/buzz.html

Buzz the Fly is cute and often sardonic, but sometimes the jokes and gags are way off the mark. Sometimes you feel like you're reading someone else's private inside jokes. Still it's worth a pop. There are new strips every day, previous strips, and jumps to all sorts of interesting sites created by, added to by, and enjoyed by The Rendering Plant Inc., including The Virtual Lightwave Demo, Cybersight, and the Meg Ryan Home Page.

EXCERPT:

Steve Ward lives in Lincoln, Nebraska. Aside from drawing Buzz the Fly, the 40-year-old cartoonist designs and markets Sidekicks pet greeting cards.

BuzzNet

http://www.hooked.net/buzznet/index.html

The Net seems to be made for pop culture. So if you want to know the buzz, check out BuzzNet magazine. There are sections on fiction (Pulp), music (Beats), travel (Action), art (Gallery and Art in Words), and technology.

The Cabinet of Dr. Casey—The Horror Web Page

http://www.cat.pdx.edu/~caseyh/horror/index.html

Even if you're not a big fan of horror movies, you're bound to have a good time at The Cabinet of Dr. Casey. From a graphic standpoint, this self-styled Horror Web Page is a pleasantly gloomy site that looks really sharp if you use an advanced Web browser. And the site is full of interesting information about horror movies and literature. Don't miss the hilarious list of things you SHOULD NOT DO if you find yourself in a horror movie.

EXCERPT:

If you realize that the people in your town/county are having their minds taken over by some strange force, alien or otherwise: DO NOT call the police as they A) are either already taken over themselves and will turn you in or B) will not believe you and laugh at you. Either way, you must handle the problem yourself.

CakeTimes

http://iiif.dgp.utoronto.ca:80/caketimes/

It's intriguing to load up a page with the date, a question mark, and an in-line graphic image of a crouching woman in lingerie with "the magazine that never gets colds and has a great tan" written underneath. The links lead to some hip, retro '50s snappy banter and graphics with only a shadow of wit, eccentricity, and playful teasing. A little more cake and a little less pseudocool fiddle faddle would make this site worth more of your time.

EXCERPT:

Perfect 1985-style power-salmon with post-World-War II hollandaise sauce on cancer-causing radium 1930's plates borne by ponytailed toxic Velveeta-tanned retro ex-biker teens.

California Election Info.

http://www.election.ca.gov/

There's not as much happening here now as there was in December 1994, but this site will be very active again during the next election. Still there's a lot of good information here for those interested in California politics. And there's a multilingual focus that demonstrates that California's government is in touch with its population. The only thing this page lacks is a way for California surfers to register to vote.

California Museum of Photography

http://cmpl.ucr.edu/

This is how a museum page should look: thick and dense. There's enough

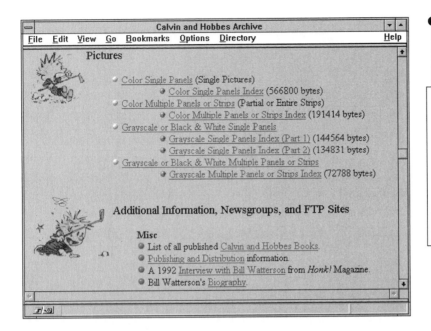

Pictures

- Color Single Panels (Single Pictures)
  - Color Single Panels Index (566800 bytes)
- Color Multiple Panels or Strips (Partial or Entire Strips)
  - Color Multiple Panels or Strips Index (191414 bytes)
- Grayscale or Black & White Single Panels
  - Grayscale Single Panels Index (Part 1) (144564 bytes)
  - Grayscale Single Panels Index (Part 2) (134831 bytes)
- Grayscale or Black & White Multiple Panels or Strips
  - Grayscale Multiple Panels or Strips Index (72788 bytes)

Additional Information, Newsgroups, and FTP Sites

Misc
- List of all published Calvin and Hobbes Books.
- Publishing and Distribution information.
- A 1992 Interview with Bill Watterson from *Honk!* Magazine.
- Bill Watterson's Biography.

here in the links to explore for hours, maybe even days. In addition to features of museum collections and work by students of all ages, this is a site of sophistication, complexity, and thoughtful aesthetics, unlike much of the pseudo-cool web kitsch.

EXCERPT:

We plan to offer a range of historical images and contemporary art works designed specifically for Internet presentation.

Calvin and Hobbes Archives

http://www.eng.hawaii.edu/contribs/justin/archive/index.html

This archival site provides completely cool and comprehensive access to Calvin and Hobbes strips, news, chatter, indexes, archives, and all things related to Calvin and Hobbes. Calvin and Hobbes fans will get a kick out of the design of the page and the interwoven in-line graphics—a really beautiful display. There are thousands of Calvin and Hobbes cartoons and links to all sorts of newsgroups and related pages. This is one of the best sites on the web.

Candela

http://www.digimark.net:80/bluepearl

Many sites on the Web have a white bread feel about them. Here's a site with an Hispanic slant to it. Touted as a place for Latinos to "hang out, create, communicate, and take action," Candela has music reviews and fiction—including its own soap opera—and The Slosh Factory, where you can drink all you want and never have to worry about being caught DWI.

EXCERPT:

Hey Latinos, it is time we create our Hispanic cyberspace station and this is it.

CandyLand

http://www.mcs.com/~candyman/home.html

Though CandyLand embodies the anarchistic spirit of many hackers, surfers, and lurkers on the net, the Candyman himself, the site's host, is rude, offensive, and paranoid. Those qualities alone are not cause for a low rating, but Candyman is not very helpful either. His page is user unfriendly. Still hardcore surfers may choose to tarry a bit here to find hacker tips of the trade, free AOL subscriptions, BBS news, and other information.

Cannes.On.Cyber

http://www.cyber.ad.jp:80/~cannes/

Couldn't get to Cannes for the film festival this year? Don't despair; it's all online at Cannes.On.Cyber. Catch up on the daily news; find out which films won; read articles, movie reviews, and interviews with actors and film makers; crash the parties; hear all the latest gossip about the movie world; and check the festival day's schedules to see what you missed. The next best thing to being there (or maybe even better—it's free!).

EXCERPT:

Look, it's DELON with MONROE!!!

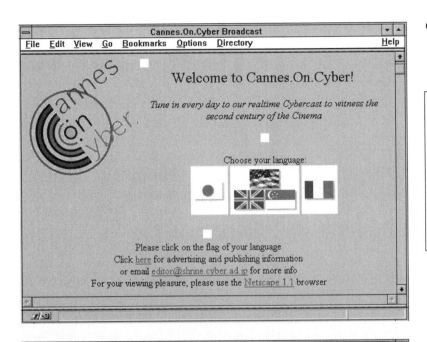

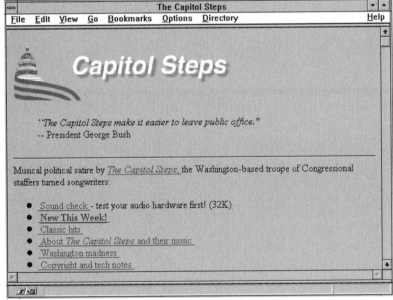

The Capitol Steps

http://pfm.het.brown.edu/people/mende/steps/index.html

Catch up on the doings in Washington, DC as interpreted by The Capitol

Steps, a troupe of current and former congressional staffers who take a musically humorous look at the issues of the day. Check the What's News! section for a weekly news highlight along with a song and links to background information on the news or Washington Madness.

EXCERPT:

The Capitol Steps, the only group in America that attempts to be funnier than the Congress.

Cappella Sistina

http://www.christusrex.org/www1/sistine/0-Tour.html

Part of a project to disseminate images of and information about works of art found in churches, cathedrals, and monasteries around the world, Cappella Sistina features 325 JPEG images of the art of the Sistine Chapel, along with a master plan of the chapel that helps locate each painting. Included in the collection are scenes from the lives of Christ and Moses, portraits of the Popes, and Michelangelo's famous ceiling. Lots of links to resources related to Christianity and Christian art.

EXCERPT:

....The chapel is rectangular in shape and measures 40.93 meters long by

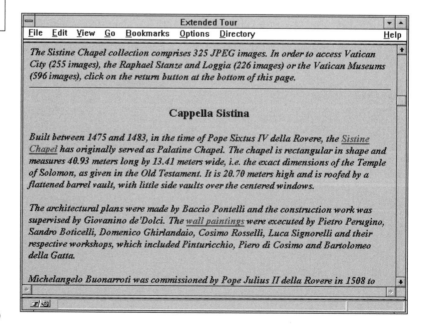

Are you COOL? To be truly COOL, someone ELSE must determine this for you. This is why the COOLBOARD exists. This is a group of people who do nothing but evaluate, cogitate and pontificate on this subject. These are individuals who would have appeared on the lecture circuit at any major university, but were too COOL to show-up. But you can have access to them through this page! You can be in the OFFICIAL Who's COOL registry.

Who's Cool in America Project:
http:/www.getcool.com/~getcool/cool

13.41 meters wide, i.e. the exact dimensions of the Temple of Solomon, as given in the Old Testament.

The Capt. James T. Kirk Sing-a-long Page

http://www.ama.caltech.edu/~mrm/kirk.html

For die-hard William Shatner fans, here is a place to listen to snippets from his one and only album. Also contains information on albums by other Star Trek notables, namely, Mr. Spock, Data, and Uhura.

EXCERPT:

Don't take my word for it: listen to the genius of Kirk for yourself.

Captain Jim: The Online Comic Archives

http://www.mbhs.edu/~dsandler/cj/

Captain Jim is a cult god nee comic book hero nee cartoon character. Set in the really-big-number century, Captain Jim explores the cosmos, fixes his hair, deals with his sidekick (who looks like a Duracell battery with eyeballs) and spoofs his own genre. Try the links to Issues Directory; Latest Issue; Announcements; Help on CJ Nav Buttons; Other CJ Art.

Carlos' Coloring Book

http://robot0.ge.uiuc.edu/~carlosp/color/

This might be fun if you like to color in the lines or if you don't have your own box of crayons, but there really are lots better places to go. Carlos provides six different pictures, and you can color them in with your choice of 10 colors. Not much of a selection, nor much of a site.

Carousel

http://www.access.digex.net/~rburgess

If carousels are your thing, check out this collection of carousel art, history, magic, photos, audio clips, images, and poetry. Link to famous and beloved carousel sites like the Holyoke Merry-Go-Round; The New England Carousel Museum; Washington National Cathedral Carousel; The Herschell Factory Museum; Gustav Dentzel Menagerie Animals; and the National Carousel Association. If you get dizzy, Zoom in on Roller Coasters!

CartooNet

http://www.pavilion.co.uk/cartoonet/

Your gateway to European cartoon arts organizations, festivals, museums, education, and cartoonists, CartooNet features a gallery of cartoons by organizations and individuals (pros and newcomers); cartoon news, including events listings; a marketplace for collectors, publishers, sellers, and others; and the Cartoon Arts Network and other cartoon arts organizations and resources.

"**W**HAT ASPECT OF THE INTERNET CONCERNS YOU MOST? WHY?"

"Commercialization of the web, making digital cash transactions. I think it will ruin the net, possibly bring metered usage, and it will change the atmosphere from that of fun and hip to commercial and shallow." Scott Willsey, scottie@teleport.com

"The great incentive for exploitation conflicting with the desire to keep it free of external controls. You can get and do anything on the net and that's about the most exciting and scariest thing you can have. Internet is society in Anarchy." Shad Augenstein, augenstein.5@osu.edu

CYBER CULTURE Magazine:http://www.cvp.com:80/cyber/

Casey's Top 40

http://www.WorldLink.ca/KOOLCFRA/casey.htm

Casey counts 'em down at KOOL-FM 93.9's Casey's Top 40. Yes, listeners, it's Casey Kasem's list of the 40 most popular songs on the radio this week. If you're expecting to find Casey's facts about the hits or spellbinding stories about the artists and their music, go turn on your low-tech radio. All you'll find here is the list of songs.

Cat Fanciers

http://www.ai.mit.edu/fanciers/fanciers.html

Whether you breed cats or show cats, you'll find something of interest at Cat Fanciers, such as FAQs on cat breeds, colors, and diseases; a glossary; essays; a bibliography; show schedules; online cat clubs; and links to the rec.pets.cats FAQ, veterinary resources, rescue/shelter information, and cat picture sites, feline home pages, and cat-related commercial sites.

The Cathouse Archives, LTD.

http://cathouse.org

Cathouse is the home of the alt.folklore.urban archive as well as the rec.autos.sport.NASCAR image archive. Cathouse also brings you one-stop shopping for other essentials like British Comedy on the Internet and John Switzer's Rush Limbaugh Radio Show Summaries. Throw in some jokes and you have it made. Don't forget to link to Legends; British Comedy; NASCAR; Literature; Rush Limbaugh; Movies; Humor; and FTP Archives.

EXCERPT:

The Cathouse.org archives, the best "waste-of-time" site on the Internet.

The cathouse.org Urban Legends Archive

http://cathouse.org/UrbanLegends/

Has cat food really been relabeled and sold as tuna? Has anyone ever really been poisoned by a poinsettia? Do alligators really live in the New York City subway tunnels? Get the real truth about these and lots of other urban myths and folktales at the Urban Legends Archive. Amaze your friends—tell them the real story about Walt Disney's frozen head....(Note: This site was heavily under construction at the time of this writing, hence the low rating. Once completed, this should be a cool site.)

EXCERPT:

Contained here are debunkings of common urban legends and information pertaining to the people and other sundry items that are the entity AFU.

Cave Paintings at Vallon-Pont-d'Arc

http://dmf.culture.fr/culture/gvpda-en.htm

Always wanted to see some Paleolithic cave paintings but didn't have a time machine or a ticket to France? Here's the next best thing. Thanks to the French Ministry of Culture, photographs (with supporting text) of cave paintings discovered in December 1994 are available to anyone with access to the Web.

EXCERPT:

...The cavern also harbours the remains of around a hundred bears, either in their hibernating places or in an alternative position....

CBS Eye on the Net

http://www.cbs.com

If you want to keep your eye on what's happening at CBS, this is the site. You can check out the new seasonal schedule, read the viewing guide for the week, catch the story of the day from CBS News, and even order some CBS souvenirs. How about this? Links to CBS Sports; Late Show with David Letterman; Late Late Show with Tom Snyder; Black Rock; Remotes; Eyewear; CBS News.

EXCERPT:

Hey, do you want to get more information about CBS and its programs, participate in interactive tests, and receive a 10% discount on your first purchase at the CBS Store?

CBS News Up To The Minute

http://adware.com/uttm/welcome.html

Missed last night's newscasts? Check out UTTMlink, CBS News Up to the Minute online, for overnight news coverage, the latest Internet and CD-ROM developments, movie reviews, women's health reports, parenting tips, and what's up in space. Use the Reporter's Resource Shelf and see how CBS Newspath operates. You can also check '95 hurricane information.

EXCERPT:

Now UTTMlink gives you a second chance to hear selected interviews and features in RealAudio. If you missed it last night, visit our new Second Chance Page.

CDnow!

http://cdnow.com/

CDnow!, the Internet music store par excellence, has almost every album made in the U.S. You can search the store by composer, title of the album or composition, performer, conductor, record label, primary instrument, genre, or any or all of the above. Everything's a lot cheaper than at your local record store because, as CDnow! says, it doesn't have to pay for floor space. And the maximum total shipping and handling for any U.S. order is $4.94, no matter how many items are in your order.

Celebrity Snack Palace

http://www.interport.net/~krayn/

Having a rough day? Want to revel in some surliness? Surf over to the Celebrity Snack Palace and join an ego trip of rants and rages. Find out the song list for a celebrity's last Valentine party or listen to a celebrity answering machine message. Some of the language is a bit harsh and may be offensive so proceed with caution. Netscape (ver 1.1) and a 14.4 modem recommended.

EXCERPT:

There ain't no celebrities, the snacks ain't fresh, and it sure ain't no palace.

Charlie's Place

http://www.tardis.ed.ac.uk/~charlie/index.html

The main attraction at Charlie's Place is Charlie's Virtual Anthology. Here you'll find many of Charles Stross' science fiction stories previously published in various magazines and anthologies as well as links to Fiction; Nonfiction; Writing; and Miscelanea.

EXCERPT:

I've sold a fair number of science fiction stories to various magazines and anthologies. As I don't seem likely to sell a collection in the near future, given the state of the market, I'm putting some of them online.

Chesley Bonestell Art Gallery

http://www.secapl.com/bonestell/Top.html

The space-scene art of Chesley Bonestell has appeared in movies of the '50s; major publications such as *Life*, *Scientific American*, and *Astounding Science Fiction*; documentaries such as "The Conquest of Space" and "Beyond Jupiter," and now resides in an interactive art gallery on the World Wide Web. You'll also find a biography of Bonestell and facts about each of his space-scene paintings.

EXCERPT:

The astronomical artist and illustrator, Chesley Bonestell, is well known for his paintings of space scenes. His paintings were more than works of art for they changed the future of space exploration.

63

Chicago Mosaic

http://www.ci.chi.il.us/

The Windy City takes to the Net in Chicago Mosaic, a collection of information about Chicago events, landmarks, neighborhoods, architecture, museums, shopping, restaurants, sports, festivals, travel and tourist stuff, community policing, city services, news from the Mayor's office, and even how to establish a home business in Chicago.

EXCERPT:

The project [Chicago Mosaic] is nourished by a mutual belief that these technologies hold the potential to remove many of the barriers to communication that have been historically associated with time, space, language, and physical ability....

Chile-Heads Home Page

http://www.netimages.com/~chile

Put some spice in your life. Jump over to the Chile-Heads home page and

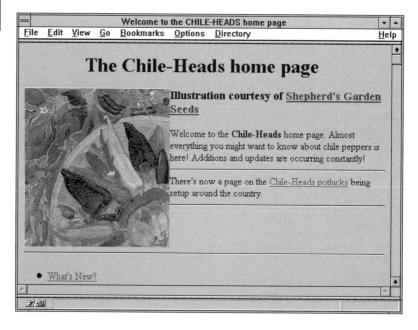

find out how to eat, grow, harvest, and preserve those spicy, little peppers. Hot links to Access the Chile-Heads Archives; Identify that Unknown Chile; Eating, Recipes, Restaurants, and Festivals; Growing, Harvesting, and Preserving peppers; Science, Botany, and Chemistry; and Other Hot Topics.

EXCERPT:

Almost everything you might want to know about chile peppers is here!

Christmas in New York

http://www.mediabridge.com/nyc/xmas/

Can't get enough of a good thing? A visit to Christmas in New York will thrill you year-round with the sights of the Christmas season. Photos highlight the bright lights and spirit of the holidays. Also links up to The Paperless Guide to New York City—NYC Current Events for a general update on what's happening in the Big Apple.

EXCERPT:

For one short month, New York City becomes a pleasant and cheerful place where a higher spirit makes New Yorkers smile.

Chrysler Technology Center Tour

http://www.chryslercorp.com/

In the words of your virtual guide on this tour of Chrysler Corporation's cyberspace headquarters, "If you want to see technology at its best, you've come to the right place, Guest. We've got five of the industries' most advanced testing centers. Not to mention three stunning concept cars. Plus, we can show you how we're taking care of the environment with our alternative fuel ideas and recycling programs...."

EXCERPT:

Get prepared to experience what many consider to be the most technologically advanced vertical development operation in the world....

A Nexis search of newspapers, magazines and television transcripts turned up 1,205 mentions of cyber in the month of January, up from 464 the previous January and 167 in January 1993.

Philip Elmer-DeWitt, in *Time*

Church of SPAM

http://www.primenet.com/~swiggy/

Read the Books of SPAM, sing the Hymns of SPAM, obey the Ten SPA-Mandments, memorize the Tenets of the Church of SPAM, and perhaps you will ascend to SPAM heaven. If your soul is in need of uplifting, view the sacred SPAM cartoons. And if you're new to the Church, be sure to read the FAQ.

EXCERPT:

Here at the Church of SPAM we care about your immortal soul... and so that your survivors cannot say we are out to take advantage of you, we recommend that you read our Disclaimer.

CIA Home Page

http://www.odci.gov/

Gather some intelligence of your own at the CIA Home page. This site gives you historical background on the CIA, as well as press releases, statements, testimony, and speeches. You can also find a list of CIA publications and link up to the CIA On-Line Career Center, if you're looking for a new career.

EXCERPT:

Much of the intelligence we produce is based on openly available information such as that which is carried on the Internet.

CineMaven Online

http://useattle.uspan.com/maven/

Can't decide which movie to see tonight or which video to rent? Check CineMaven's movie and video reviews. And if you happen to live in the Seattle/Tacoma area, you can even find out where your chosen movie is playing and the show times. But if you'd rather read instead, CineMaven has some articles on the movie biz and a list of Top 10 movies, arranged by year.

EXCERPT:

As a syndicated movie reviewer, Doug has been heard on the radio in the Seattle area for several years. His call-in shows have been a popular forum for movie fans....

City of Bits

http://www-mitpress.mit.edu/City_of_Bits

This book is about the future, so if you plan to be here in 20 years, spend a

little while now exploring the City of Bits. Someday you'll be living in it. One of the most interesting features of City of Bits is the Reader's Choice Web Sites, where visitors may create links from each featured chapter of the book to sites they feel are relevant.

Clay Shirkey's Home Page

http://www.panix.com/~clays/

Clay Shirkey is the author of "Voices from the Net" and an HTML enthusiast. This page is stocked with as much HTML information as Shirkey can muster and excerpts of his writing, as well as a list of Clay's 5 favorite HTML resources. The links go to My Current Web Projects; HTML Information List; Home Page Guides; URL Info; HTML Forms; Information for Information Providers.

EXCERPT:

If I were stranded on a desert island with 5 URLs, this is what they would be...

Climbing Archive

http://www.dtek.chalmers.se/Climbing/index.html

Before you head up that mountain pass, check out the Climbing Archive for guidebooks, songs to climb by, equipment, and techniques, as well as *Ravage Climbing Magazine*. Link to Guidebooks; Climbing Directory; Climbing Stories; Climbing Songs and Poems; Commercial Information; Hardware; Climbing Pictures; Technique & Training; *Ravage Climbing Magazine*.

EXCERPT:

We cater to both trads and rads, so you will probably find what you're looking for.

Codpiece International

http://www.teleport.com/~codpiece/

This is the home of Codpiece International, and we ain't talking fish here.

For those in the dark, a codpiece is a medieval article of men's clothing. As to its use and appearance, you'll have to visit the site or check the links to What Is New at Codpiece International; What Is a Codpiece; What Is the "Bring Back the Codpiece" Campaign; What Is Codpiece International; The Codpiece International Catalog; What Is the Codpiece Resurrection Society; Codpiece-Related Items on the Web.

EXCERPT:

Indulge your bulge.

Coghead Corner

http://www.teleport.com/~bazzle/coghead.shtml

Lots of stuff here for mountain-biking friends and fans, including trail guides (some with photos and maps), the IMBA rules of the trail, an explanation of the trail-rating system, a stolen- bike database, a directory of bikes-for-rent shops in the Portland, Oregon, area, the weather forecast for Portland, and links to mountain-biking organizations and other resources for cyclists.

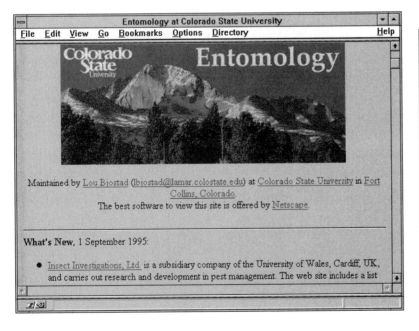

EXCERPT:

Located in the hills of NW Portland, Forest Park is undoubtedly the city's coolest park....

Collection of 3D Pictures

http://fmechds01.tu-graz.ac.at/heidrun/3d/3dpic2.html

This site offers GIF format graphics files for viewing and/or downloading as well as free software for creating 3-D images in DOS or Windows. Each file presents a full-color 3-D image. The pictures are presented without descriptions, but there is an option to preview a smaller image prior to loading the complete file.

Colorado State University Entomology

http://www.colostate.edu/Depts/Entomology/ent.html

There are bugs in every computer system, but the ones at Colorado State shouldn't crash your system. This site gives you the lowdown on the CSU Entomology Department, as well as information of interest to entomologists everywhere. You can find images, job listings, publications, upcoming meetings, and links to other sites like Buzz the Fly, An Entomological Comic; CSU Entomology; The Center for Insect Science Newsletter; and Upcoming Events in Entomology.

Comedy Central's Totally Free Web Site

http://www.comcentral.com/

Designing a homepage is easy; comedy is hard. If you don't believe it, Comedy Central's Totally Free Web Site will prove it to you. You'll see some intriguingly garish graphics with the assistance of an advanced browser. But you'll also have to slog through some utterly unfunny efforts at "hip, cutting-edge humor." You're better off watching a Monty Python rerun.

Comic Relief

http://www.ws.pipex.com/comic.relief/

Comic Relief is a British web site brought to you by the organization whose goal is to generate laughs for a worthy cause. Comic Relief helps poverty-stricken people in Africa and the United Kingdom by arranging comedy fundraisers. The organization's home page provides a tasteful combination of serious information with amusing suggestions for ways you can sponsor a Comic Relief fundraiser.

EXCERPT:

The cash you earn for Comic Relief pays for 100's of brilliant projects. None of the money you raise, not one penny, is spent on our fundraising costs—every single p. goes to work, making a difference to some of the poorest people in both Africa and the UK.

The Comic Strip

http://www.unitedmedia.com/comics/

United Media, which syndicates many of America's best newspaper comic strips, has put together an excellent web site for comic strip fans. Folks in search of a chuckle will find many popular daily strips at the Comic Strip site, while serious fans will find vast amounts of background information about their favorite comics.

EXCERPT:

From Dilbert's '90's style satire to the timeless charm of the Peanuts gang to Steve Benson's Pulitzer Prize-winning editorial perspective, unitedmedia.com is home to the Web's largest and most comprehensive collection of contemporary comic art.

Comics n' stuff

http://www.phlab.missouri.edu/~c617145/comix.html

Biff! Bop! Ah, the sounds of superheroes. You can find them along with a cast of thousands (or at least a whole bunch) of comic characters at this site. Comics 'n Stuff has links to lots of online comics, as well as comics related stuff, like the Calvin & Hobbes web page, and a chat room. The index is searchable by title so if you're looking for someone special, you don't have to wade through hundreds of entries.

Computer Music Journal

http://mitpress.mit.edu:/jrnls-catalog/comp-music.html

Good place to learn about the skills and technologies of digital sound and the musical applications of computers. The site gives you the abstracts and index of the latest issue, as well as the archives of past articles and table of contents. You can even sample some computer music sounds and check out software.

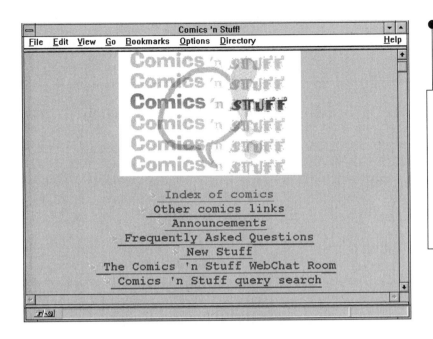

EXCERPT:

A must for the serious computer music researcher.

Comstock Web Site

http://www.com-stock.com/dave

Excitement is building as the 1996 Summer Olympics draws closer. This web site provides Atlanta Olympic information resources, training sites and venues, and links to other Olympic sites. You can even check out the rental market around Atlanta. Athletes and spectators can link to 1996 Centennial Olympic Games Hotlist; Corporate Sponsors with 1996 Olympic Web Pages; Atlanta Olympic Information Resources; Outstanding Homes for Rent; Olympic Venues and Training Sites Outside of Atlanta; Olympic Pins and tons more.

EXCERPT:

Atlanta...Come celebrate our dream.

Conde Nast Traveler

http://www.cntraveler.com/

This lively travel information web site continues the tradition of serious, hard-hitting journalism begun by the print version of *Conde Nast Traveler*. You'll see gorgeous pictures of exotic locations, as well as editorials warning against unsafe ferryboats. Even the *Conde Nast Traveler*'s listing of other travel-related web sites doesn't just provide you with online addresses—they also tell you what they like or dislike about the other sites.

EXCERPT:

It's a new concept built on the sound principles behind *Conde Nast Traveler*, the magazine. That is to say, it's a source of worldly, opinionated travel advice, albeit in a wholly new, constantly updated, infinitely interactive form.

Condom Country

http://www/ag/com/Condom/Country

The name of this web page pretty much speaks for itself. You can browse the catalog and order merchandise on-line, but this is not just a catalog site. You'll also find government information on practicing safe sex, instructions on how to use a condom, and even a history of the condom. There are also links to related sites. The only problem with this site, ironically, is that it's often down.

EXCERPT:

Howdy pardners, and welcome to Condom Country, home to the largest assortment of condoms and other below-the-belt-buck'l items on the Web.

The Confession Booth

http://anther.learning.cs.cum.edu/priest.html

Now you can relieve your guilt without even going to church. Simply fill in the form provided by the digital priest at the Confession Booth and submit.

Electronic democracy is far from perfectly democratic, given the high relative cost of computer equipment, phone service and information fees. Recent demographic surveys of the Internet reveal an electronic citizenry that is predominantly white, male, educated and well to do. But there are countless resources available to those who want to make the effort to keep tabs on the new Congress, a new Governor or a new City Council. Computer-based communications allow individuals and grassroots activist groups to be almost as politically connected as lobbyists and political action committees.

Peter H. Lewis, in *The New York Times*

Your penance will be posted along with your confession on the Scroll of Sin. If you're feeling especially pious, check out the links to Barrels Full and Tankfuls of Sins.

EXCERPT:

Bringing the net to its knees since 1994.

The Connected Traveler

http://www.well.com/user/wldtrvlr/

Visit the sights and sounds of exotic places through the eyes of Russell Johnson and his traveling friends. Well worth the visit just to read the list of fractured English signs from around the world. Links travel to Dispatch from the Borneo Underground; Jan's Nightmare; Poles Apart, Wherein Georgia Hesse Comes Out on Top; J-Michel Cousteau on Responsible Tourism; and more.

EXCERPT:

Take a look and listen to Georgia Hesse as she makes her assault—scotch and snowda in hand—on the North Pole.

The Conservative Link

http://www.moscow.com/~bmdesign/TCL/TCLintro.html

This home page is a well-designed, entertaining hangout for political conservatives. The Conservative Link will guide you to right-of-center resources all over the Internet, including links to popular conservative talk-radio hosts. It also provides links to some liberal homepages, just to be fair.

EXCERPT:

If you are a conservative American who is tired of the status quo...if you are sick of being categorized as a mind-numbed dittohead robot...if you want to back up your political beliefs with facts...then you will enjoy The Conservative Link.

The Contest Catalogue

http://www.catalogue.com/contest

Are you still waiting for Ed McMahon to come to your door, check in hand? Why not try some other contests while you wait. Though the stakes aren't generally quite so high, you can still have some fun. The contests are broken down by type, so if you're a trivia buff, you can go right to Trivia. Other game links include Games; Scavenging; Creativity; Raffles; and Traditional.

EXCERPT:

We at catalogue.com, incorporated are keeping an up-to-date list of all the contests, sweepstakes, raffles, and giveaways we can find on the Web.

Contours of the Mind

http://online.anu.edu.au/ITA/ACAT/contours/contours.html

This site is the companion to an exhibit held in Australia in July 1994 and aims to forge links between computer music and computer animation. Look for a blend of visual art, science, and music all related to the themes of fractals, feedback, and chaos. You can link to Fractals in Nature; Cellular Automata; Synthetic Fractals; Strange Attractors; and Chaotic Dynamics.

EXCERPT:

Contours of the Mind will be a celebration of fractals, feedback, and chaos, and a unique blend of visual art, science, and music.

Cool Word of the Day

http://www.dsu.edu/projects/word_of_day/word.html

Expand your vocabulary. Every day you'll find a new word like "entomostracan," "marsupial," and "cynosure." You can submit words for possible inclusion and review past Words of the Day if you are really ambitious. If you're studying for SATs, this is an easy way to start.

EXCERPT:

We encourage you to submit a cool word!

Covered Bridges

http://william-king.www.drexel.edu/top/bridge/CB1.html

People who enjoyed *The Bridges of Madison County* might want to visit this homepage dedicated to covered bridges. But they probably won't visit twice. This overly sentimental web site, which is supposed to evoke the good ol' days, includes plenty of photos, but they're often quite big and take long time to download. Tourists might profit from the site's list of covered bridges, but the overall design and concept is pretty dull.

EXCERPT:

Covered bridges symbolize small-town America. Something from the nineteenth century, a little archaic and strange to nineteen-nineties eyes, picturesque and sentimental, "kissing bridges" recall a time when life was simpler and closer to the land—if only in our dreams.

Crash Site

http://bazaar.com:80/Crash/

If you need to go the extreme, visit the Crash Site, home to extreme music. Find information about groups like Femme Fury or The Watts Prophets, along with soundtracks from the likes of Lollapalooza. There's also art and literature for the savage at heart. Links to other extremes like Music; Politix; Art Sabotage; Snowboarding Zombies; and Crass Commercialism.

EXCERPT:

The world of unhindered voyeuristic desire. Where the idea becomes image and the real is imaginary.

Crayola

http://www.crayola.com/crayola/

You can almost smell that waxy aroma when you visit the Crayola web page. Of course Crayola just isn't crayons anymore, and Binney & Smith

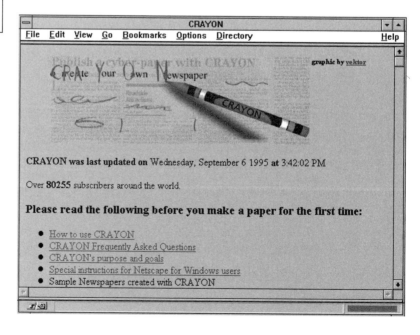

introduce you to their whole product line. But this site is more than a big commercial. You can learn how crayons are made, get a history of Crayola, and even learn how to get those paint stains out of your shirt. Colorful links to Colorful News; Crayola Trivia; Fun Stuff from Crayola; Stain Removal Tips; and Welcome to Crayola.

EXCERPT:

While you are here, you'll find lots of fun, colorful, and useful things to see and do.

CRAYON

http://www.eg.bucknell.edu/~boulter/crayon/

An innovative and interactive homepage, CRAYON gives you the tools to assemble your own online newspaper by using excerpts from news sites throughout the Internet. For instance, you can pick world news from the *London Daily Telegraph*, business news from the *San Francisco Chronicle*, and sports from ESPN, then dump it all into one neatly organized file to read at your leisure. CRAYON is a great idea—as amusing as it is useful.

The Creative Internet

http://www.galcit.caltech.edu/~ta/creative.html

This self-proclaimed interactive playground features the Asylum, a space for expressing your opinions in a variety of outlets, as well as The Mechanical Bull, a free-for-all post-your-link-here kind of place. The Creative Internet lets you be just that, creative. Also contains a dandy Websurfer's Handbook that will help you to at least talk the talk, and a number of fun links to Insomnia Records Catalog; and Universal cHANnEL8.

EXCERPT:

Bearing the demented seal of approval.

Crossing the Line

http://hamp.hampshire.edu/~jtsF93

Crossing the Line is proof positive that the enterprising spirit is alive and well on the Internet. The homepage belongs to a gifted computer artist, who shows off his work in hopes of landing a job when he graduates from college in 1997. He should have no trouble. This site is crammed with beautiful images that download relatively fast. Web-surfers in need of a break will find some nice eye candy here.

EXCERPT:

Here is an image of a brain that I was doing for a job that I had, but it turned out that the client didn't need a brain, he already had one. So I took the brain I spent a week and a half on and put it on a silly background and then on my homepage. So I hope you like it.

Crossroads

http://info.acm.org/crossroads/

Want to get the skinny on what the next generation of computer geniuses are talking about? Crossroads is the site for you. It's an online magazine produced by a leading society of computer professionals, and it features work by computer science students. Generally, the web site has an appealing, fresh design, but the articles tend to be a bit pedestrian.

EXCERPT:

Crossroads is primarily an educational magazine. We strive to bring our readers articles that will pique their interest in a wide variety of computer-related areas. Columns representing the diverse opinions of our readership; reviews of books, software, and conferences; and articles designed to assist students in making educational and career decisions appear in every issue.

CRS4 Animation Gallery

http://www.crs4.it:80/Animate/

This site would be very cool if it ran in Mosaic. But it only runs in Netscape. As is, there's some amazing stuff here, but only people with Netscape can see it. CRS4 is into applied mathematics, parallel computing, scientific visualization, and lots more. It jumps to whole worlds of science for people with the right browser program.

CTHEORY

http://english-server.hss.cmu.edu/ctheory/ctheory.html

An online journal, CTHEORY is full of scholarly musings a wide range of topics from technology to philosophy to culture and the media. Remarkably, quite a few of the articles are not abstruse or technical so they may be read and enjoyed by serious laypeople. Don't look for pretty pictures here—just challenging ideas.

EXCERPT:

CTHEORY is an international, electronic review of books on theory, technology and culture. Sponsored by the Canadian Journal of Political and Social Theory, reviews are posted periodically of key books in contemporary discourse as well as theorisations of major "event-scenes" in the mediascape.

Cults: The A-Z Index

http://www.observer.co.uk/a-z-cults/index.html

This site explores the decline of western civilization as evidenced by the rise in cults. This is a comprehensive, in-depth explanation of cults and their beliefs, from the Branch Davidians to the Hare Krishnas, voodoo groups, and the Order of the Solar Temple. The writings seems fairly objective.

EXCERPT:

...[These groups] symbolize, in the most dramatic fashion, an abiding hunger for extreme belief in an unbelieving world.

Cupid's Cove

http://www.NeoSoft.com:80/citylink/cupid/default.html

Send your valentine some cyberlove all year round. Just pop over to Cupid's Cove and see what he has to offer for your sweetheart. You'll find coupons, online valentines, and even recipes for a special treat. If you don't have a valentine, maybe you can find one in the personals. Don't spend too much time at the kissing booth. Surf the sweet links to Internet Valentine's Day Coupons; An Online Valentine; and Virtual Tunnel of Love.

EXCERPT:

Prepare to fall in love and be romanced.

The Cute Kids Page

http://www.prgone.com/cutekids/

Parents will get a kick out of this one. The Cute Kids Page features amusing stories about children sent in by parents and relatives. After you've finished laughing, you can submit a story about your own child. The web site is attractive, easy to use, and quick to download—a charming place to visit.

EXCERPT:

Our three-year-old had a little trouble lately controlling her temper. Trying to stop her from hitting her older brother, I asked her why she did that. She replied, "because he makes my hands mad!"

Cyber Culture

http://cvp.onramp.net:80/cyber/

Cyber Culture is an online magazine that features computer-related fiction and essays. A web design company created the web site, so it comes as no surprise that the graphics are visually stunning. However, the written material, while mildly entertaining, isn't worth too much of your online time.

EXCERPT:

Cyber Culture is about Cyberspace and Netizens all around the world. We seek out strange new pages and digital civilizations...to boldly go where no one has gone before! Actually, it's a magazine about—nothing. We have no focus, nor do we want one. A focus means we limit what we care about, what we're interested in and what you'll see. We're unlimited, so to speak.

Cyber Publishing Japan

http://www/toppan.co.jp

If you want to see what cyberpublishing can do for your company, check out this site. TOPPAN Printing shows you some of their best efforts for companies like Honda Communication Network, Okamura Corporation, and Hotel New Otani Co., Ltd. Basically an online advertisement for their services, and a nice look at how to set up company web pages.

Cyberboarder!

http://www.cyberboarder.com/

Cyberboarder! is a snazzy, adventure-evoking web site that caters to surfers, snowboarders, and sailboarders. This all-purpose homepage features an attractive design and runs at a swift pace; what's more, there are plenty of good articles and stories here to entertain boarding enthusiasts. Even if you're not a skilled in the art of boarding, Cyberboarder! is worth a look-see.

EXCERPT:

Jackson Hole, Wyoming. Friday, 7:00 a.m. The temperature is already 40 degrees. You look out your bedroom window at cobalt blue skies and the red gridwork of the gondola pylons framed by the rising gray and white snow-covered Tetons. Yes! A truly awesome day and nothing to do but play in the snow!

CyberCafe

http://www.cybercafe.org/cybercafe

If you want a place to uphold your dignity and creativity, this is the one. CyberCafe gives you a chance to create, behave and express yourself in an assortment of mediums such as radio, TV, telephones, fax, and their own bbs. No real content but a chance to explore the unusual.

EXCERPT:

CyberCafe aims to promote/create spaces/situations in which people can create/behave/express/experience in ways unavailable in currently existing places.

Cybergrrl

http://www.cybergrrl.com

First there were Valley Girls. Then there were Riot grrrls. Now there are Cybergrrls. Although this self-proclaimed Cybergrrl includes a lot of her own stuff (articles, favorite things, and advice) you'll also find some great resources on dealing with domestic violence and other important grrl issues. Good links to Finding Your Way; Places to Go; People to See; Things to Read; and Good Causes/Important Stuff.

EXCERPT:

Don't forget to surf with Cybergrrl.

Cyberia

http://houston.infohwy.com/index.htm

Cyberia is an excellent place to begin an evening of Web-surfing, especially if you're an Internet newbie who's not sure where to visit first. This web site features links to hundreds of other homepages with information on just about every topic you can think of. Cyberia does a commendable job of bringing the links together in one place and organizing them so that they're easy to find and use.

Cybertimes

http://cybertimes.com/Welcome.html

A feature of Cybertimes Magazine, this site pitches products from their catalog, movies from New Line Cinema, like "Dumb and Dumber," and artists from Rhino Records. Lots of links.

Cybertown

http://www.cybertown.com/cybertown/

Cybertown, a content-rich and multi-purpose web site, was created by an innovative Internet marketing firm. The concept is to imitate a Anytown, USA, in cyberspace. There's a shopping mall, a nightclub, a town newspaper—even a seedy, dangerous part of town. Throughout Cybertown there are links to numerous other interesting web sites. The impressive use of graphics is offset by some design mistakes—for example, reaching some "neighborhoods" requires paging through three or four unnecessary links.

EXCERPT:

The purpose of Cybertown is to create a virtual community where people can have fun, be entertained, learn things and explore the best of the Earth Internet.

Cyberwest Magazine

http://gemini.netway.net:80/cyberwest

The American West...that romanticized place of adventures. Explore the pages of *Cyberwest Magazine*. You can read the news of the West, see what events are coming up, view some great scenery, or read up on some of the places to visit. Go West with links to News West; Events West; Digital West; Reckoning; and Cyberwest.

EXCERPT:

Don't mind the neighbors, but never trust a city slicker.

The Cyrano Server

http://www.nando.net/toys/cyrano.html

Are you at a loss to describe the depth of your love for your sweetheart? Fear not, Cyrano will rescue you. If you've got a forms-capable browser, all you have to do is submit some vital information about your sweetie, and Cyrano will respond with an eloquent love letter. Then you can mail it off to your beloved and pretend that you wrote it, just like in the classic play *Cyrano de Bergerac*.

EXCERPT:

Just fill out the following form and submit it to Cyrano. Cyrano will present you with the perfect letter for your beloved. Download it and mail it to them, or use the "mail" function of your browser to send off your electronic serenade. Your beloved will be swept away with romance, laughter, or confusion.

Dahlin Smith White

http://www.dsw.com/home.htm

Dahlin Smith White is an advertising agency specializing in the technology industry. It also provide an Internet presence for its clients. For the casual user, White provides a slightly zany forum for creativity: a doodle pad. It is possible to download a form to doodle on and then return it via e-mail. It's different!

EXCERPT:

At DSW, we believe you can't sell technology if you don't understand it. That's why everyone who works at DSW uses a computer (or two). In fact, we have more computers than employees.

Daily Work by an Ordinary News Photographer

http://www.metronet.com/~arose/today/workhome.html

Want to know what it's like being a newspaper photographer? Check out Allen Rose's site. Each day, Allen posts the photos which he has submitted to the news desk of the *Fort Worth Star-Telegram*. Why? Well, to generate feedback and maybe get some feedback on how he handled an assignment. He also keeps his photo portfolio and resume available, just in case.

EXCERPT:

I'm still trying to become the best photographer I can, and all viewpoints are valid and requested.

There are concerns that any Internet voting effort won't really track the voice of the people.

"The demographics of the Internet are particularly skewed in the case of gender, education, etc.," said Scott Fritchie, technical coordinator for the Minnesota Electronic Democracy Project, a volunteer group exploring Internet issues.

But, said Stanton McCandlish, online services manager for the Washington-based Electronic Frontier Foundation, "The real potential here is for grassroots organization and information dissemination."

Debra Aho Williamson, *Advertising Age,* June 26, 1995.

DansWORLD Skateboarding

http://web.cps.msu.edu/~dunhamda/dw/dansworld.html

Watch out, here come the skateboarders. Whether you're new to the sport, making a comeback, or a veteran, here's the place to find all sorts of skateboarding info. There are photos, merchandise, articles, even a history of skateboarding. Skate over to other links like Multimedia Features; The Industry Section; Articles; and Other Stuff.

Dark Planet

http://nickel.ucs.indiana.edu/~lusnyde/cover.html

There wasn't a whole lot to see at Dark Planet—a new science fiction 'zine—during a recent visit. Some eye-catching homepage graphics indicate that this web site has a promising future, but for now there are only a few stories to tantalize you. Dark Planet may be worth another visit, once the planned further expansion takes place.

EXCERPT:

I started this [home page] to test the "if you build it, they will come" philosophy, and you, too, can be a part of the experiment! If you're a writer, read the guidelines below and send me your stuff. If you're a reader, send me e-mail and tell me what you'd like to see here. Once I've amassed enough submissions I plan to release a new version of this every 1-2 months.

The Dark Side

http://www.dnx.com/vamp/

An O.K. home page that features links to many gothic web resources; the Siouxsie and the Banshees Home Page; some decent photo art; and to an eclectic set of 'zines on topics like art and poetry, computer hacking, and cyberpunk. Too bad the author doesn't identify himself/herself somewhere in here.

EXCERPT:

...This area is simply my area to experiment with HTML and my hobbies and interests. Then I found it actually got me a job! ...

Darpan

http://www.ncsa.uiuc.edu/People/pmishra/darpan

India. The word itself evokes exotic images. Darpan is published by students at the University of Illinois at Urbana-Champaign, and they devote their online magazine to visual and literary reflections on India. Check the links to Editorial; Prose; Poetry; Graphics; Credits; and Copyright.

EXCERPT:

We have tried to make Darpan a visual and literary treat.

Daytona Beach - Spring Break '95

http://www.america.com:80/mall/store/springbreak.html

Essentially an online advertisement for Daytona Beach, this site provides a mild amount of information and directory assistance for the area. A single home page offers information about concerts, night clubs, health clubs, Sports Illustrated Beach Club, accommodations, group travel, contact information, weather, and the obligatory FAQ list. Since the break is over, much of the information is dated.

DealerNet—The Virtual Showroom

http://www.dealernet.com

Cars? We got 'em. Along with boats, and RVs. Consumers can find information on new and used cars, get an online insurance quote, even sell your own car. Cool links to drive around to Dealers; Makes and Models; Used Cars; Special Interest Automobiles; and Virtual Consignment. Also view video footage of current models.

EXCERPT:

Find a dealer, make a service appointment, order a part, find out how to get there from here or ask a question.

Deep Style

http://zipzap.com/deepstyl/cover.html

If you're into dense philosophical ruminations and slice-of-life essays, then this online 'zine is just right for you. Pseudo-polemical in tone, Deep Style contains some interesting first-person articles—a woman recalling her abortion, a man describes his battle with a mugger—but there's nothing else especially memorable here.

EXCERPT:

Deep Style is not scientific. We do not specialize in talking about society. Like a God, society cannot be discussed well, because it is not a thing, but a

Online demographics (average age: 39) favor music over movies, as does bandwidth (at least for now).

Jeff Jensen, in *Advertising Age*

motion. Society figures in literature as the castrate's amnesiac memory of his lost organ: the discreet object studied by scientists, the fiction that artists pretend to represent.

DejaNews Research Service

http://www.dejanews.com

It's big, it's fast, it gets results. It's DejaNews, your tool for slogging through mountains of information from the largest collection of indexed Usenet archives. Now you can make a query and find that recipe for hot pepper jelly you saw months ago on the chile pepper newsgroup. So verify your deja vu with DejaNews.

EXCERPT:

The information is out there—now there's a way to find it.

The Den of Chaos

http://ucsu.colorado.edu/~anschutz/music.html

The Den of Chaos provides you with an eclectic collection of hypertext links to such topics as feminism, German culture, rock music, and humor. These are all sites that you can through other web searching techniques, but some users will find a handy shortcut in the links organized at The Den of Chaos.

EXCERPT:

You have just entered the Den of Chaos, where you can find entertainment, enlightenment, and adventure.

Andrew H. Denton Web Archive

http://www.eunet.ch/People/ahd/home.html

Andrew Denton presents his renderings in what he calls Engulf and Devour. Here you'll find images of aliens, dragons, dinosaurs, and aquatic things. You can also read what his friends think about the artist who creates his Internet art near Santa Cruz, California.

EXCERPT:

After years of releasing my artwork on the Net, I've been happily rendering away in my little house south of Santa Cruz, California.

Destination: Unknown!

http://www.vnet.net/dest/destabo.html

Destination: Unknown! is another web site that lists links to other interesting homepages on the World Wide Web. Logically arranged and easy to use, the opening page promises pointers to web sites on art, computing, science, news, and government, among other things. As it turns out, however, Destination: Unknown! is very poorly maintained. You'll find lots of bad links and pointers to sites that no longer exist.

EXCERPT:

Welcome to Destination: Unknown! This WWW site was founded to take you to some of the BEST destinations on the Net!

Detroit News Direct

http://detnews.com

Now you don't even have to send the dog out to bring in your newspaper. Just fire up your modem, pour that first cup of coffee, and check out the *Detroit News*. It's got all your standard newspaper fare: news, weather, and lottery numbers.   Just click and you're there. No more ink-stained hands! Link to Horoscope; Notes from the Net; Death Notices; Cyberia; Editorials; and Outside Interests.

EXCERPT:

Delivers the news you want to your e-mailbox.

The Diabetes Home Page

http://www.nd.edu/~hhowisen/diabetes.html

As you might gather from its title, the Diabetes Home Page presents a convenient, yet comprehensive resource for information about diabetes. In addition to providing their own information, the web site also contains links to various other Internet resources for diabetics and their families. Overall, the home page is easy to read and use, and it downloads quickly.

EXCERPT:

The purpose of this page is to provide everyone (specially those whose Pancrei have opted for early retirement) with information concerning diabetes.

Digital Gallery

http://ziris.syr.edu/home.html

This Digital Gallery houses collaborative Internet art projects (including the hypermedia project—Digital Journeys) and other computer-related art works. Visitors explore and respond to various themes and are invited to submit JPG or GIF images, text, poetry, short stories, MPEG or Quicktime movies, or audio files. The journeys are thus open-ended, depending as they do on user input and collaboration.

Digital Illusions

http://www.mcs.com/~bcleach/illusions/index.html

Digital Illusions calls itself an online magazine, but it's really just a collection of links to other folks' pages. However, if computer graphics is your thing, this is a good site to visit. This homepage has tracked down some of the best graphics pages that can be found scattered across the Web. What's more, Digital Illusions is well designed, and looks quite sharp on advanced browsers like Netscape 1.1.

EXCERPT:

Digital Illusions is an online magazine covering all aspects of computer graphics and animation. From modeling to film special effects we cover it all.

Digital Photography

http://www.bradley.edu:80/exhibit/index.html

An arts organization in Peoria, Illinois, formed a partnership with Bradley University to produce this World Wide Web gallery of photographs produced by computers. There's some pretty stunning work at this exhibit, underscoring the fact that computers are capable of serving an aesthetic purpose. The images are copyrighted, so you can't reproduce any of them, but visitors are encouraged to download pictures for their own viewing.

EXCERPT:

This juried exhibition sought entrants worldwide from artists working in "digital photography." For the purposes of this show, "digital photography" was defined as two-dimensional work which "originated in a 'lens-imaging' device and was then brought to completion on a computer."

Digital Planet

http://www.digiplanet.com/

This home page basically serves as an advertisement for a multimedia design company, but it's well worth viewing if only for the phenomenal graphics. Digital Planet also offers links to other homepages that they have helped to create, including the web sites for movies like *Apollo 13* and *Species*. All in all, this site gives you a preview of some of the best in commercial Web site development.

EXCERPT:

Digital Planet, a leading producer of interactive entertainment, is creating bold, innovative content for a new medium...stretching the boundaries of multimedia and giving the 20 million-strong Internet audience an experience they won't find anywhere else.

digital wave photography gallery

http://catalog.com/exhibit/

Another creative World Wide Web exhibit of digital photographs. A recent visit turned up a fascinating series of black-and-white pictures of self-described "gangsters" in a New York neighborhood. This site is a bit light on content, but it's unaffected design serves to accentuate the thought-provoking aspect of the photographs.

The Dilbert Zone

http://www.unitedmedia.com/comics/dilbert/

A home for all things Dilbert, including this Sunday's cartoon, an archive of past Dilbert cartoons, Dilbert's early history, a photo tour of how the artist creates Dilbert, a newsletter archive, instructions on joining Dogbert's New Ruling Class, and how to find a Dilbert-carrying newspaper in your area. Send the artist a photo of yourself with a sock puppet, and he'll post it here—honest.

EXCERPT:

I think you'll agree we're using the Information Superhighway to its fullest potential: simulating the excitement of being invited to somebody's house to look at their photo album...

dimFLASH eZine

http://turnpike.net/metro/futrelle/index.html

Wow! It's a rare accomplishment when an online magazine succeeds at being both visually stunning and extremely well-written. Kudos to David Futrelle, a writer for the socialist magazine *In These Times*, for organizing such professional and stylish model for all other 'zines to emulate. Bar none, dimFLASH is an exceptional online 'zine, with a sharp, attractive visual style, and genuinely funny writing. Not to be missed.

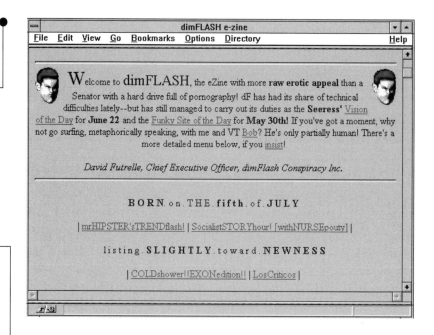

dimFLASH e-zine

File   Edit   View   Go   Bookmarks   Options   Directory   Help

Welcome to dimFLASH, the eZine with more **raw erotic appeal** than a
Senator with a hard drive full of pornography! dF has had its share of technical
difficulties lately--but has still managed to carry out its duties as the **Seeress'** Vision
of the Day for **June 22** and the Funky Site of the Day for **May 30th!** If you've got a moment, why
not go surfing, metaphorically speaking, with me and VT Bob? He's only partially human! There's a
more detailed menu below, if you insist!

David Futrelle, Chief Executive Officer, dimFlash Conspiracy Inc.

B O R N . on . T H E . fifth . of . J U L Y

| mrHIPSTER'sTRENDflash! | SocialistSTORYhour! [withNURSEpouty] |

listing . S L I G H T L Y . to ward . N E W N E S S

| COLDshower!!EXONedition!! | LosCriticos |

EXCERPT:

Welcome to dimFLASH, the eZine with more raw erotic appeal than a senator with a hard drive full of pornography!

Dining Out on the Web

http://www.ird.net/diningout.html

Looking for someplace to dine besides the standard squat-and-gobble fare?
Check out Dining out on the Web for a list of restaurant guides to speed you
on your way. You'll only find restaurants here, no cafes, pubs, etc. Most of
the listings are actually guide sites. Mostly North American, but some international, and even a few reviews.

EXCERPT:

Enjoy life. Eat out more often.

Diogenes' Links to the Ancient World

http://www.snider.net/lyceum/

Need help with that term paper on the ancient Assyrians? Help is on the way in the form of Diogenes' Links to the Ancient World. This academically inspired web site features a collection of links to numerous Internet sites that contain information on the ancient world. Greek, Roman, Egyptian, and Jewish resources are listed here, among others. What Web-surfer in their right mind *wouldn't* want to spend an evening brushing up on the history of Western Civilization just for ha-has?

Dirty Linen

http://www.dirtynelson.com/linen/

Dirty Linen's homepage is basically a teaser site for fans of the print version of the folk music magazine. At this web site, you can view excerpts from the latest issue of *Dirty Linen*; articles from previous issues; and record and book reviews. The site has a handsome graphic design and its pages download quickly.

EXCERPT:

The Magazine Of Folk, Electric Folk, Traditional and World Music.

Dirty Sole Society

http://www.erinet.com/brubro/dss/

Most of us kick off our shoes at least once in a while, but here are some die-hard folks who want to go barefootin' all the time. If this is your idea of fun, stop by. You can find out about other barefoot hikers, check out upcoming activities, and look into the newsgroup alt.lifestyle.barefoot. Check out links to What's This All About?; Activities; and Barefoot Hikers.

EXCERPT:

Set your feet free and your mind will follow.

Discover Magazine

http://www.enews.com:80/magazines/discover/

The *Discover Magazine* home page features articles and other information from the popular science magazine. The site serves as a good reminder of how useful and informative a very simple site can be. There are few splashy graphics here; just links that bring up articles which have appeared in the magazine. The bottom line is that this is a easy-to-use web site, packed with good reading for "curious and intelligent adults."

EXCERPT:

Welcome to the online home of *Discover*, the magazine of science and technology; their wonders, their uses; their impact upon our lives. *Discover*'s goal is to offer curious and intelligent adults a lively and literate look at our quest to understand ourselves and the universe around us.

Discovery Channel Online

http://www.discovery.com/

The Discovery Channel Online is an online guide to their programs, but includes much more. You can play "What is it?" and guess the identity of unusual items from the Smithsonian. You can visit the Discovery Store, a search service called Knapsack, and read lots and lots of articles based on or related to current TV stories.

EXCERPT:

Originally produced interactive stories with film, music, photography and illustrations.

The Doctor Fun Page

http://sunsite.unc.edu/Dave/drfun.html

Need your daily laugh fix? Tune into the Doctor Fun Page and see what the Doctor has found to amuse himself today. You'll find the day's single panel cartoon, and you can catch up on the ones you missed for this week, as well as previous weeks. Lots of links to more fun: Today's Doctor Fun; Other Doctor Fun Mirrors and Archives; and Information about Doctor Fun.

EXCERPT:

Doctor Fun is a dull boy. Why not check out some real fine upstanding characters?

Dr. Internet

http://tweb.gactr.uga.edu/steve/drnet.html

Dr. Internet is a cyberspace Ann Landers, providing advice for the life problems that follow people onto the net—questionable relationships, broken hearts, insulted egos, etc.

EXCERPT:

...Problems formerly associated with the three-dimensional world are emerging again in cyberspace.....Egos get crushed and hearts get broken....

Dog Soup

http://www.tcp.co.uk:80/~rat/

Dog Soup is a small collection of original stories. Here's the beginning of one: "You wake up one bright sunny morning to find a strange parcel lying outside your door, with a note attached to it saying merely, 'Dog Soup.'"

EXCERPT:

...Cautiously you take it inside and tear away the paper and string to reveal a number of strange and intriguing objects. What could it mean?

Doggie Information on the Web

http://www.io.com/~wilf/dogs/doggy_info.html

Yup, the Web has gone to the dogs, at least as far as this site is concerned. If canines are your thing, then check out all you can learn about them on this home page. You can find links to pages on various breeds, learn about dogs as aids to the physically disabled, ask Dr. Jim, order custom laser-engraved gifts for your pooch, and find out how dogs help the physically disabled. Don't miss the Dr. Jim Humphries Home Page.

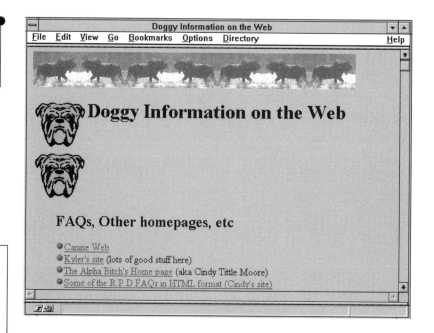

The Dominion

http://www.scifi.com

To boldly go... Well, science fiction isn't just *Star Trek,* although that along with many other shows appear on the Sci Fi Channel. The Dominion is the Sci Fi channel online. You can browse through the programming schedule, read about science fiction, download images and audio and video, and talk to other like minded folk on the bulletin board. Use links to trek to Sci-Fi Originals Within Pulp and the Orbit Zone.

EXCERPT:

The Dominion is the Sci-Fi Channel On-Line...and then some.

Downtown Anywhere

http://www.awa.com

Some claim downtown is dead, but it's alive and well on the Web. This commercial site helps businesses set up a storefront on the Web and even offers real-time credit card and voucher processing. Shop the links to All about Downtown Anywhere; Main Street: Shopping and Services; Travel Center; People; Sports Arena; and Post Office.

EXCERPT:

Downtown Anywhere, a "virtual salon for the marketplace of ideas" with a secure and real economy.

The DRC Virtual Gallery

http://dougal.derby.ac.uk/gallery/drc-gallery.html

Art imitates nature, and in this case, nature is the electronic world. The Virtual Gallery introduces you to what can be done in the world of electronic art and gives you a place to discuss it, too. Look for information on books and photography and link to the What's New and Visitor's Guide; Visitor's Book; Photography; Electronic Art; Virtual Reality Art; and Public Art.

EXCERPT:

Art meets technology.

Dream Works

http://www.teleport.com/~bskoda/dreamworks.shtml

Bill Skoda likes to experiment with film, print, and advertising, and his personal home page features pictures of cars and unusual artworks. Bill also includes links to other TelePort sites.

Drywall

drywall@atsprimenet.com

You can't tell the players without a program, and now you can't tell your rock groups without a Web page. So, here is one for the group Drywall. You'll get information on their album, tour dates, your standard tacky trinkets, and assorted off the wall articles. Their Panel of Experts section was rather disappointing though, since most of them were out to lunch, literally.

EXCERPT:

It came from Los Angeles, and nothing could stand in its way!

DTF

http://www.hh.se/home/stud/t/92/mn/c/html/startx.html

DTF is a site started by a bunch of Swedish college students and is devoted to a college student's most serious pursuits: beer, good times, and parties. You'll find a calendar of beer-related fests from around the world, games, and jokes. There are also links to other fun places, as well as to related beer sites like Beer, Beer, Beer and When's the Next Party? SKOL!

EXCERPT:

DTF, the choice of a drunk generation.

The Duckman Information File

http://bluejay.creighton.edu/~jduche/duckfaq.html

You've seen the show, now visit the web site. Duckman, that arrogant, self-ish duck detective, can be found here, along with the other characters of this series. You can read show synopses, check out some graphics, even hear some sound bites. Don't forget to stop by the store for your Duckman merchandise.

EXCERPT:

Duckman is a crabby but lovable dreamer who longs for a world of black and white, a world that makes sense...an old fashioned guy who just want to crack the BIG case and be left alone!

Ecola's 24-Hour Newsstand

http://www.ecola.com/ez/newshome.htm

Finally, a newsstand where an angry proprieter won't yell at you for skimming the reading material. It's Ecola's 24-Hour Newsstand—a home page dedicated to helping you find good stuff to read on the World Wide Web. The sole purpose of this web site is simply to list newspapers and magazines that operate their own web sites; however, Ecola's Newsstand boasts a strikingly comprehensive library of links, which is well-organized and easy to use.

The Electric Postcard

http://postcards.www.media.mit.edu/Postcards/

Having a wonderful time. Wish you were here. Now you don't even have to walk to the post office for a stamp. Send your postcards electronically. The postcard rack contains 27 categories of images such as Van Gogh, or Graffiti. Easy to use, and a bit classier than regular e-mail. Pick the card you like, write your message, and send it off. The Electric Postcard will notify the recipient to come to the Pick-Up Window.

Electronic Gourmet Guide

http://www.2way.com/food/egg/index.html

This site is enough to make you work up an appetite. Get great tips on food

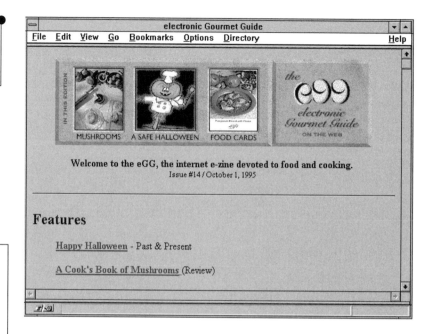

preparation, drinks, and using the bounties of the season. Read the mouth-watering feature articles such as Traveler's Cuisine and take a peak at how some of the nation's classiest hotels are serving travelers these days. Links to lots of tasty features and columns as well as Quick Tip; Did You Know...?; Toasts & Quotes; and Food Sites Around the Web.

EXCERPT:

Welcome to the EGG, the internet e-zine devoted to food and cooking.

Emily Stern's Web Page

http://bradley.bradley.edu/~ebs

The Web is a vanity press for writers and also a means for artists to open their own galleries. Ms. Stern offers not only her own art work but also that of her students. Her area of expertise is graphic design, so you'll find lots of examples of posters, logos, and menus and links to Typography; Art Gallery; and Student Gallery.

Canine Companions for Independence has come a long way since Bonita (Bonnie) Bergen, CCI's founder, pioneered the service dog concept in 1975. Although many people told her she would not succeed, Bonnie trained a black Labrador Retriever named Abdul in her home, and later placed him with Kerry Knaus, a quadriplegic woman from Sonoma County, California.

Since then, Canine Companions has grown from a virtually unknown at-home operation to an agency with five centers around the nation. CCI is now recognized world-wide as the authority in service dog education.

Doggy Information on the Web,
CCI (Canine Companions for Independence)
http://www.io.com/~wilf/dogs/doggy_info.html

The Endless *Star Trek* Episode

http://trek.resultsdirect.com/trek.htm

The series that can't be killed has its own neverending story on the Web. The Endless *Star Trek* Episode is just that. You can submit your own chapter or vote on entries submitted by other Web Trekkies. Each week you read the story so far and then answer the questions and add your thoughts to the story. The plot definitely thickens on this one.

EXCERPT:

Join the rest of the net.trek.citizens in creating the endless Star Trek episode.

Enfolding Perspectives: Photographic Collage

http://www.art.net/studios/visual/simran/enfolding-

Part of the Art on the Net site, Enfolding Perspectives contains photographic collages, charcoal and pastel landscapes, self-portraits, and masks by Simran Singh Gleason. Gleason's goal is to create spaces that wrap around the viewers and enfold them into the picture.

EXCERPT:

I call the show "Enfolding Perspectives" because I am trying to create perspective spaces that wrap around the viewers...@source:Enfolding Perspectives: Photographic Collage

The Enhanced for Netscape Hall of Shame

http://meat.europa.com

The best of the worst! This Hall of Shame pokes not so gentle fun at all those jumping on the Netscape bandwagon. You can see nightmare pages enhanced with background textures and colors to make a salamander shiver. There is also the Hall of Shame Homepages, where you can submit your own worse Netscape-enhanced page.

EXCERPT:

Best of the worst. How sickly ironic. There is nothing good about these homepages!

Entertainment Weekly

http://pathfinder.com/ew/Welcome.html

Entertainment Weekly is Time Inc.'s offering to the Net for entertainment information. You'll find feature stories, reviews, and bulletin boards to chat with others. There's also a search feature that lets you search all of Pathfinder, the site that includes *Entertainment Weekly* as well as other Time-Warner publications and music.

Enzian

http://magicnet.net/enzian

Alternative cinema is alive and well and living in central Florida, at least according to the Enzian Theater. Its home page provides information on the Florida Film Festival, the Enzian Theater and Film Society, and links to other film-related sites. Good spot to visit to talk about films, festivals, and the cinema experience.

EXCERPT:

Do you like to talk about films, film festivals, film makers, or the cinema experience in general?

ESPNET Sportszone

http://espnet.sportszone.com

Now you can not only watch your favorite sports on ESPN and then read about them on the Web. ESPNET gives you all the sports news you want: from baseball to boxing to wrestling and college teams. You can also submit questions to ESPN's interview shows and take part in live chats with some of your favorite sports stars. If you still need more sports stuff, link to Select Sport; Zoned Out; Sports Talk; or The ESPN Studios.

EXCERPT:

ESPNET SportsZone presents live chat! Here's your chance to go one-on-one with other fans, or take on the crowd.

The ETEXT Archives

http://www.etext.org/

The ETEXT Archive is one of the largest collections of somewhat off-beat electronic texts on the Internet, with about 225 small-press or independent publications and uncountable political, religious, and legal essays, treatises, and other works produced by more than 60 organizations. You can link to Sports (home of Dorian Kim's baseball archives) or to Legal (legal documents and essays). And there's plenty more.

EXCERPT:

There are many controversial files on the site that I do not endorse in any fashion, and some that I hope nobody endorses....

A man goes to an exotic tropical island for a vacation. As the boat nears the island, he notices the constant sound of drumming coming from the island. As he gets off the boat, he asks the first native he sees how long the drumming will go on. The native casts about nervously and says "very bad when the drumming stops."

At the end of the day, the drumming is still going and is starting to get on his nerves. So, he asks another native when the drumming will stop. The native looks as if he's just been reminded of something very unpleasant. "Very bad when drumming stops," he says, and hurries off.

After a couple of days with little sleep, our traveller is finally fed up, grabs the nearest native, slams him up against a tree, and shouts "What happens when the drumming stops?!!"

"Bass solo."

The Drums and Percussion Page: http://www.cse.ogi.edu/Drum/

Everything Extreme

http://www.duke.edu:80/~cperhun

If you like living life on the edge, check out Everything Extreme. You can link to skydiving; hang gliding; windsurfing; car racing; snowboarding; extreme ski; and rock climbing. Enjoy pictures and some film clips, too. Just remember, don't try these activities while sitting at your computer.

EXCERPT:

Every person considering trying any of the extreme sports on these pages is strongly encouraged to first obtain the proper instruction, and performs any extreme actions at their own risk.

ExploraNet

http://www.exploratorium.edu/default.html

The Exploratorium's web server features online versions of some of the hands-on science museum's 650 exhibits and projects, general information about the museum and its programs, an events calendar and schedule, a gift shop, list of museum publications, a digital library of scientific images and sounds, an ask-a-science-question feature, and links to the Exploratorium's FTP and Gopher servers.

EXCERPT:

The Exploratorium is a museum of science, art, and human perception with over 650 interactive "hands on" exhibits....

Exploring Architecture and Private Lives via the WWW

http://mercury.rti.org/house.html

Are you one of those people that love to check out people's houses as you walk down the street? Well here you go... It's open house at John and Sandie's and you're invited to take a virtual walk through. John's been busy making digitized stills of all their rooms so come right around back and walk in.

EXCERPT:

This is an experiment, and is kinda cool if I do say so myself.

The Eyesore Database

http://www.is.co.za/andras/music/eyesore/eyesore.html

Eyesore is a hypertextual discography documenting all artists affiliated with the 4AD record label both in the U.K. and in the U.S. Tune in to the 15-minute weekly radio show. The interactive database contains lists of groups, idents, titles, years, tracks, and people, along with the 4AD FAQ and an archive of messages to the 4AD-L list.

EXCERPT:

A fifteen minute weekly radio show featuring me babbling and playing a few tracks from bands on 4AD is available....

The Face of Venus Home Page

http://stoner.eps.mcgill.ca/~bud/craters/first.html

Indulge your dreams as you stare into the face of Venus, the planet, not the goddess. You can learn about Venus and what her surface is like. Check out the crater and corona atlases and even search for a particular type if you desire. There's also an introduction to volcanic, tectonic, and impact structures on Venus and you can search the interactive corona database.

EXCERPT:

Learn about the surface of the planet Venus through hypertext documents and the interactive databases...

Fair Play

http://rmii.com/~jkelin/fp.html

Running even longer than the OJ trial is the media trial of Lee Harvey Oswald. If you have any doubts, check out the e-zine *Fair Play*. As they say, "The American people are the only jury the Lee Harvey Oswald will ever have," and according to these folks, the jury is still out. Each issue contains articles and editorials related to John F. Kennedy's assassination. There is also a JFK bibliography, and links to other JFK related sites.

EXCERPT:

We regard *Fair Play* as essentially one big Op-Ed page.

"The truly great thing about publishing electronically is E-mail," Mr. Perkins said. (Dan Perkins writes "This Modern World," under the pseudonym Tom Tomorrow.) "E-mail allows for direct reader feedback, and to be able to get that kind of response as a creator is fantastic."

Todd Krieger, *The New York Times,* **January 8, 1995.**

The Fashion Page

http://www.charm.net/~jakec

Need to know what's cool in clothes? Here's the e-zine for all those that want to know what's hot and what's not in the world of fashion. Take a look at the current season or the upcoming one. Learn a little clothes history, check out the fashion bibliography, or read feature articles on a variety of fashion-related topics.

EXCERPT:

...How to be cool and wear the latest in Trash Flash.

The FBI's Current Ten Most Wanted Fugitives

http://www.fbi.gov/toplist.htm

Save yourself a trip to the post office. Now you can view the FBI's 10-Most-Wanted fugitives right from your own computer. Choose your felon, click, and get the complete run down of his or her dastardly deeds. Also includes a FAQ that explains the history of the program and the addresses and phone numbers of all FBI field offices.

EXCERPT:

Warning: if you have any information concerning these fugitives, please contact your local FBI office.

FEED

http://www.emedia.net/feed

FEED is essentially a series of links to related topics and is designed to show some of the potential for hypertext publications. This e-zine offers articles full of links to sound files, video clips, and other FEED articles or sites across the Web. You can debate with the expert panel or even link into a bulletin board system threaded to the debate topic.

EXCERPT:

Feed, after all, is a creature of the World Wide Web, born and bred in the binary soup of zeroes and ones.

Female Bodybuilder Home Page

http://www.ama.caltech.edu/~mrm/body.html

Find out who's who in the world of female bodybuilding! For those who enjoy that "pumping iron" look, check out this home page for all the information you'll ever need on all the top female bodybuilders, many of whom have their own home pages. There are also links to related sites. Join the Women's Bodybuilding Forum by sending a message to femuscle-request@atslightning.com saying "subscribe femuscle."

EXCERPT:

Don't know who's who in the world of female bodybuilding? Check out the House Recommendations.

Ferret Central

http://optics.rochester.edu:8080/users/pgreene/central.html

We all know there are gophers on the Net, but now there are ferrets, too. If you have one of these pets, or want to know about them, check out Ferret Central for medical information, essential equipment for your pet, history of ferrets, and care information. Listen to the sound of ferrets wrestling. Links take you to places like the Swedish Ferret Society and the NetVet ferret page.

EXCERPT:

In a fit of curiosity, I've collected some mostly useless statistics about Ferret Central, the FAQ, and the Photo Gallery.

The Festival

http://www.interport.net:80/festival

The Sundance Film Festival in Park City, Utah, is an annual affair. This past January, it went live on the Web. The festival is a chance for American film artists to showcase their works. This site has information on the films, the city, background on the Sundance Institute and Festival, and links to Sundance Film Festival Awards; Films; Buzz; Stuff; Lay of the Land; Mail; and The Making of...

EXCERPT:

Our view is not intended to be the official comprehensive report, but rather to create a virtual Festival experience.

50 Greatest Conspiracies of All Time

http://www.webcom.com/~conspire/

Did Americans really land on the Moon? Was Jack the Ripper really a prince? And just how many gunmen were on that grassy knoll? If questions like these keep you awake at night, then sneak on over to the 50 Greatest Conspiracies of All Time. With excerpts from the book of the same name, links to other conspiracy-related sites on the Internet, archives, news, and images, this is where all the really cool conspirators hang out.

EXCERPT:

From mind control to brainwashing and back, this book covers it all. You'll find it irresistible. STRANGELY irresistible. In fact, you feel a sudden URGE to BUY a copy NOW. YOU ARE GETTING SLEEPY. SLEEPY. BUT NOT TOO SLEEPY TO PLACE A BOOK ORDER (ordering information listed below).

What is Ebola virus?

The Ebola virus is a member of a family of RNA viruses known as filoviruses. When magnified several thousand times by an electron microscope, these viruses have the appearance of long filaments or threads. Ebola virus was discovered in 1976 and was named for a river in Zaire, Africa, where it was first detected.

What do we know about the recent outbreak of Ebola virus infection?

The recent Ebola virus outbreak is centered in Kikwit, Zaire. (Kikwit is a city of 400,000 located 400 kilometers east of Kinshasa, the capital of Zaire.) The outbreak appears to have started with a patient who had surgery in Kikwit on April 10, 1995. Members of the surgical team then developed symptoms similar to those of a viral hemorrhagic fever disease....At the request of Zairian health officials, medical teams from CDC, the World Health Organization, and from Belgium, France, and South Africa are collaborating to investigate and control the outbreak in Zaire.

The Ebola Page
http://ichiban.objarts.com/ebola/ebola.html

Film.com

http://www.film.com

If you want to be your own movie critic, get your facts from Film.com. You can read about the latest releases, check out the new stars, and find a list of film festivals around the world. There is information on home video and laser disc releases and even a video store database and search service. Use links to go to The Movies; Spotlight Reviews; The Home Front; Cinecism; and The Festival Circuit.

EXCERPT:
Bringing a critical perspective to the world of film.

Final Frontiers

http://www.microserve.net/~trek/

Your chance to be a member of the Federation or a Klingon or a Frenghi. An interactive *Star Trek* role-playing game in which each player is a very small part of space society. *Star Trek* comes to life—this is all about battles, diplomacy, and commerce. This Web page gets you to the game.

EXCERPT:

Final Frontiers is a low bandwidth virtual reality (AR) game....The setting is the Universe created by Gene Roddenberry and populated with Humans, Klingons...and a bevy of other races.

Doug Fine: Unedited

http://www.well.com/user/fine

According to Doug, writing is his only marketable and legal skill. Mr. Fine presents samples of his writing at this site. Included are his first e-mail message, his favorite pieces of journalism, upcoming pieces, a "Scratch Your Head of the Month" feature, and "Hero/Heroine of the Moment" (in which Fine relates anecdotes about individuals with whom he has been impressed).

EXCERPT:

Doug discovered at an early age that about the only skill he had that was marketable and legal was his writing...

Fineart Forum Online

http://www.msstate.edu/Fineart_Online/home.html

FineArt Forum serves as the news service of the Art, Science, and Technology Network (ASTN), a virtual organization whose members meet in cyberspace. They are there to serve artist interested in applying technology to art. You can read the current issue, check out old issues, visit the gallery, or link to other fine arts sites.

EXCERPT:

FineArt Forum is a electronic news service that covers art and technology.

Firehorse

http://peg.peg.apc.org/~firehorse/welcome.html

A well-designed and fairly-quick-to-load 'zine from the folks down under. The Australian publishers have good information for you on credit-card safety and banking on the net. Check out the weekly Tecknomad feature that chronicles the travels of a guy trekking around Australia. An art gallery includes the graphic works of a number of aboriginal artists, and other sections cover literature, food, and music. Pretty neat.

EXCERPT:

Believe nothing, no matter where you read it, or who said it, no matter if I have said it, unless it agrees with your own reason and your own common sense.

Yuval Fisher's Home Page

http://inls.ucsd.edu/y/

Another Web surfer who thinks everyone will be interested in his pedestrian home pages and his favorite links. Those links include classifieds, news, computers, games, etc., and it's really not that interesting.

EXCERPT:

My tabloid WEB (and other diversions).

Flicker

http://www.sirius.com/~sstark/

Bored with Tracy and Hepburn? Had enough of Hollywood's starlets?

...**m**ost liken trying to find information on the Internet to taking a drink from a firehose...

Kate Murphy, in *Houston Business Journal*

Here's an excellent location for fans of alternative cinema. Flicker offers pithy descriptions of the latest underground films, along with good quality still images from the movies. The site also tells you where you can go to see these underground movies.

EXCERPT:

...Find films and videos that transgress the boundaries of the traditional viewing experience...provide cutting edge alternatives to the media information technocracy.

Flightless Hummingbird: A Pseudo-Periodical

http://www.umich.edu/~rmutt/

This site that makes no sense and is proud of it. It features information on famous surrealist artists like Andre Breton and Luis Bunuel, presented with infuriating—and fascinating—randomness. For weirdness on the installment plan, check out No More Words, a "non-glossary" featuring seemingly random links to incidents in the lives of these very strange artists.

EXCERPT:

Just as all matter will eventually fall into a black hole, so all knowledge, all art, all thought will be sucked into an intellectual singularity....

Fluffy's World

http://www.xensei.com:80/users/wayward/Fluffyhome.html

"Fluffy" is Cathy Faye Rudolph, rabbit fancier and one-time genetic engineering researcher. Now she runs her own electronic publishing business, Wayward Fluffy Publications, and displays her wares at Fluffy's World.

Her graphic work is impressive. There's some splendid calligraphy and eye-catching cyberscapes, while the essays and stories are rather more cute than cool. Still, the pages are attractive and well designed, and it's a good visual rest stop for the casual surfer.

Fluxus Online

http://www.panix.com/fluxus/

Named after the influential post-Dada art movement, Fluxus is another haven for esoteric art with drawings and photos and downloadable videos devoted to the avant-garde.

EXCERPT:

Fluxus is the wry, post-Dada art movement that flourished in New York and Germany in the 1950s and '60s...

Fly With Us!

http://www.mig29.com/mig29/

This is a site for Top Gun wannabes only. It's an advertisement for a Moscow company that wants to sell you a supersonic flight of fantasy in a high-performance Russian fighter jet. Prices range from $3,000 to a sky-high $50,000.

EXCERPT:

The thrill of supersonic flight in one of the world's finest flying machines is now available to a select few.

Fool Site of the Day

http://gagme.wwa.com/~boba/fool/fool.html

A silly site that's a nice change of pace from serious Web surfing. The April Fool simply picks out some pleasantly silly site he's discovered on the Web and plops it down on this page. You never know what he'll turn up. So wherever you go, there you are.

EXCERPT:

Please consult your psychiatrist if you use this page often. Hermetically sealed, and kept in a number four mayonnaise jar...

Fortean Times on line

http://www.mic.dundee.ac.uk/ft/ft.html

This site is a teaser for *Fortean Times* magazine, a publication that specializes in such news of the weird as UFOs, crop circles and spontaneous human combustion. The *Fortean Times* site contains only a few of the articles published in the print version, which sells for $30 per year. But the site features an amusing clickable map of the UK. Point and click at any part of the British Isles to read bizarre—and supposedly true—tales from that region.

EXCERPT:

Three lighthouse keepers vanished from their posts on Eilean Mor.... Some believed they had been snatched by fairies, others that they had fallen victim to a gigantic freak wave.

40 Tips to Go Green

http://www.ncb.gov.sg/jkj/env/greentips.html

Wash dishes with a basin of water instead of under a running tap. Use a bucket instead of a hose for washing the car.... If your fridge is set too cold—even 5% colder than necessary—it's using 25% more electricity than it should.... Use mugs instead of disposable paper cups.... This site contains 37 other earth-friendly habits. Don't forget: every day is Earth Day.

Through the Car (or 'The 3 Second Car Jacking'). There is little peace in the land of Mentos, as yet another teen is faced with a distressing problem. While crossing the street, he is separated from his friends, and nearly from his legs by an over anxious motorist. Finding himself needing to traverse the street, but without a normal means to do so, he again thanks his lucky stars he remembered the freshmaker. His supply is reduced by one, but his freshness is increased exponentially. Opening the rear door, he climbs through the auto, while the driver looks over his shoulder in astonishment. Upon exiting, the youth shrugs at the motorist, Mentos in hand. Although a bit shaken, the passenger acknowledges the care free youths with an approving glance as he speeds away. "Wait till the wife hears of my brush with freshness!"

The Mentos Page: www.best.com/^dijon/tv/mentos/mentos-faz.html

Fractal Explorer

http://www.vis.colostate.edu/~user1209/fractals/index.html

The Fractal Explorer is a web site attached to a powerful graphics workstation. The computer generates fractals—colorful, abstract images produced by complex mathematical equations. Visitors to the site can take a look at some of these remarkable images, but unless you're enthralled by the mathematics, it gets stale fairly fast.

EXCERPT:

...Fractals are infinitely complex, the closer you look the more detail you see.

Frankenstein, or The Modern Prometheus

http://www.medio.net/lit/frank/index.html

The copyright has expired on Mary Shelley's classic novel Frankenstein, so anybody can put it up on the World Wide Web. That's what Medio Multimedia has done here, but why? This online book gives you nothing you couldn't get more easily from a cheap paperback.

EXCERPT:

Abhorred monster! fiend that thou art! the tortures of hell are too mild a vengeance for thy crimes....

The Franklin Institute Virtual Science Museum

http://sln.fi.edu/

This superb site, run by the well-know Philadelphia museum, is ideal for parents, teachers, and curious kids. The exhibits are few in number, but rich and detailed. An exhibit on Benjamin Franklin featured pictures, audio and video clips, a list of Franklin's famous sayings, and vast amounts of historical information. The overall design of the site is equal to its contents. Very impressive.

EXCERPT:

It's not quite the real thing, but a visit to our Virtual Museum should satisfy your yearning for learning about science....

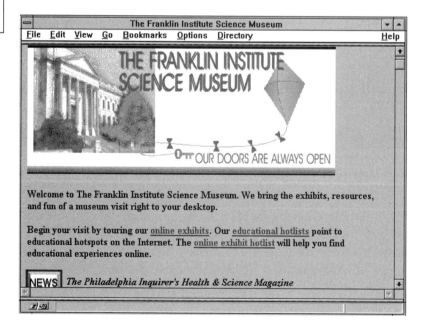

The Free Art Website

http://www.mccannas.com/

Laurie McCanna is a graphic designer who specializes in creating graphical user interfaces, splash screens, and software icons. Her website showcases some of her work and provides resources about typeface design, graphic design, and Corel products. You'll find pointers on creating type with Corel as well as downloadable TrueType fonts and icons, mostly in .zip format for PCS (although there are also a couple of UNIX files here).

The Fridge

http://www.wbm.ca/users/kgreggai/html/fridge.html

Gross...Don't open that door! If your fridge hasn't seen a wash cloth in eons, you might recognize some of the mold-ridden monsters on this page. Grudge becomes art with images of various foods and all the neat stuff they grew. Visitors are encouraged to write their own horror stories. Link to Stuff I found before; Mushrooms?; Bread?; Fish?; or Potatoes? for inspiration.

EXCERPT:

This page is intended entirely for entertainment value only.

Friends

http://geminga.dartmouth.edu/~andyjw/friends

Friends, the ongoing sitcom about a group of 20-something friends who live in the Big Apple has its own Web site. Surprise, surprise, there's an episode guide, star info, and of course, stuff to buy. Check friendly links to Drinking Game; Favorite Quotes; Photo Gallery; Friends Mailing Lists; Friends FTP Site; The Friends Zone; Friends Zone T-shirt FAQ; and more.

EXCERPT:

So no one told you life was gonna be this way.

The Froggy Page

http://www.cs.yale.edu/homes/sjl/froggy.html

Admirers of amphibians will enjoy this collection of frog-based fact, fiction, and frivolity. There are plenty of frog pictures and sound clips, classic stories about frogs, and links to serious scientific research on frogs. And be sure to peek at *Slime Magazine,* featuring true frog stories straight from the pond.

EXCERPT:

On the Internet, nobody knows you're a frog.

FUSE'9

http://www.worldserver.pipex.com/fuse94/fuse94.html

This one's exclusively for typography buffs. The site is operated by *Fuse,* a British magazine devoted to the creation of new computer typefaces. There are some attractive images here, but the writing holds little appeal for general audiences.

EXCERPT:

Launched in 1991, *Fuse* is an interactive magazine that sets out to challenge our current ideas about typographic and visual language...

Future Fantasy Bookstore

http://futfan.com/home.html

A well-designed commercial site run by a California science-fiction bookstore, in cooperation with Digital Equipment Corp., the big computer company. You can search the shelves for works by your favorite author, but you can't order the books on-line—phone, fax, and mail orders only. There are also many links to other science fiction resources on the Net. Too many spelling mistakes in the text detract only a little from the site's overall quality.

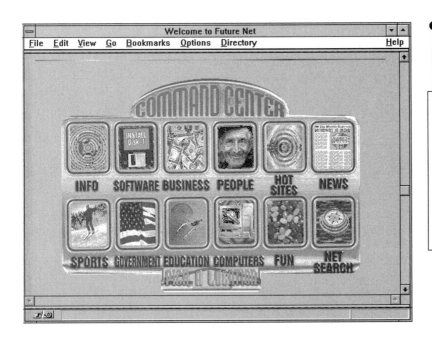

Future Net

http://www.fn.net/

Future Net is a whimsical intro to the wonders of the Internet. While there is a text-based version, for those that do not have graphical browsers, it's strong point is the visual layout. Bright, attractive, and compact, with two rows of six of buttons for access to topics like Business, People, Hot sites, News, Sports, Government, Education, Computers, Fun, and Netsearch. The one drawback is that it is a very busy site, and difficult to get to sometimes.

Future Pirates Inc.

http://www.fpi.co.jp/Welcome.html

A glimpse at pop culture in Japan. This site touts the video games and animated cartoon work of Tsuyoshi Takashiro, creator of the popular Wacky Races game. Half the stuff here is in Japanese, which comes out looking like hash on English-language browsers. But there are a lot of amusing graphics.

EXCERPT:

...Takashiro lived in parks and (depending upon the weather) his car.... He was just "groovin' to the feel of things."

G-Spot Magazine

http://www.hardnet.co.uk/gspot

G-Spot is a new wave electronic lifestyle magazine covering the new, emergent, post-nerd, technoglam way of living. What's all that mean? If you have to ask, this magazine isn't for you. But if you can party till dawn and believe that rock's not dead yet, try links to Alternative Peepshow; Artie Phartie; Bargain Bin; Clubzone; Happy Fashion; Hard Media; and more.

EXCERPT:

Can you be a vegan, follow Jesus, enjoy hardcore sex, and party till dawn?

Game Bytes

http://sunsite.unc.edu/GameBytes/

Hard-core videogamers will love this site. It's an online magazine that features images from the latest games, plus reviews written by avid players. The prose has the breathless tone of a 16-year-old—which makes it just right. Game Bytes is also available via e-mail and ftp.

EXCERPT:

The game is loads of fun....you must destroy all of the digitized actors before they destroy you.

Games Domain

http://wcl-rs.bham.ac.uk/GamesDomain

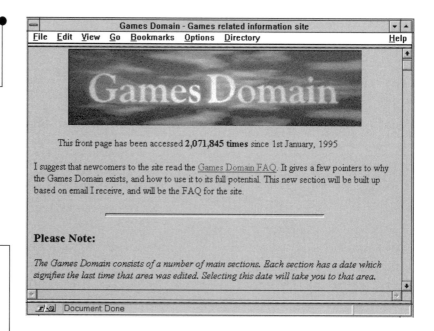

Games Domain - Games related information site

File   Edit   View   Go   Bookmarks   Options   Directory   Help

Games Domain

This front page has been accessed **2,071,845 times** since 1st January, 1995

I suggest that newcomers to the site read the Games Domain FAQ. It gives a few pointers to why the Games Domain exists, and how to use it to its full potential. This new section will be built up based on email I receive, and will be the FAQ for the site.

_____

Please Note:

The Games Domain consists of a number of main sections. Each section has a date which signifies the last time that area was edited. Selecting this date will take you to that area.

Document Done

Games Domain is a one-stop center for electronic game enthusiasts with links to thousands of gaming resources scattered across the Internet. You can download free games, find cheat sheets to get you over the tough spots, and even learn programming tips for writing your own games. A well-designed site, easy to use and crammed with information.

EXCERPT:

The site is designed to be a central reference point for all things "games-related" on the Internet.

Gargoyle Home Page

http://ils.unc.edu/garg/garghp4.html

A smattering of information about gargoyles, dished up as a class project by a couple of students at the University of North Carolina at Chapel Hill. In case you're wondering...gargoyles are those ugly stone creatures who inhabited the great cathedrals of the Middle Ages, This site has the feel of a homework assignment—competent, but not all that well-developed.

EXCERPT:

Welcome. You are about to meet a peculiar race of creatures which inhabited the great cathedrals of the Middle Ages...

Gateway to Darkness Gothic Web Server

http://coe1.engr.umbc.edu/~vijay2/home.html

This glimpse into the grim world of gothic horror won't send too many shivers down your spine. It's just a disjointed collection of images, audio clips, and text files. The fragments are lying here and there for you to plow through, instead of being woven together into a well-designed Web site. Not a lot of fun here.

EXCERPT:

"As far as we can discern, the sole purpose of human existence is to kindle a light of meaning in the darkness of mere being."—C.G. Jung

GEARS

http://gears.tucson.ars.ag.gov/

The U.S. government spends millions on honeybee research, and at this site they share some of what they've learned. It's a fun place to visit, with lots of pretty pictures and entertaining stories about bee research. Youngsters can visit the Internet Classroom to learn bee basics.

EXCERPT:

...Somewhere high in the Tualang canopy, a seventy year-old Malay honey-hunter and his...grandson were readying their gear to gather honey from giant Asian bee colonies.

Geek Chic

http://access.advr.com/~geekchic/

This site celebrates the joys of being a computer nerd, but with far less originality and wit than you'd expect from a true geek. There's a nice listing of films and books that prominently feature computer buffs and some amusing evidence that Andy Warhol and Marcel Duchamp would have been geeks if they'd understood math. But for the most part, it's a gag site with only one gag to its name.

EXCERPT:

I never have problems getting girls, once they see my pocket protector. I often have to fight them off!

Generality

http://www.generality.wis.net//Generality.html

A moderately interesting art site, mainly because you can visit the Pixel Pushers gallery and view the interesting and offbeat pictures hanging there. Some efforts at humorous writing don't work well, but the art makes up for it.

EXCERPT:

Window cleaner is in fact an excellent beverage, straight up with a twist, or splashed over the rocks....

Giantess Collages

http://cnj.digex.net:80/~esc/collage1.html

A lot more interesting than *Attack of the 50-Foot Woman,* the giantess collages found here will make you wonder how on earth the artist created them (her tips, notes, and FAQ are included). They might even make you smile a little.

EXCERPT:

...Because they are physically impossible, they [giantesses] work well as icons that ask you to suspend disbelief.

The Gigaplex

http://www.directnet.com/wow/

A spectacular site, full of movie reviews, interviews with famous actors and writers, audio and video files and plenty of photos and graphics. Too many, in fact. Loading up a page can be a real pain, because of all the art. Still, it's a great place to visit when you're looking for fun.

WELCOME TO THE GIGAPLEX!

File   Edit   View   Go   Bookmarks   Options   Directory   Help

THE GIGAPLEX

A billion pleasures await you!

It's the land of a billion pleasures...It's a whopping 600-plus page Web-magazine devoted to arts & entertainment!

Glass Wings

http://www.aus.xanadu.com/GlassWings/welcome.html

A well-meaning but mediocre site. There are a few short stories, some soft-core porn essays about sex, and a collection of rather lame jokes. In short, nothing to get excited over.

Fasten your seat belts folks...And prepare yourselves to teleport down the galactic glass web at the speed of light and thought.

Global Chat Service

http://webchat.service.digital.com/webchat/chat.html

Here's a place to chat live with folks from all over the planet—for the cost of a local phone call. This site also offers connections to other chat lines covering every thing from Muslim issues to skateboarders.

EXCERPT:

The discussion topics range from Web Chit-chat, thru online classes, on-the-spot technical forums, impromptu discussions of world issues, and business conferences for people throughout the globe.

GNOME'S Science Vessel

http://marie.mit.edu:80/~gnome/

If you're having trouble finding any useful information on the Internet, then it's high time you hopped aboard GNOME'S Science Vessel. This self-styled info-navigator was created with the intention of acting as a one-stop directory to locate dozens of other information sources, ranging from online dictionaries to the latest World Wide Web indexes. GNOME'S Science Vessel even provides some basic guides to the online world for Internet new-bies. This site belongs on every Web-surfer's hot list.

EXCERPT:

Information, the Final Frontier. These are the voyages of GNOME's Sci-

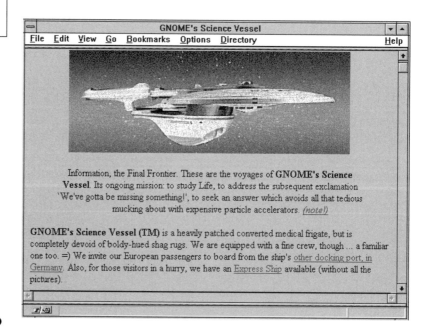

> The annual revenue generated from remote gambling from home and elsewhere through on-line systems eventually could grow to $10 billion in the United States alone.
>
> Jason Ader, Smith Barney analyst, in *The Detroit Free Press*

ence Vessel. Its ongoing mission: to study Life, to address the subsequent exclamation "We've gotta be missing something!," to seek an answer which avoids all that tedious mucking about with expensive particle accelerators.

Godzilla

http://www.ama.caltech.edu/~mrm/godzilla.html

Here's Godzilla in all his glory fighting the ultimate battle: Godzilla vs. Web. Yes, right here on the Net you can learn more than you ever wanted to know about Godzilla and find a brief description of all 22 movies, attendance figures, pictures and posters, win/loss statistics, the inevitable merchandise hawking, and links to related sites.

EXCERPT:

This page is designed to both glorify the world's greatest film star, as well as to inform the masses of the new adventures of Godzilla.

Goldsite Europe

http://www.cityscape.co.uk

Cityscape is an Internet provider that also has its own web page. You can find today's edition of *The Scottish Daily Record,* a brief guide to some sites around the Internet, as well as a listing of free advertisements from Cityscape customers. Try your luck in Situations Vacant and check the link to Directory and News Services.

EXCERPT:

Your one-stop Internet Information Site.

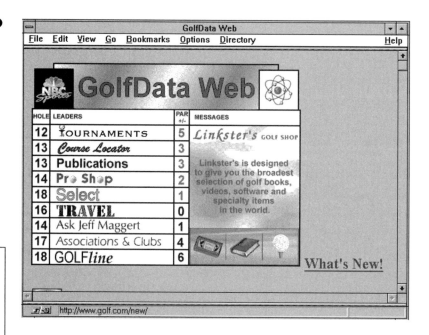

http://www.golf.com/new/

GolfData Web

http://www.golf.com/

It's a hole-in-one for golfers. This site devoted to golf is so good you may miss your tee time. It's crammed with facts and statistics about the game, including the latest tournament scores, player biographies, and information about courses throughout the U.S. There's even an on-line pro shop where you can buy the latest gear.

EXCERPT:

The goal of GolfData Web is to become the leader in online golf information and entertainment....

Good Quotes from Famous People

http://www.cs.virginia.edu/~robins/quotes.html

The site is pretty simple, the ideas are not. Each quote includes the person's name and historical period. The site author is always accepting new quotes. Stop in here and then try to impress your friends with big thoughts.

EXCERPT:

"Glory is fleeting, but obscurity is forever."—Napoleon Bonaparte (1769-1821)

GORP—Great Outdoor Recreation Pages

http://www.gorp.com/

If traveling the Web isn't exciting enough and you yearn for clean fresh air, this site is your guide to some real adventure. It's crammed with travel information, mostly for people who want to stray from the beaten path. Backpackers, cyclists, scuba divers and hang gliders are welcome. But there's plenty of information and fun here for everybody else.

EXCERPT:

Great Outdoor Recreation Pages contains a wealth of information on what to do and where to go in the great outdoors! ...

Grafica Obscura

http://www.sgi.com/grafica/

This is a compendium of technical notes, pictures, and essays all dealing with computer graphics. The information is highly technical, so if you're just a casual browser, you won't find much here. But serious, hard core graphics designers will probably benefit from a visit.

EXCERPT:

Welcome to Grafica Obscura, my computer graphics notebook. This is a compilation of technical notes, pictures, [and] essays...

Gramercy Press

http://www.mci.com/gramercy/intro.html

Here's the Web site for an imaginary publishing house featured in the TV commercials of long distance phone company MCI. It's meant to tout MCI's Internet and computer networking services, but it's also a fun place to visit. You can follow the ongoing story of Gramercy Press' battle to survive and prosper and check out the secret identity of their hottest author, Marcus Belfry.

EXCERPT:

Click on any window of the building to enter, and you'll find yourself in somebody's office. Feel free to stay as long as you wish...

Graphics on the Web

http://bw.cea.edu.zooop

This site contains links to Web sites serving as resources for graphical page designs. While not a comprehensive list, the database can be useful for finding resources and suggestions for designing WWW home pages. You might even end up with your very own home page.

The Graphix Exchange

http://www.rust.net/TGX_WWW_pgs/TGX.html

Looking to hire a good commercial artist? You're in the right place. Artists from around the world post their addresses and qualifications here. Click on the artist's name and you can automatically request more information via e-mail. Some of the listings even include a link to the artist's own Web page, where you can see samples of his or her work.

EXCERPT:

Here you will find some of the best illustrators, graphic designers, photographers, animators and other graphic-related professionals...

The Great God Contest

http://www.islandnet.com/~luree/contest.html

Here's a page Joseph Campbell would appreciate. The Great God Contest lets you pit the god of your choice against all the other gods. The god to complete all three challenges is the winner. Along with the contest, you will find a bibliography of materials on various religions (know thine enemy, so to speak) and a review of common beliefs among religions.

EXCERPT:

Right here on the Internet, we will attempt to bring a final resolution to all religious wars, controversy and hypocrisy.

The Green Cart Magazine

http://www.greencart.com//

A rich, heavy e-zine centered about the artistic and literary life of Vancouver. The writing is solid stuff, compared to the frivolity of many zines. But the site design is hampered by way too many arty graphics, which drag out download time.

EXCERPT:

...The Green Cart promises to provide a platform for the arts community, and a place for art appreciators to explore all styles and mediums of art.

Greenpeace WWW Information Page

http://www.cyberstore.ca/greenpeace

Greenpeace has been around nearly a quarter century and now proclaims its presence on the Web with a site that explains the history of the organization, its latest hot topics and campaigns, and enables you to learn about the Greenpeace ships. Go to the Berlin 1995 UN Climate Summit and to Greenpeace in Amsterdam for the inside story on this international organization.

EXCERPT:

Greenpeace was conceived in 1971 when members of the Don't Make a Wave Committee in Vancouver, Canada, renamed their organisation the better to proclaim their purpose.

GridPoint

http://www.paranoia.com/~manson/gp/

A site for hackers and phone phreaks, full of interesting and often illegal information about breaking into computer networks or stealing free phone calls. Not a place for honest folk.

EXCERPT:

GridPoint was patched together by Packet Rat. It is a junction of information geared towards the inquisitive net wonderer.

Grouchy Cafe

http://www.echonyc.com/~cafephrk/cafe.html

A sparse, singularly uninteresting site. It contains little except the mental ramblings of its creator, who identifies herself only as Cafephreak. Someone with an exceptionally interesting mind could pull this off, but it doesn't work here.

EXCERPT:

Think about bald women....They are sort of naked. I think they are brave. Bald women aren't afraid to be who they are....

H's home page

http://www.designsys.com/champ/

Heather Champ's personal Web site is weak on content, but it's pretty. The high points are the graphics found on almost every page—they're unusually good. The text content is rather limited, but there are lots of good links to other interesting places, including Web sites especially for women.

EXCERPT:

These pages were lovingly created while under the influence of Pet Shop Boys - GO WEST (the cd with every version imaginable)....

Halifax Police Department

http://www.atcon.com/HPD/hpd.htm

Here's a site run by a Canadian police department. You can get a list of unsolved murders (there aren't many) and learn how to tip the cops to crime in Halifax. The site suffers from being Canadian—they just don't have as much crime to report as Americans. The home page is a little graphics-heavy and will slow down the casual browser.

EXCERPT:

The City of Halifax is still a safe place in which to reside. In the last forty years there have been only ninety homicides....

T he new game online—at least among those users who are handy with both modems and soldering irons—is to wire up computers with cameras, microphones, robot arms and all manner of sensors to make something cool and really useless that everybody can enjoy.

Philip Elmer-DeWitt, in _Time_

Hang Gliding

http://cougar.stanford.edu:7878/HGMPSHomePage.html

Experienced and wannabe hang gliders and paragliders can zoom into this site. There's information on supine flying and sailplanes; lots of how-tos; glider designs; listings of schools, clubs, and manufacturers; and some helpful phone numbers. Links to weather sites, other aviation sites, and hang-gliding comics round out this server.

EXCERPT:
A WWW server for the foot-launched flying community.

Happy Puppy's Games Onramp

http://happypuppy.com/games

Happy Puppy Software started its own WWW site to provide games and games info to Net users. It also lets them introduce you to some of their own games too, but the selling is kept to a minimum. Lots of links for game players: Hit PC Games; PC Cheats and Patches; Macintosh Games; Game Developers Page; Nifty 50 PC Game Survey; and Ask Charlotte.

EXCERPT:
The best place on the Web to get hit games and info.

Hawaii Home Page

http://www.hawaii.net/

Pretty much a collection of links to other pages on Hawaii. This site has a clean, simple design that lets you navigate fast to obtain tourist information and the lowdown on how do business in Hawaii. Links also to state and local government databases.

Healthwise

http://www.columbia.edu/cu/healthwise/

Healthwise is a quick-loading web site dedicated to health education for an expanding worldwide community. The home page has some interesting links, including such useful tools as a Q&A forum and a newsletter. However, despite some nice graphics and link titles, there's not much on the home page to draw the average surfer forward into the links. Healthwise's chief links include: Go Ask Alice, New Announcements, Healthwise Highlights Newsletter, Columbia University WWW Server.

EXCERPT:

Healthwise is the Health Education and Wellness program of Columbia University Health Service. We are a team of professional and peer educators committed to helping you make choices that will contribute to your personal health and happiness, the well-being of others and to the planet we share.

The Heart Preview Gallery

http://sln.fi.edu/tfi/preview/heartpreview.html

Follow blood as it travels through the heart and learn how to take care of yours in this comprehensive collection of views, sounds, and operating details of your most vital organ. Like your high school human anatomy text, only a lot more fun. Statistics, tips for a healthy heart, exercises and loads of additional resources.

EXCERPT:

Explore the heart. Discover the complexities...Learn how to have a healthy heart....

Hell—The Online Guide to Satanism

http://www.marshall.edu/~allen12/index.html

A clearinghouse for information about Satanism—a creed that isn't really about worshiping Satan, but rather about rejecting any sort of God. As such there's a lot of railing against religion here, and it gets pretty negative. But if you're interested in Satanism, this is a very hot spot indeed.

EXCERPT:

In 1966 Anton Szandor LaVey declared the dawning of a new age....The Church of Satan was born.

High Five

http://www.best.com/~dsiegel/high_five/high_five.html

A superbly designed web site with a simple mission: To encourage superb web site design. Every week, Siegel picks out a Web page that rises above the ordinary, and honors it with a High Five award. And for those who don't make the cut, High Five offers lots of tips on how to create excellent Web pages.

EXCERPT:

Promoting fine design and high style on the Web for the benefit of surfers around the world.

Hinterlands

http://pubweb.acns.nwu.edu/~sid/hinterlands.html

A Northwestern University student shows off his talents on this Web site. He even posts his own resume, which is impressive. So is the site. A bit

In St. Louis, Missouri, Brian Gottlieb has wired his telephone to display to Internet users the hour and date of his most recent phone call. Paul Haas in Ypsilanti, Michigan, has hooked a computer to his refrigerator and hot tub to report their respective temperatures. In Pittsburgh, Pennsylvania, Michael Witbrock uses a voice synthesizer to let online visitors "talk" to the cat that likes to sleep in the warmth of his modem.

Philip Elmer-DeWitt, in *Time*

thin on textual content, but laden with interesting graphics, as well as audio and video files.

EXCERPT:

Every month I will post a sample from a different song written and performed by Chris Mills....

The History of Rock 'n' Roll

http://www.hollywood.com/rocknroll/

A big, fat site linked to a TV documentary on rock history. You can spend a lot of time here downloading pictures of rock stars, listening to audio clips, and watching movies. Avid fans will love it. This is a lavishly produced site, put together by experts.

Hokeo Hawaii

http://www.visit.hawaii.org/

This Hawaiian tourism site suffers from the kind of laid-back attitude that comes easy on the islands. The pages are so loaded with graphics that it may take you several minutes to view each one. Updating is infrequent. Still, there are lots of good links to tourism information.

EXCERPT:

...A friend describes a sunset off Waikiki. We hear the twang of a steel guitar....Golden beaches and golden people.

Hollyweb

http://www.ingress.com/users/spease/hw/hollyweb.html

An unemployed UCLA graduate with an honors degree in film production created this site, and why doesn't somebody hire this guy? His web site is very good—even with its attractive graphics, it loads up fast, and everybody will enjoy reading the selection of trendy Hollywood news and gossip.

EXCERPT:

The Hollyweb is envisioned as a place for people with an interest in film to offer opinions, share film knowledge, and talk about the film industry....

Hollywood Archeology

http://mosaic.echonyc.com/~hwdarch/

The Whitney Museum of American Art sponsors this site. It has little to do with Hollywood, except for a very good recent piece on old-time movie character actor Mike Mazurki. But unless you're into post-modern writing, there's not much here.

EXCERPT:

Being free to sell art since winning my fight with the IRS, I arranged for a presentation of the Fat Bat to Hank Aaron at Dodger Stadium....

Home Recording Rights Coalition

http://www.digex.net/hrrc/hrrc.html

A good example of a web site devoted to political advocacy. If you're wor-

The hot spot this past holiday season was the Rome Lab Snowball Cam, which advertises itself as a robot arm, ice machine and camera setup that invites Internet visitors to heave snowballs at engineers working at an Air Force base in Rome, New York.

Philip Elmer-DeWitt, in *Time*

ried about protecting your right to record music or TV programs, this site is a clearing house for information on the issue. Lawyers, politicians, and telecommunications industry professionals can learn a lot here.

EXCERPT:

The HRRC is...dedicated to preserving your right to purchase and use home audio and video recording products for noncommercial purposes.

Hot! Hot! Hot!

http://www.hot.presence.com/hot/

Not for the meek of tongue. The on-line catalog of a Pasadena hot sauce shop offers dozens of products with names like Jamaica Hellfire and Bat's Brew Hot Sauce. You can burn your mouth with links to Gifts of Fire that are arranged according to Heat Level/Origin/Ingredients/Name.

EXCERPT:

We want to welcome you to the Internet's first "Culinary Headshop!"...We have over 100 products of fire and the list is always growing.

Hotwired

http://www.hotwired.com/

A cool and comprehensive 'zine. Everything from travel and technology news to chat groups, games and images, and electronic classified ads. For the on-line generation, it serves many of the purposes that a newspaper did for American families in the past.

EXCERPT:

HotWired's five channels are like five different doorways into the digital revolution....

How far is it?

http://gs213.sp.cs.cmu.edu/prog/dist

In case you needed to know, this site provides distances, as the crow flies, between any two points in the United States. It also provides a map showing the two places, using the Xerox PARC Map Server. Are we there yet?

EXCERPT:

This service uses the University of Michigan Geographic Name Server to find the latitude and longitude of [any] two places....

HTML Validation Service

http://www.halsoft.com/html-val-svc/

A helpful service for Web site builders to make sure they are using a legal URL address. This site will help you determine if your idiom and/or syntax conforms to the HTML 2.0 specification.

EXCERPT:

This form is intended to be used by folks who are wondering whether some idiom or syntax is legal according to the HTML 2.0 specification....

The Hub

http://web.syr.edu/~jbarnold/intro.html

The experimental Web pages of a Syracuse University student. Very clear graphics, with a heavy emphasis on memory pigs that take all day to load. Many links, too.

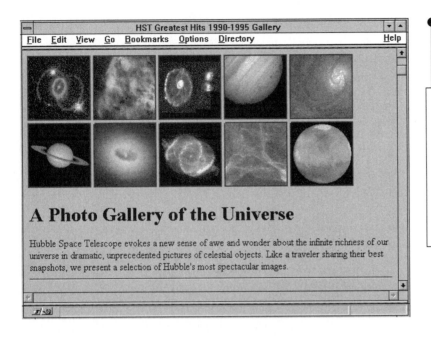

A Photo Gallery of the Universe

Hubble Space Telescope evokes a new sense of awe and wonder about the infinite richness of our universe in dramatic, unprecedented pictures of celestial objects. Like a traveler sharing their best snapshots, we present a selection of Hubble's most spectacular images.

Hubble Space Telescope's Greatest Hits 1990-1995

http://www.stsci.edu/pubinfo/BestOfHST95.html

Amazing images from far, far away are featured at this tribute to the achievements of the Hubble Space Telescope. The main screen showcases 10 of the best Hubble images, with hundreds of others available in the archives. Lengthy descriptions of the images and full-text press releases accompany the GIF, TIFF, and JPEG images. Scan the skies for Supernova 1987A: Halo for a Vanished Star, The Orion Nebula: Stellar Birthplace, and Ring around a Suspected Black Hole in Galaxy NGC 4161.

EXCERPT:

Hubble Space Telescope evokes a new sense of awe and wonder about the infinite richness of our universe in dramatic, unprecedented picture of celestial objects....

HypArt—The Project

http://rzsun01.rrz.uni-hamburg.de/cgi-bin/Hyp.sh

If only the United Nations could cooperate like this. Web users from around the globe collaborate here on a common theme, and everyone contributes very colorful computer illustrations. A painting is always in progress and anybody can contribute.

E X C E R P T :

The thought is to create a single picture together with other people from all around the world.

Hype Electrazine

http://www.phantom.com/~giant/hype.html

A 'zine featuring cartoons, music clips, and an occasional interview, mainly with on-line techies. Links to some strange Soundz/Toons/Stuff/Utils.

hyper@ctive

http://hyperactive.com/

A great stop for computer game players You can link to News; Previews; Reviews; Play Guides; Missing Stuff; and Features. The reviews will help you weed out the stuff that just wastes your time.

E X C E R P T :

Strap your favourite karate symbol around your head all you PC fighting fans because here comes FX Fighter....

hyperFuzzy

http://www.hyperfuzzy.com/

An oblique 'zine offering suggestions for music aficionados, essays and other forms of creative writing, and a worldwide chat group.

E X C E R P T :

Anyone who enjoys his computers or video games has been forced, at one time or another, to defend the very existence of technology.

Hyperreal

http://hyperreal.com/

A guide to rave parties, including the latest in music, media attention given to ravers, a calendar of major, upcoming raves, and a guide to recreational drugs. If you don't know what a rave party is, skip this web site. You probably won't be interested in it or the links to Rave Culture Archives; Music Resources; Electronic Publications; Chemistry; and Media Clips.

EXCERPT:

...Our mission is to give a home to alternative culture, music and expression.

Hyperweb

http://www.hyperweb.com/

An Austin-based shortcut to good web sites. Provides direct access to many sites on many topics, from food to politics to on-line commerce. Check the links to Promenade; Rest Stops; Residents Information; Library; and What's New.

EXCERPT:

...There is a world full of uncharted Internet space yet to be explored by us or any one person....

I

I Am Online

http://www.molson.com/canadian/

The place to come for anything and everything Canadian, I Am Online features a chat pub; the Canadian concert calendar; the Hockey Hall of Fame, with daily stats and a nationwide pool during hockey season; a compendium of provocative news, odd facts, humor, and cultural commentary derived from member submissions; and much, much more. Guests may browse freely, but membership (free) is required to send and receive Webmail, post a personal profile, contribute to the chat groups, and vote on the site's various opinion polls.

EXCERPT:

We're aiming to build the closest knit community on the World Wide Web....

Ideal Order Psychic TV

http://www.parnasse.com/ideal.htm

This man claims that every week he disrupts national evening newscasts by employing the powers of Zen to make the cameras glow. He claims to have interrupted three presidential debates in 1992 using the same technique. Goofy.

EXCERPT:

My intent is infinite and immaculate in its beautifully chaotic illuminative interventions; wreaking havoc with light....

We have to look at gaming as probably the largest untapped source of potential revenue and interactivity throughout the world today.

Nelson Goldberg, president of Gaming & Entertainment Television, a marketer of electronic gambling games, *The Detroit Free Press*

IHTFP Hack Gallery

http://fishwrap.mit.edu/Hacks/Gallery.html

This site presents a digest of hacks committed over a period of years at MIT or by MIT students or personnel. To qualify as an ethical hack, the hack must be safe, not damage anything or anyone, and be funny. The gallery exposes a list of hacks arranged by topic, location, and dates. Each is an enjoyable read and represents an innocent prank pulled off cleverly.

EXCERPT:

The word hack, when used here at MIT, usually refers to a clever, benign, and "ethical" prank which is both challenging for the perpetrators and amusing to the MIT community.

Imagex Design WWW

http://sandpiper.rtd.com/~imagex/index.html

Enter this web site and you enter an advertisement, albeit a really cool advertisement. You'll see the interactive portfolio of the WWW design talents of Imagex, an award-winning design firm. Enjoy the neat graphic images from a professional Web site builder—they're free. Or link to information about the company's services.

EXCERPT:

...Providing professional creative services for the Internet WWW community...

Imaging Radar Home Page

http://southport.jpl.nasa.gov/

NASA and JPL give you a prime seat on the Space Shuttle thanks to this home page. The high point is the cool views of the earth's features straight from Shuttle cameras. There are lots of neat shots from all over the globe, including San Francisco Bay, volcano views, and rain forest overheads. You can enhance the journey with 3-D movies.

EXCERPT:

Find out how to obtain radar images of many areas around the globe....

info HIGHWAY

http://www.gold.net/info-highway/

A technical magazine about the Internet written in conjunction with the folks at Newsbytes. Easy to navigate and suited to users of all major computer types. Covers all the news from the computing and computer communications industries.

EXCERPT:

In conjunction with Newsbytes, we bring you the most navigable IT news service on the Net....

The Information Supercollider

http://www.eecs.harvard.edu/collider.html

Click a button and this supercollider puts a random image from cyberspace on your computer screen. Imagine the odds against having your own home page pop up here. Worth a brief look and then move on.

EXCERPT:

...The collisions release small but massive information particles, scattered in all directions....

Inkspot

http://www.interlog.com/~ohi/inkspot/

A virtual Franklin Planner for children's writers, this site seems to list more than you would ever think to ask. Find libraries, publishers, and agents and then post and read items on the message boards.

Inquisitor Magazine

http://mosaic.echonyc.com/~xixax/Inquisitor/

Lots of articles on technology themes, cultural icons that have changed our lives, media criticism, and a fun, real-life diary of what it's like to exist in the Big Apple. The links are enticing: Inquisitor; The 90210 Weekly Wrap-Up; and New York Diary.

EXCERPT:

A content-dense, quarterly guide to media, art, culture, and technology.

Insect Nest

http://www.interport.net/~rexalot/insectnest.html

Try this one in the dead of winter for a creepy, crawly reminder of summer. Point and click on the bugs. Hear them chirp. After an encounter like this, you might stop counting the days until you return to the beach.

EXCERPT:

Come in! See and Hear Them Sing.

Intelligent Gamer Online

http://igonline.escape.com/

This site calls itself the biweekly journal for the mature gaming community.

The Internet is the Holy Grail of billboards.

**Don Carpenter, president of Onestop Desktop, which will have a
graphical presentation online within the month.**

So if you are that kind of a game player, you might want to investigate the features, reviews, discussions, and technical information available here.

Interactive Graphics Renderer

http://www.eece.ksu.edu/IGR

Do you need tools to help you build your own Web page? Here's the place to find an easy-to-use interface for designing customized graphics. Lots of choice when it comes to color, size, and object so the result looks like a real custom job.

EXCERPT:

Here you will find a multitude of objects, colors, sizes and other options...to produce the bullet or line that you would like on your home page.

Interactive Movie Reviews

http://batech.com/cgi-bin/showmovie

Public movie ratings strictly by the numbers. Internet surfers, broken down into male and female categories, rate the most recent flicks at the box office. This would be a top-notch site if it made a little more information available. A few comments would be a big improvement.

EXCERPT:

The best movie reviews are the ones you pick. We thank you for your participation in our efforts bring the Internet users an honest movie review...

Interactive Patient Home Page

http://medicus.marshall.edu/medicus.htm

Play doctor here. This site is really designed for medical students, but everyday web surfers can also read about the patient's chief complaint and then get an additional history, perform an exam, and review lab reports and x-rays in order to make a diagnosis and suggest a course of treatment. Calling Dr. Welby.

EXCERPT:

A truly unique Interactive World Wide Web Program that allows the user to simulate an actual patient encounter. This teaching tool for physicians, residents and medical students...

International Interactive Genetic Art

http://robocop.modmath.cs.cmu.edu:8001/htbin/mjwgenforml

This site is an interactive art exhibit in which a set of pictures is displayed on the page and the user rates each one on a scale of 0 to 9. After each 10 votes, the results are tallied and used by a genetic algorithm to create new pictures. You'll have to wait a while to see the changes, but it's worth the wait.

Internet and Comms Today

http://www.atlas.co.uk/paragon/ict1.html

Internet and Comms Today may be Britain's best-selling Internet magazine, but it's not the Internet's best web site—at least not yet. Offering only a few links, there's not as much on this page as in the print magazine. It's hardly "encyclopedic" as it claims to be. The posted articles are okay, but the page will improve when more information-filled files are added. Main links include Video Conferencing, Getting MUDdy, JANET, Service Providers, and Computing.

EXCERPT:

Welcome to the *Internet and Comms Today* home page, the site of Britian's best selling Internet magazine. Over the next few months, we plan to construct the perfect binary companion to the print magazine, with lead features and reviews from past issues, together with sneak peaks at forthcoming ones. The aim is to build up an encyclopedic well of knowledge on all things Internet.

Internet Art Museum for Free

http://www.artnet.org/iamfree/

IAMfree is a "first of its kind" museum dedicated to bringing the Internet community a wide range of contemporary media including literature, music, photography, and motion pictures. All art displayed at IAMfree has been created exclusively for this museum and is free (for noncommercial use). The museum is operated by the Artists for Revolution Through Technology on the Internet (ARTnet). Membership is IAMfree is free and you can join online.

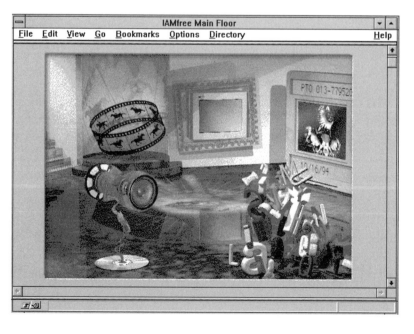

internet
entertain-
ment
network:
hollywood
online

"Greenpeace will continue to put ourselves between the whalers and whales for as long as we can stay here in Antarctica," said Greenpeace whales campaigner Kieran Mulvaney. "But we obviously can't stop the whale hunt by ourselves. It's up to the 23 governments and their citizens who created the sanctuary this year to convince Japan to stop its hunt and call back its whaling fleet."

Greenpeace International:
http://www.greenpeace.org/whales/wahling.html

EXCERPT:

IAMfree has embarked on an ever-changing series of exhibits in modern art, bereft of the pitfalls and commercialization that is currently stifling art.

Internet Documentation (RFC's, FYI's, etc.) and IETF

http://ds.internic.net/ds/dspg0intdoc.html

No need to go here, unless you are among the growing number of Internet architects. While government is a nasty word on the Internet, somebody has to preserve some sense of order. This site includes much of the work, debate, and publications of the many folks involved in the building of the Internet.

EXCERPT:

The Internet Engineering Task Force (IETF) is the protocol engineering, development, and standardization arm of the Internet Architecture Board....

Internet Entertainment Network: Hollywood Online

http://www.hollywoodnetwork.com

The Internet Entertainment Network is a vast list of paths to all sorts of

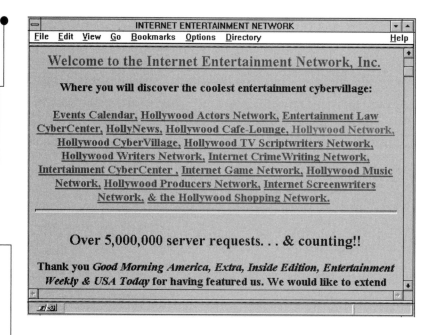

INTERNET ENTERTAINMENT NETWORK

File   Edit   View   Go   Bookmarks   Options   Directory   Help

Welcome to the Internet Entertainment Network, Inc.

Where you will discover the coolest entertainment cybervillage:

Events Calendar, Hollywood Actors Network, Entertainment Law
CyberCenter, HollyNews, Hollywood Cafe-Lounge, Hollywood Network,
Hollywood CyberVillage, Hollywood TV Scriptwriters Network,
Hollywood Writers Network, Internet CrimeWriting Network,
Intertainment CyberCenter , Internet Game Network, Hollywood Music
Network, Hollywood Producers Network, Internet Screenwriters
Network, & the Hollywood Shopping Network.

Over 5,000,000 server requests. . . & counting!!

Thank you *Good Morning America, Extra, Inside Edition, Entertainment
Weekly & USA Today* for having featured us. We would like to extend

entertainment services and subject areas, including networks for screen and
TV writers, producers, and other folk who flock to Hollywood. Chief
among the great services at this web site is a prodigious movie database
which contains facts on all facets of the movie industry. What's more, you
can shop, play games, and participate in community chat areas. As far as
home pages go, this one's dense, rife with myriad links and extensive expla-
nations of what you're getting into before you click.

E X C E R P T :

Welcome to the Internet Entertainment Network Inc. where you will discover the coolest entertainment cybervillage.

Internet in a Baby

http://www.wideweb.com/baby

Internet in a Baby was deservedly named Cool Site of the Day on April 2,
1995. Click on a part of the baby and travel to some of the net's most
unique destinations. (Bet you never would have thought on your own about
visiting the Mr Edible Starchy Tuber Head Page.) For those in need of a little help, there's a cheat-sheet page and an extensive bookmark page with
useful links to reference, government, HTML resources, and much more.

EXCERPT:

We proudly present the next generation, the ultimate user interface, the only Internet product that even a baby could use: Internet in a Baby.

Internet Island

http://hisurf.aloha.com

Having trouble scraping up change for that Hawaiian vacation? Surf over to the Internet Island. Download the picture postcard for the day, check out the local shops and restaurants, and when you're ready to hit the beach, check the weather and surf report. There's also local news here and a bulletin board for posting messages to other island visitors. Oh, and what's a trip to Hawaii without a lei? Get your virtual lei and enter the monthly contest for an "I got Lei'd on Internet Island" t-shirt.

Internet Movie Database

http://www.cm.cf.ac.uk/Movies/moviequery.html

Pop up a big bowl of popcorn and grab a soda, because we're off to the movies. The Internet Movie Database contains more than any one person could ever know about movies, from the silent era to the present. You'll find details of "tens of thousands" of films, some of which are still in production; biographies of actors, actresses, directors, and other important folks; ratings; and reviews.

EXCERPT:

Enough information to melt even the brain of a black belt in movie trivia.

Internet Published Comics

http://www.reed.edu/~rseymour/home/comics/comics.html

An unofficial bibliography of comics available for the reading pleasure of net surfers. Links to 13 comics as well as access to the Finnish Comics Society web page. There are also full-color sample comics to chuckle over.

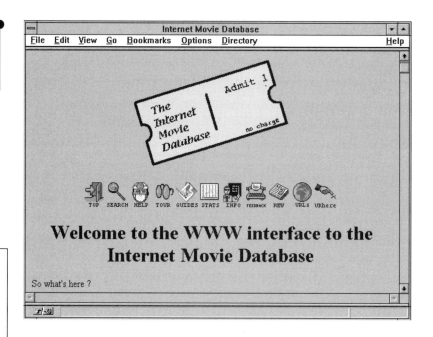

Internet Resources

http://www.brandonu.ca/~ennsr/Resources/

This site has links to online materials that will be useful to Internet trainers and anyone who wants to learn about online resources. There are mailing list directories, search tools, Internet book reviews, and links to Internet consultants. Internet Resources has won awards from both Cool Site of the Day and Point Survey, which ranked it within the top 5% of all web sites.

Internet Roundtable Interviews

http://www.irsociety.com/

The Roundtable presents multimedia interviews, each followed by a moderated audience-question-and-answer period. Guests range from physicists to current-affairs authors and from experts on the online community to true crime authors. Check the home page for a handy schedule of upcoming guests. If you miss an interview, transcripts and biographies of guests are also available in HTML format. The Roundtable uses WebChat server software so all you need is your web browser.

Check out the Internet calling card assembled by Eve Astrid Andersson, a student at the California Institute of Technology, which includes a Martian version of herself — with green skin and two antennae — grinning out into cyberspace....

"It's like a huge billboard for yourself," said Andersson, 20, whose page has brought her marriage proposals, a horde of regular cyber pen pals and job offers. There's even an Eve Andersson Home Page fan club.

Fern Shen, *The Washington Post,* **April 25, 1995.**

EXCERPT:

The Internet Roundtable is...a window into the insights of the policymakers, innovators, authors, and artists who shape today's political world.

The Internet Sleuth

http://www.intbc.com/Sleuth

The Internet Sleuth makes finding the particular piece of information that you what a little bit easier. This site is a one-stop search facility that uses forms that let you take advantage of many of the major Internet search engines without having to travel to each one. There is also a list of hundreds of useful hotlinks arranged in alphabetical order and by subject. These links are all search engines or listings of other databases.

Internet Travel Network

http://www.itn.net/cgi/get?ita/index/

Calling all travelers! ITN lets surfers access a national reservation system that draws its information from the Apollo system used by travel agents across the country. Real-time airline pricing and seat availability is here and free 24 hours a day for all commercial airlines worldwide except South-west Airlines, which operates its own web site (http://www.iflyswa.com/). ITN does not sell tickets but acts as an interface between Internet users and registered travel agents who can book your trip. There is no charge to the user and many of the agencies will waive ticketing fees.

E X C E R P T :

...Real-time [travel] information straight from the same source used by over a third of the world's travel agents.

Internet Underground Music Archive

http://www.iuma.com/

IUMA presents full-length music (stereo and mono) of more than 600 inde-pendent bands, 33 different genres of music from a cappella to hip-hop to world beat, as well as spoken word recordings. Featured works can be downloaded as excerpts (.au format) or as compressed full-length record-ings (MPEG format). Many artist biographies are included as well as e-mail addresses to contact them with comments. Start with the guided tour that shows off the featured links at this site.

Internet World Home Page

http://www.mecklerweb.com/mags/iw/iwhome.htm

Internet World sets a pretty high standard for what an online magazine should look online. Acting as a kind of virtual archive, *Internet World* not only provides access to issues of its own magazine, but it also serves as a clearinghouse for many other internet services and useful sites. The web site even gives you the opportunity to order Net Gear—purchasable items for the fashion-conscious surfer. Overall, this homepage offers all sorts of news and information for the surfer keen to stay in the know.

E X C E R P T :

Internet World Extra: Because Paper Isn't Enough.

The Internet WorldWide Classifieds Service

http://www.worldwide-classifieds.com/classifieds/

A well-designed and colorful online classified section. It's even capable of displaying photo ads. Rates are cheap — $2.75 for a basic, one month ad. You pay via credit card for both the ads and purchases. One glitch: many of the categories are currently vacant. The site claims nearly a 1,000 hits a week (not tremendous by Web standards).

InternetMCI

http://www.internetmci.com/

The first thing you encounter when you hook up to InternetMCI are two Mosaic stand-in icons for two larger hypertext maps. The hypertext MCI map is some of the leading edge web work, and the links lead to all sorts of useful information for newbies and veterans alike. Maybe the best thing is that there's no Friends & Family program here, so you don't need to "name names" to MCI. Instead, you can get 25 tips on navigating the net or learn the history of MCI and the Internet.

InterSex City/The Point of No Return

http://www.intersex.com/

InterSex City is a subscription-based service "designed to provide you with all the services of any real metropolitan area." The Red Light District is restricted to users aged 21 years and older, who must provide an e-mail address for billing. The charge for Red Light District access is currently $19.95/month. Limited visitation is allowed but you still have to register. In the unrestricted area (The Main Drag) there's a pretty good hotlist arranged by subject and links to businesses of various sorts.

Think of home pages as digital dorm rooms, furnished with just about anything: scantily clad supermodels, the home page maker's dog (click to hear him howl), reproductions of the Dead Sea Scrolls, essays on black history.

Fern Shen, *The Washington Post,* April 25, 1995.

Intrrr Nrrrd

http://www.etext.org/Zines/Intrrr.Nrrrd/intrrr.html

This e-zine is an online tribute to punk rock (er...."rawwwk"). There's a plethora of album covers, short reviews, and audio clips, as well as schedules of tours in Chicago, the Bay Area, and Michigan. Other links include downloadable Internet resources, Intrrr Nrrrd souvenirs and various .gifs.

EXCERPT:

INTRRR NRRRD Salvaaayshun! Saving Souls with Punk Rawwwk Since August 1994.

Ion Science

http://www.injersey.com/Media/IonSci/

ION Science is a weekly magazine that explains the latest trends in science and nature to people who are not rocket scientists. Some topics from recent issues are stress, memory, coho salmon depletion, and a ranking of "the most miserable U.S. cities" for summer heat, and plenty of past issues of ION Science are also available.

EXCERPT:

ION Science's professional writers and artists will demystify complex topics because we don't think you have to be a rocket scientist to gain insight into the natural world.

IRC *Cheers* Channel Gallery

http://www.enterprise.net/kipper/cheers.html

If you're into IRC (Internet relay chat) and you're a huge fan of the TV show *Cheers*, then you may enjoy this site. You'll find tips for finding the *Cheers* IRC channel, hints for proper behavior when chatting, and a virtual brick wall with graffiti by the denizens of the *Cheers* channel. If you've never heard of IRC and Sam and Diane are your favorite news anchors, go to the nearest major airport and hang around a real *Cheers* bar. You'll have more fun.

EXCERPT:

The very first days were strenuous...I remember clearly....whole nights passed like minutes...real world beers vanishing... but IRC caught me...I'm addicted now and will be on forever....

J

It's impossible to know how many of the 75,000 sites on the Web are home pages created by individuals (rather than by organizations or businesses), but schools in the Washington area and across the country report that courses teaching HTML, the programming language necessary to make a page, are booked solid this year.

Fern Shen, *The Washington Post,* April 25, 1995.

Japan Edge

http://www.ces.kyutech.ac.jp/student/JapanEdge/e-index.html

Japan Edge is an alternative culture page with links to underground music, art, literature, and fashion. Users can see main information in either English or Japanese. Many of the links lead to pages in Japanese. Much of the culture section leads to Japanese adults-only sites.

EXCERPT:
...This archive introduce Japanese street/underground culture information. Now you are making connection to here.

Japan Window

http://jw.stanford.edu

The Japan Window project was developed to research human-computer interaction, Japan-information content, multilingual computing, and Japanese technology management. The site is aimed primarily at American users. Topics include Living and Travel in Japan; Japanese Government; Japanese Science and Technology; and Business and Finance. There is also a section called Kids Window for the K-12 set and a number of home pages in Japanese.

Jazz: The 1950s - Records & Photography

http://bookweb.cwis.uci.edu:8042/Jazz/JPRA6.html

If you want to learn about jazz, at least during the 1950s, stop by this site. Stop and hear some tunes, check out the books on the period, and find photographs and information about the musicians of that time. Explore some of the jazzy links to Publications & Exhibitions; The Jazz Photography of Ray Avery; The Lighthouse All Stars; Nightclubs, Festivals, & Concerts; and Recording Sessions - Los Angeles.

EXCERPT:

Jazz: the 1950s - Records and Photography, provides some historical anchors to the jazz scene of the mid 1950s, and traces the growing popularity of jazz through magazine articles from this period.

JazzWeb

http://www.nwu.edu/jazz/

Lots of jazzy information, including a hypertext chart illustrating the history of and relationships between styles of jazz, with essays; biographies, discographies, and reviews of jazz artists; performances, including festivals, venues, and regional jazz events; jazz instruments; jazz in the media; jazz art; jazz education and musicianship; retailers; and links to other jazz-related resources.

EXCERPT:

The end goal of the JazzWeb is to contribute to the fantasy of finding all answers to all questions on demand....

The Jihad to Destroy Barney on the WWW

http://deepthought.armory.com:80/~deadslug/Jihad/jihad.html

Barney sure isn't the most popular dinosaur in cyberspace. Yet another site for Barney bashers. You can find the FAQ for alt.barney.dinosaur.die.die.die, information about the war against Barney, and even a bit of fiction. There's Jihad Art; Jihad Software; Jihad Codes; Jihad Literature; and Barney Fun Page.

EXCERPT:

Barney must die, all else is irrelevant.

J.V. Jones

http://www.imgnet.com/auth/jjones.html

This is the web site of the nationally renowned science fiction author, J.V. Jones, author of *The Baker's Boy*. Here you can read excerpts from the book (the prologue and first two chapters); read reviews of Ms. Jones' work, as well as a short biography; and be graced with the wisdom of Bodger & Grift, "the two strangest medieval guards on the net."

EXCERPT:

"[Baker's Boy is] a complex tale of sorcery and swordsmanship, intrigue, and affairs of the heart." —Library Journal.

Michael Jordan Page

http://gagme.wwa.com/~boba.mj.html

This web site provides an on-line tribute and fact omnibus devoted to Michael Jordan, the Bulls, and the NBA. Included are Michael's Statistics; Career Summaries; links to other Michael Jordan pages on the World Wide Web; information about the Chicago Bulls; Bulls Statistics; Scoreboard returns for the playoffs; "Top 10 Reasons for MJ's Return;" Sports Cards; Bulls Roster; NBA Today; and links to other National Basketball Association web sites.

Finding well-designed Web sites and pages is...a little like watching cloud formations. Just when you think you've spied something beautiful and interesting—it changes. That's because everyone on the Web is checking out what everyone else is doing and changing what they've done, accordingly.

Anita Dennis, *Publish,* **September, 1995.**

EXCERPT:

This is the Michael Jordan page....If you are really into Michael or the NBA, you can spend hours at this site.

Journal of Buddhist Ethics

http://www/psu.edu/jbe/jbe.html

This online scholarly journal promotes the study of Buddhist ethics. The journal covers ten areas of ethics, including Vinaya and Jurisprudence; Medical Ethics; Philosophical Ethics; and Human Rights. (The publication accepts submissions, subject to peer review.) Also of interest at this site is the Global Resource Center page, which has many links to other Buddhist studies Internet resources.

JRNY

http://www.columbia.edu/~newmedia/JRNY/

These pages are the project of graduate students at Columbia University developed as an experiment in "non-linear media." An image map leads the user to articles and images relevant to the NYC Area, such as crime, fashion, transportation, and restaurants.

EXCERPT:

The Center for New Media is a working laboratory for journalists, film makers, engineers, educators, publishers and others to develop new and innovative forms of storytelling and multimedia information delivery....

Juggling Information Service

http://www.hal.com/services/juggle/

Anything you might want to know about juggling is here at JIS: news; pictures (still and motion); shopping at the Juggler's Mall; events listings; magazines - including a full archive of Juggler's World; simulation software; and links to other jugglers' home pages and associations. And if you follow the link to Barry Bakalor's personal page, you can see a picture of him juggling with Alan Greenspan.

Jumble

http://odin.chemistry.uakron.edu/cbower/jumble.html

If all else fails, cheat! The Jumble home page is an ingenious and valuable site for word puzzle enthusiasts who might be looking for a little shortcut to solve tough puzzles. The beauty of this web site is that it will automatically unscramble scrambled words or offer solutions to tough crosswords. The home page is plain and unadorned, so it downloads fast for those of you are impatient for answers.

EXCERPT:

If you're like me, the scrambled words and crossword puzzles in the newspaper are an exercise in frustration tolerance. No longer! Let the computer do the work!

Justin's Links From the Underground

http://www.links.net/

Links From the Underground contains a wealth of information, from the frivolous to the sublime. The Underground Content page includes: sex, drugz, spirituality, net nuggets, eye candy, music, literary links, science

sites, communities, commerce, line law, and news. If you want to survey the full spectrum of Internet culture this is definitely the place to look.

EXCERPT:

I know the web is getting big when Internet World beats me to covering an offbeat site.

K

Kaleidospace

http://kspace.com/

Kaleidospace is a multimedia art studio where the user can view and purchase works by medium—acrylics; lithographs; metal assemblages; mixed media; ocean life; oils; pencil; photography; serigraphs; and watercolor—or by subject—abstract; chaos; English nursery tradition; florals; inspirational vision; landscapes; Mexican & Latin American; New Age; seascapes; shadow world; sports art; still life; travel-pop culture; wildlife; and women.

EXCERPT:

In its short history, Kaleidospace has become one of the most popular sites on the Internet - with 10-40,000 visitors daily and real sales when most groups are still debating Internet commerce.

Keepers of the Lists, The

http://www.dtd.com/keepers/

Here's a little competition for David Letterman. The Keepers of the Lists is a site where Internet users can read and contribute to a variety of top (fill-in-the-number) lists. Each day the Keepers post a new theme, such as Top Episode Titles for the New TV Show "The Brady Bunch X-Files" or Top Brand New Events for the Atlanta Olympics. Users can vote yea or nay on each list item and can add new items to the list at any time.

EXCERPT:

We are a secret society dedicated to the creation and maintenance of lists.

The most wonderful thing about the Net is its very existence: there has never yet been such a large gathering of people over which no one had clear authority. And although many people think that the Usenet humor groups are nothing more than places to swap jokes, they are, in reality, the leading edge of the wave of modern evolution. So rest assured that when you spend your time to read jokes on the Net, you are not just idling away a few idle minutes. Rather, you are watching human progress in action and participating in what is truly a revolution in the history of mankind.

Harley Hahn and Wendy Murdock, *Boardwatch*

Kerry's Home Page

http://www4.ncsu.edu/eos/users/k/klsmith2/mosaic/index.html

This is the personal page of an engineering freshman at NCSU with a collection of sounds and pictures from Animaniacs, as well as a link to probably the largest Animaniacs collection online. There are also pages of links for DOOM, various other interactive games, Movies and Pics; Sounds and Music; and TV and Movies. If you like personal pages of college students, give it a try.

Kev's World

http://www.cris.com:80/~Mppa/s2f/kevin.shtml

You don't need to turn to the funny papers for your laugh of the day. Just hop over to Kev's World and view the cartoon of the day. Kevin Nichols has been drawing newspaper cartoons for 10 years and now entertains the web world with some of his creations.

Kibo

http://rescomp.stanford.edu/~asuter/kibo/kibo.html

What is Kibology? Well, it's a philosophy of the Net that helps keep us from getting too, shall we say, ostentatious. Branching off from the alt.religion.kibology newsgroup, the Kibo page takes a hard and funny look at any thread that seems bizarre, outrageous, and takes itself too seriously.

EXCERPT:

There are places where people can be pretentious and radical and cyber-punkian and all that. Then there are the places where we make fun of them, like here.

The Kids in the Hall Show

http://www.usit.net/public/jmbell/kith/kith.html

Yes, another TV spinoff page, this time for *Kids in the Hall,* a sketch comedy TV show known for its offbeat irreverent characterizations of men and women. As usual, you will find episode lists, updates on recurring characters, transcripts, and sound files.

Kids Internet Delight

http://www.clark.net/pub/journalism/kid.html

This page grew out of a demonstration about the Internet for children. It sports links to 50 sites of kid-appropriate material that might be of interest to children and their parents. It's a good safe site for kids to use.

EXCERPT:

Gathered here are anchors to sites that children and their parents might enjoy.

Kids' Space

http://www.interport.net/kids-space

Here's a spot for kids of all ages. Kids Space is set up to allow children to "authentically experience the Internet." Kids Space encourages visitors to send in their pictures, stories, music, and letters. Good kid links to What's New; Kids Gallery; Story Book; On Air Concert; Beanstalk; Outside; Mail Office; and Doctor's Help Office.

EXCERPT:

Kids Space is everybody's home page.

KidsCom

http://www.spectracom.com/kidscom/indexl.html

Here's another site for kids where they can feel right at home. The site is well monitored and provides a safe environment for kids to be kids. They can find a pen pal, ask questions of the resident Net expert, Scott Yanoff, play games, write stories, decorate the Graffiti wall, and even talk about their pets.

EXCERPT:

We knew that before you sit your young one in front of KidsCom, you would want to check things out first, so please take some time to explore this special adults preview section....

Kingswood Kranium

http://www.kingswood.com/

Kranium is an online magazine created by writers, art directors, and programmers at Kingswood Advertising in Pennsylvania. There are really cool graphics, a parody corporate brochure (if you look hard enough you'll find a real one, too), humorous lists, an advice column (Just Ask Shecky), and "Links to Other Sites That Will Get on Your Nerves."

"The television is still the most powerful medium for influencing consumers in our culture," said Mr. Renker (a founding partner of Guthy Renker).

"The power of the Internet will be to enable consumers to access television's products conveniently. The television will create the need; the Internet will fulfill it."

Kim Cleland, *Advertising Age,* **August 7, 1995**

EXCERPT:

Creative Creed: When you come right down to it, creative brilliance is at the heart of all great advertising....

The Klingon Language Institute

http://www.kli.org/

This site is the home of KLI, the Klingon Language Institute, which was founded in January 1992 and grew to more than 750 members in 20 different countries by the summer of 1994. Here you can see how Klingon is written and hear it pronounced; learn about different KLI projects (examples are Bible translation and the Shakespeare Restoration project); read through archives of the KLI mailing list; and get info on joining the organization.

Aidan Christopher Kolar

http://chemviz3.ncsa.uiuc.edu/aidan.html

Aidan is a true '90s kinda kid—his baby book is on the web. Proud mom and dad have posted baby photos, updates on Aidan's progress, and even a guest book for Aidan to read when he learns how. Aidan's baby book was the Cool Site of the Day on 11/24/94.

4 March 1995 Aidan starts eating solid foods. His favorite food is peas, though he also likes pears mixed in with cereal.

Stanley Kubrick Page

http://www.lehigh.edu/~pjl2.kubrick.html

This is a multimedia tribute to Stanley Kubrick, supplemented by sound samples, film clips, images, biographical information about the director, and data about each of his films. Links to the Internet Movie Database and Voyager Film Clips are neatly incorporated on each page. You'll recognize lots of link names Paths of Glory; Lolita; Dr. Strangelove; 2001; A Clockwork Orange; Barry Lyndon; The Shining; and Full Metal Jacket.

Kyosaku

http://cs.oberlin.edu/students/djacobs/kyo/kyomain.html

Kyosaku is an e-zine "dedicated to endangered concepts." Here you will find images and writings such as "Ode to Grape Nuts," "Freakish Frank, Former Marine," and "A Fear of Small Round Things." Submissions are welcome, and subscriptions to the print version are available for $5 per year (4 issues).

EXCERPT:

Artistic rebellion is the least blatant but most gratifying means of spitting on society's shoes.

L

John Labovitz's e-zine list

http://www.meer.net/~johnl/e-zine-list/

John Labovitz updates his directory of electronic journals available on the net on a monthly basis. The list is available in both HTML and text versions. Additions are welcome, and there's a form to submit your e-zine if you have one to add to his list of more than 400 sites. In addition to the e-zine list, there's a page with resources related to hypertext and electronic publishing.

EXCERPT:

Over the last year and a half, the list has grown from 25 entries to over 250, an indicator of the huge growth in popularity of not only the net in general, but grass-roots/amateur/personal publishing as well.

Las Vegas Online

http://www.infi.net/vegas/online

Las Vegas, here we come—and Las Vegas Online is the first stop! Hosted by KLAS-TV (Channel 8), these pages have 24-hour news, weather, and sports, as well as links to entertainment, shopping, tourism, and an introduction to gaming. Businesses planning to relocate in the Vegas Area will find useful data on the labor force, foreign trade, and economic statistics. Individuals planning a move will find tons of useful facts about services, taxes, schools, and area recreation.

EXCERPT:

This year, more than 30-million people are expected to visit Las Vegas. Las Vegas Online is the first stop on your journey.

You've reached the top page of Las Vegas Online, presented by KLAS-TV (Channel 8; CBS affiliate) in Las Vegas, Nevada.

Our mission is to create the premier Las Vegas information source on the internet. We've built a one-stop resource where you should be able to find all the information and insights on Las Vegas you could ever need. If there's anything you can't find here, e-mail pikelny@vegas.infi.net and we'll answer your questions and/or add the information to our service.

Begin your journey by clicking on a choice below.

Last Files From The News

http://web.cnam.fr/Images/Usenet/

This site is really unfocused. There are many random images on many topics such as animals and cars, but the layout is poor and the source of the pictures is obscure. If you like to view pictures with a clear theme, go somewhere else.

The Last Homely House

http://www.bu.edu/~aarondf/

Modeled after J.R.R. Tolkien's world (there's a GREAT Tolkien resource page here), The Last Homely House leads you through the Internet maze with creative prose and beautiful images. Each page represents a room of the house. There's a library; a Hall of Fire (poetry and literature); a Games Room; a Kitchen; a Map Room (starting points for net exploration), an

THE LAST HOMELY HOUSE

File   Edit   View   Go   Bookmarks   Options   Directory   Help

Welcome to the Last Homely House

Aaron Fuegi , Proprietor

Click for beautiful full size JPEG (282K) or another image of Rivendell (394K JPEG)

You walk across the ford and up the steep path towards the Last Homely House, which shines in the midst of a beautiful woods and lies just in the shade of the tall mountains. You sense a great

Audio/Video Gallery; and a Hall of Excellence for the author's favorite links.

EXCERPT:

...this house was once said to be "a refuge for the weary and the oppressed, and a treasury of good counsel and wise lore."...Aaron quietly says that he has tried to have the house continue to live up to its reputation and, he hopes, has been reasonably successful.

Late Show with David Letterman Home Page

http://www.cbs.com/lateshow

Want to know what's coming up on Letterman? You can find out at this CBS site. You can see a list of that night's guests, check out cast bios, catch up on the latest news. There's photos, merchandise, and best of all, a complete archive of Late Show Top Tens.

EXCERPT:

Your source for daily Top Ten lists.

Electronic networks are rapidly supplementing and sometimes even supplanting traditional job-search methods. The
cost is low, and going on-line can be very effective; both
job hunters and corporations can cast a wider net than
with traditional methods, and the pool of job seekers tends
to be high-quality.

Bronwyn Fryer, *Working Woman*, March, 1995.

Latvis' RockData

http://www.skoji.uta.fi/~latvis/rockdata.html

Latvis' RockData is an online gateway to the Finnish music scene—mostly
rock, but folk and jazz make occasional appearances. Much of the text is in
Finnish but the concert schedules (very up-to-date) are easily interpreted.
There is a truly impressive directory of the entertainment industry in Fin-
land, replete with phones/addresses for sound and lighting companies, mas-
tering services, agents, clubs, and artists.

LavaMind

http://www.best.com:80/~lavamind

Gazillionaire is a game for all ages that is described by Family PC as "one of
the most addictive and educational business simulations around." Players run
a trading company in a science fiction environment and try to amass profit.
You can't actually play the game here but you can take a virtual trip through
the seven planets of Kukubia and meet some stranger-than-fiction characters.

Le WebENIC

http://www.enic.fr/webenic/webenic.html

This web site is a starting point for web exploration developed by French engineering students. The pages are available in either French or English and include a number of search tools, such as the World Wide Web Worm and a clickable world server map. Also included are a hotlink to the CIA, a books and libraries page, career sites, sex-oriented sites, and Pizza Hut's online delivery in Santa Cruz, CA. Could you ask for anything more?

EXCERPT:

You can find anything and everything on the Web. The WebENIC knows where to look....

Le WebMuseum

http://sunsite.unc.edu/wm/

Le WebMuseum with its vast collection of art works and sound clips that can be viewed, heard, and downloaded received the Best Use of Multiple Media Award at the CERN WWW'94 conference. The Famous Paintings exhibition, which includes works from the Gothic era through the 20th Century, can be searched by artist or by theme and includes a virtual a hypertext lesson in art history. The audio portion of this site has clips of classical works in .au format, as well as links to other multimedia sites.

One of the legal barriers to telemedicine, a much-touted application of the information superhighway, is the question of whether a physician consulting with a patient in another state should be licensed in that state. Last year, Kansas required out-of-state physicians to be licensed in Kansas if they use telemedicine to treat in-state patients....The transborder nature of on-line traffic means that an aggrieved party or prosecutor can pick the jurisdiction with the toughest law against a particular conduct, a practice known as "forum shopping."

Mitch Betts and Gary H. Anthes, in *Computerworld*

EXCERPT:

The ever-expanding WebMuseum network is now welcoming 100,000 visitors every week, delivering over 5 million documents!

The Timothy Leary and Robert Anton Wilson Show

http://www.intac.com/~dimitri/dh/learywilson.html

From the Psychedelic Experience to Gilligan's Island and the Eight Circuit Model, this page offers a mind-boggling potpourri of info about Timothy Leary, the father of psychedelia and LSD, and Robert Anton Wilson, who the page authors label as "one of the most profound and important scientific philosophers of this century." Tune in, trip out.

LeClub International

http://yucc.yorku.ca/home/leclub

The archives haven't been updated since November 1994, but the hotlist of 25 sites makes LeClub worth visiting. Some fun links include The Mother of All Archives and Comedy Central. LeClub also links with interactive entertainment on the Net, including quicktime video comedy skits, the Seinfeld Home Page, and sites to make your own virtual greeting cards.

EXCERPT:

We simply want to make computing fun and more human friendly.

Lego

http://legowww.homepages.com

Lego is one of the most popular toys in the world, and this site is an online repository for Lego resources. There are many downloadable images, Lego trivia and history, and links to other Lego sites on the net. This site is not affiliated with INTERLEGO A.G.

EXCERPT:

Children (and adults) in Europe alone play Lego 5 billion hours a year.

Les Miserables Home Page

http://www.ot.com/lesmis

This site is dedicated to *Les Miserables* in both its stage and literary versions. The novel page has a biography of Victor Hugo and a link to Project Gutenberg where the full text of *Les Miserables* can be downloaded (3.2Mb). A link to Professor Christopher Fox's Introduction to French Literature has recently been added to this page. The musical page includes a playbill, sound clips, graphics, a complete libretto, and tour dates.

Letter R.I.P.

http://www.dtd.com/rip/

Play a game of hangman with Dr. Fellowbug and Zeppie the Zombie (he's the one hanging on the dungeon wall). If you pick a wrong letter, the illustrious doctor proceeds to amputate. Dr. Fellowbug will cheer you with commentary as you play. Be sure to click on Zeppie, too.

EXCERPT:

Heavens to Betsy! These arms pop off just like the ones on my Barbie!

Letters from ABroad

http://www.compulink.co.uk/arc/abroad.htm

Take a peek into the lives (and mailboxes) of Doreen and Birdie—two girls from New York City who met while working in the secretarial pool of an international ad agency, Way Cool, and then got transferred. Birdie's in Boston; Doreen's in London. Doreen's ex- is seeing the cutthroat assistant personnel director in New York but still professes his love. Birdie keeps an eye out on this side of the Atlantic.

EXCERPT:

This is your chance to do the unthinkable....snoop in the private mailboxes of 2 very crazy young women...

LIFE

http://pathfinder.com/life/lifehome.html

This site has *LIFE* photo essays, and the photos are awesome; after all, this is *LIFE*. There is also a Virtual Gallery where you can view thumbnail images and order the items via a toll-free number. Items for sale include notecards, posters, calendars, books, and CD-ROMs. You can also subscribe to *LIFE*.

EXCERPT:

LIFE of course does more than present discrete photographic moments. The magazine was also a pioneer when it came to telling stories in still images. *LIFE*, in effect, created the photo essay.

The Lighthouse

http://the-tech.mit.edu/Weather/

This site, provided by The Tech, MIT's oldest and largest newspaper, has weather forecasts for more than 250 U.S. locations and nearly 60 foreign cities as well as a national weather summary. U.S. locations can be requested by city, state, or airport code. Once your request is displayed, you can add that page to your personal hotlist so you'll always go straight to your local weather report. Generally the reports you receive reports are less than an hour old.

The Link Digital Campus

http://www.linkmag.com/

This site is a virtual campus with news and resources for college students. Click on the campus map to travel the web. Links include various college newspapers around the country; a pub with games and sounds; a bookstore; a stadium where you can check out game schedules, scores, and standings; a theater where you can preview movies and read reviews; and a library and student union with other web resources.

Lite-Brite

http://www.galcit.caltech.edu/~ta/lb/lb.html

The favorite design tool of generations now lets you be an artist on the web. Go to Lite-Brite and create your own masterpiece. Each month there is a featured work, and you can check out all the previous months works. Take a Random Walk or visit the Gallery to view other Favorites.

loQtus

http://pubweb.ucdavis.edu/documents/quotations/homepage.html

Here's the site that can help you write that banquet speech or check on who said "One if by horse; two if by sea." LoQus provides links to Quotations Resources; Archives; and Series. Might not be the most exciting net site, but can come in handy when you need to check a phrase.

Legal experts say the industry should be worried. Already, Prodigy is facing a libel suit because of a message sent on its system attacking a company. The courts said Prodigy could be liable.

"It's an impossible situation," Post says. [David Post, a cyberspace law analyst at Georgetown University Law Center] "The court's message to service providers is if you screen messages, you become liable for the content of the messages. On the other hand, Congress comes along and says you've got to monitor."

Haya El Nasser, in *USA Today*

EXCERPT:

Please note that Jack makes no warranty and cannot be held responsible for the use...of these ideas....

Los Angeles Webstation

http://www.losangeles.com/

It's a big city out there, and someone's got to help you get around. Use this site as your guide to movies and cinemas, traffic updates, weather forecasts, entertainment, and the dozens of media outlets in the City of Angels. (Keep your street map handy.)

Lurker's Guide to *Babylon 5*

http://www.hyperion.com/lurk/lurker.html

This site offers a copious amount of material related to *Babylon 5*, a popular television series. You can link to sites that review past episodes and preview the current show, sell *Babylon*-related merchandise, and analyze the characters and plot. Also try out Novels; Writers; Directors; Foreign Schedules; Production History; and Fan Clubs.

EXCERPT:

The Lurker's Guide is a volunteer effort encompassing documents maintained by many *Babylon 5* fans....

Lycos, the Catalog of the Internet

http://lycos.cs.cmu.edu

Lycos, the Latin name for the wolf spider (a type which weaves no web, but actively hunts its food) is also the name of this net hunter. Lycos explores the Web and builds a database of all the web pages it finds every day. You can search the database or learn more about Lycos, Inc., including employment opportunities.

Mabus Homeroom

http://www.rpi.edu/~mabusj/home.html

Mabus is a list of World Wide Web sites that have multimedia content or files available for downloading. Neither comprehensive nor particularly unique, the listing is grouped loosely around the type of site or application being offered, for example, Graphics; Icons; and Textures.

EXCERPT:

Welcome Gathers. Join us in the battle for Dominia.

Apple/Examiner *MacWorld* San Francisco Home Page

http://www.examiner.com/projects/macworld/

The *MacWorld* page, or rather the Electric Examiner *MacWorld* page from San Francisco, is not the best the web has to offer. Though you get a wide range of Apple services here, including a web server, many of the links are cryptic, so you're not sure what you're getting when you click on the icon. Still there's some useful stuff here, though apparently the site is not updated frequently; in fact, it still features a "Happy Holidays" greeting presumably from the 1994 Christmas season.

Sarah McLachlan Home Page

http://www.nettwerk.com//sarpg.html

Fans of the Canadian folk-pop songwriter and musician Sarah McLachlan

Take something as innocuous as letter-writing. With cheap long-distance telephone service, people had fallen out of the habit. But thanks to the new virtual post office that vast computer networks create, tens of millions of people have rediscovered the lost art.

John W. Verity, in *Business Week*

will be fumbling towards Internet ecstasy when they discover this very complete site maintained by the artist's record label, Nettwerk Productions. Included are album covers, tour info, news about upcoming releases, song lyrics, several audio cuts, and lots more.

EXCERPT:

Sarah's intimate vocals and moody, evocative songs convey a passionate honesty rarely found in most of today's music.

Magic 8-Ball

http://www.resort.com/~banshee/misc/8ball/index.html

The Magic 8-Ball is a virtual Ouija board; it can respond to any yes or no question you ask. Responses range from "Yes" and "No" to "Very doubtful" and "Outlook not so good" or "It is certain" and "Yes—definitely." You will need to use a forms-based net browser to enter queries.

EXCERPT:

Before you seek the blessings of the Oracle, you should be aware that factions within the United States seek to deprive you of your right to free speech...

The Magic of Xanth

http://www.cs.indiana.edu/hyplan/awooldri/Xanth.html

Magic is the unofficial online home of Piers Anthony Dillingham and his

Xanth series of fantasy/science fiction books. Participate in ongoing discussions of Xanth and find images of Xanth characters, ways to contact Piers, lists of his complete works, and ways to get them.

MagicURL Mystery Trip

http://www.netcreations.com/magicurl/index.html

MagicURL Mystery Trip is a "random links" web site with a difference. While it's true that there are lots of home pages on the World Wide Web that play the random links game, this one only offers links to pages that the webmaster has checked out first. Chances are you'll travel to sites that are worth the trip. Just click on an icon, and you're transported to a randomly selected web page. Usually it's a pretty interesting site, too.

EXCERPT:

Imagine a place where every random link goes somewhere cool.... No college home pages, no MAKE MONEY FAST, no 'hi, I'm Biff, and I'm into TV!' Every link is hand selected by me, and I'm picky. Feel free to submit a link to me!

Main Sanitary Nag

http://infobahn.com:80/img/anagram.map?92,49

This interactive anagram creator accepts the user's input of a phrase or word and generates a list of anagrams, scrambled letters, and words based on the original text string. Fun for word buffs.

EXCERPT:

Na angamar si a wrod ro prhaes meda yb scarmbngi teh lesttre ni...

Make a Map with NAISMap

http://ellesmere.ccm.emr.ca/wnaismap/naismap.html

Using N-map (a Geographical Information System or GIS software engine), this site enables the user to manipulate points, lines, and areas (polygons) of any given map in the NAIS collection. The system accepts user input and produces an on-screen map. The system is forms based, so you'll need a browser that supports forms.

EXCERPT:

With NAISMap, you can view and manipulate National Atlas spatial data layers and construct your own map of Canada.

Mammoth Music Meta-List

http://www.timeinc.com/vibe/mmm

This site may be the most comprehensive music-related information site on the web. You'll find searchable information fields related to specific geographical regions; specific artists and recording labels; lyrics and discographies; instruments; styles and genres; radio stations; performances; sounds; MIDI; computer music; buying music recordings; music festivals; and music schools, libraries, and research.

EXCERPT:

...The intention is to keep this a relatively complete set of all music resources available.

> **I**n the coming digital, online world, the public libraries will: (a) languish as outdated, expensive artifacts of an earlier age, or (b) adapt and thrive as key resources on the Internet and as public on-ramps to the Information Super-highway.
>
> John W. Verity, *Business Week*

Mark's List of Internet Activity

http://eia.brad.ac.uk/mark/fave-inter.html

Handle remote-control robots, moveable cameras, laboratory equipment, and other devices all over the world from your home computer. Another link lets you look through automated telescopes. Nice stop for the curious and science minded.

Bob Marley's 50th Birthday Celebration

http://www.netaxs.com/~aaron/Marley/Marley.html/

Every genre has its king, and Bob Marley, to many, is considered the king of reggae. To keep that memory alive, you have the Bob Marley web page. It includes information about him and his family, audio clips, print materials dedicated to Bob, even information on Ziggy Marley and the Melody Makers. You'll also find links to various reggae and Caribbean sites.

EXCERPT:

This page is an ongoing celebration of Bob Marley's birthday, life, and accomplishments.

Mathart

http://www.wri.com/~mathart

View a series of digital 3-D sculptures, based on fractal art generations. The system also uses routines based on probabilities to generate lotto numbers and poetry. You can take links to Real-Time Poetry; Math-Art Fractal MUD; and Computer-Aided Rapid Mechanical Prototyping.

EXCERPT:

I am a Silicon Graphics Personal Iris 40/20G. I reside at the domicile and sculpture studio of Stewart Dickson...

Matiu Carr

http://www.auckland.ac.nz/arch/mats

This site is both a source of architectural knowledge and a teaching platform, including samples of projects, on-line models, interactive drawing programs, and software for producing rendered drawings. Go to the City Campus Model for details and examples based on the University of Auckland's City campus and to the Barcelona Pavilion, a model of the German Pavilion for the 1929 World Exposition at Barcelona.

EXCERPT:

It is now fairly readily accepted that drawing is more than a graphic expression of the thoughts of an architect, that it is in fact a part of a thought process involved in design...

Matthew and Jake's Adventures

http://www.mit.edu:8001/mj/mj.html

The "See Spot Run"-style adventures of a couple of MIT students, with text by Matthew, graphics by Jake. Jake wears a funny hat. Matthew has purple hair. Familiarity with the MIT campus not necessary. Link to your favorite story: Matthew and Jake Fly a Kite; Matthew and Jake go to the LSC Party; Matthew and Jake go to Walden.

EXCERPT:

Matthew and Jake are MIT students. They have adventures. They like the web, so they put the adventures there....

MCA/Universal Cyberwalk

http://www.mca.com/

This web site, run by the MCA/Universal entertainment conglomerate, is an awesome place to hang out. There are pages featuring the latest Universal movies and news from the Universal Studios theme parks. You can even order the latest books from Putnam Berkley Publishing. But this lavish, good-looking site is pretty hard to access, because the large number of visitors often overwhelms the server. Still, this home page is worth the extra effort.

EXCERPT:

Welcome to MCA/Universal Cyberwalk on the Internet. Here you can sample the latest products and entertainment from the MCA/Universal family of companies. Something's always happening on the MCA/Universal Cyberwalk—you'll find exciting items to explore, read, purchase, and entertain yourself.

McChurch Tabernacle

http://mcchurch.org

McChurch is a virtual tabernacle based on a fanciful (farcical?) set of tenets, online worship services, and links to various religious and quasi-religious sites. The "church" offers virtual "happy meals" for eternal salvation, along with a baptismal rite in memory of Harvey Glunkman, the McMartyr. The images are striking and more than slightly troublesome. Links to Snake Oil; Shroud of Turin Home Page; and much more.

EXCERPT:

McChurch is a REAL religion, complete with iconographic images suitable for worship, a martyred saint, snappy advertising slogans, and easy to understand spiritual truths....

Media Maniacs

http://www.crawford.com/media.maniacs/media.html

This eccentric web site offers conspiracy theories "from the future" and

> **M**arket players enjoy seeing the eternal battle between bulls and bears argued out on the level playing field of a computer screen. The Internet will become increasingly important to the market as investors discover the hidden values in cyberspace.
>
> **Dave Zgodzinski,** *Internet World*

links to musical excerpts from motion pictures, files related to liberty and the right to bear arms, and a Special Report on the National Emergency in the United States of America. The general theme supports prevailing conspiracy theories that the U.S. is being controlled by an elite group determined to disarm the populace and erode basic liberties.

EXCERPT:

Strange, apocalyptic postings originating from the future....

Media Whore Studios

http://www.phantom.com:80/~tomwhore

This site presents a series of stories about the Media Whore (called, naturally, "Tales of the Whore"). Story titles include "Send in the Clowns;" "First Person Prerogative;" "Spinning Wheels Got to Go Round;" "In the Haze of Scardozes Arm;" and others. The stories are text only.

EXCERPT:

This homepage contains content that may be offensive to some readers.

Mediamatic

http://www.mediamatic.nl

This slick quarterly digital publishes articles on media and art in simultaneous translation (Dutch and English). Each issue has a theme such as The

Ear, The End of Advertising, Storage Media, and Home. The main area is devoted to Mediamatic Magazine, but other files include conference reports, "Webside Story" (about the cultural implications of new media), and updates on media changes.

EXCERPT:

...Whatever the subject, playfulness and freedom of thought are applied to recreate unexpected insights....

Megadeth Arizona

http://bazaar.com/Megadeth/megadeth.html

Metal band Megadeth's Arizona experiences, along with information about the band's other activities, are presented in slick multimedia format. Visitors can download screen savers and postcards, musical soundbites, and digital movies from several of the files with titles like Obituary; Horrorscopes; Megabyte News; and Screen Saviors.

EXCERPT:

To record Youthanasia, Megadeth packed up and moved to Arizona where they built a unique recording studio in a warehouse on the outskirts of Phoenix....

Melvin Magazine

http://www.melvin.com

This biweekly on-line humor magazine is like a cross between *MAD Magazine* and *Time*. Its subtitle is "News for Little Dumb People." The magazine presents lunatic chronicles (some based on real events), spectacular graphics, a clever design scheme, and an emphasis on irreverence. The movie reviews are timely and intelligent (for the most part). Try Front Page News; News in Brief; Man on the Street; Today's Horoscope; and more.

EXCERPT:

Melvin is a satirical biweekly magazine published every other Monday exclusively over the World Wide Web.... Melvin uses invented names in all stories....

Metaverse Internet Entertainment Network

http://curryco.com/.a/audio/index.html

Metaverse turns your computer into a radio. First you download the free software. Then you listen to music and interviews with artists like Jerry Garcia, Santana, and Slash. Pretty neat, especially if your computer has a good sound system.

EXCERPT:

RealAudio works in real-time even over a 14.4 bps modem.

MGD Taproom

http://www.mgdtaproom.com

MGD Taproom is a virtual bar with eclectic links and information sources related to modern lifestyles and interests (with an emphasis on youth and young adult attractions). Included are MotorTalk (about motor sports); 1995 NASCAR Winston Cup Series Schedule; 1995 Indy Car World Series; Schedule 95 (races); Top Fuel Dragsters; Rusty Wallace's Career Track Records; Profiles of Racers; Cybercafe; Rock en Espanol; and much more.

EXCERPT:

Belly up. Tap into the latest in music, art, fashion, sports, nightlife, food and social issues...

Microsoft on the Web

http://www.microsoft.com

You'd expect a company like Microsoft to blow all other web pages out of your RAM, but that's not the case here. Microsoft's such a humungous corporation with so many things going on that it has trouble disseminating its company information into an easily digestible, quick-to-grasp format. Sure, there's a nifty multi-color, slick, professional, well-designed menu map, but you have to click three or four links deep before you find any substance. Until then, it's all nested lists of links, which might contain all kinds of great information. Good luck finding it. While Microsoft's dense web site presents an image of complexity worthy of a corporate mega-structure of its influence and stature, it is hardly useful for the average user who wants infotainment or something productive.

Mirsky's Worst of the Web

http://mirsky.turnpike.net/wow/worst.html

This site has been referred to as the "Gong Show of the Internet" because it has links to the absolute worst sites on the web: foolishness, inappropriate, or incompetent page designs, or meaningless links to "ether madness." Also included are Mirsky's Drunk Browsing Test; World Wide Web Drinking Game; Worst of the Web Nicknames Page; and daily entries to the WOW gallery. You need a graphical browser to view the pages.

EXCERPT:

...Mirsky's Worst of the Web prides itself on perpetuating user disorientation.

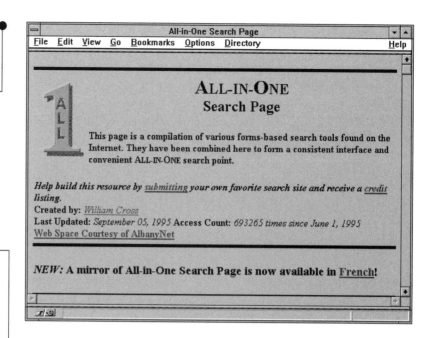

Mr. Showbiz

http://web3.starwave.com/showbiz

This web site provides a place for people with an acute need to know about celebrities, trends, movies, historical facts, heavy metal bands, television shows, and "the end of the world." You can link to your Daily Dose (this day in history, birthdays of the stars, deaths, show business calendars); Scoop (headlines of each day, entertainment news, classic columns from the fifties); Month Off (letters to the editor, chats, votes, "Ask Mr. Showbiz"); Until Tomorrow (an on-line serial novel); and tons more.

E X C E R P T :

...Cheaper than therapy, safer than the New York transit systems, Mr. Showbiz presents original and up-to-the-minute entertainment news and commentary with an attitude all its own....

MJ's Cyberport

http://metro.turnpike.net/~cyber/index.html

Michael J. Shea has set up his Cyberport for writers, researchers, gamers, and general surfers. You'll find links to places like The World Factbook and The Human Language page, as well as FTP sites, electronic magazines, and whatever else he deems of appropriate interest.

EXCERPT:

...You can go below decks and check out my biography, do some research, or go to the games room.

Mkzdk

http://www.ingress.com/~mkzdk/hub.html

This unique site presents beautiful art work, text related to new age concepts (Gaia hypothesis, future science, aliens, "biophilia" and other ideas), and an interactive "mutating" presentation that allows the user to change color and pattern schemes and navigate by pressing directional arrows. Included are galleries of beautiful full-color images, play lists of musical "mutations," gateways to relevant discussions, and much more.

EXCERPT:

We are beginning a new construction of reality, a new ideational context in

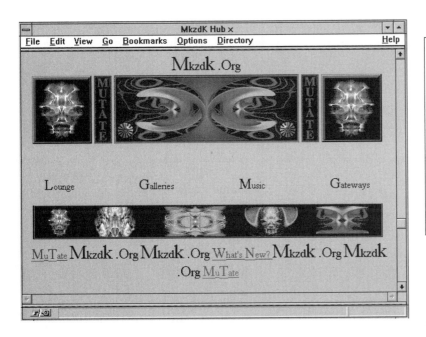

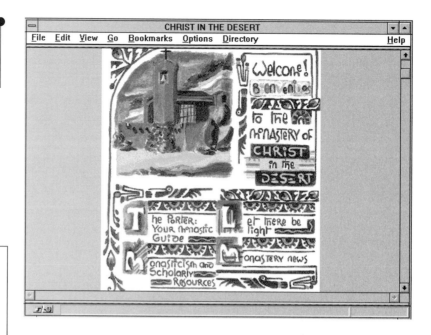

which to understand the many nested worlds, from ourselves up to the universe as a whole...

Monastery of Christ in the Desert

http://www.christdesert.org/pax.html

The Monks of Santo Domingo de Silos brought us the CD "Chant;" now the monks of the Monastery of Christ in the Desert bring you a virtual monastery. Here you can view glimpses of the lives of the Brothers, learn about the monastic life, even get a lesson about Gregorian chant. Spiritual links to Seeking God; The Porter, Your Monastic Guide; Let There Be Light; Monasticism and Scholarly Resources; Monastery News.

EXCERPT:

Get comfortable for a few minutes and let Brother URL tell you about our life.

Monster Board

http://www.monster.com

This system offers a searchable database of more than 2,200 jobs, mainly in

September 1995: Career Hunting Is In Season! The Monster Board continues to change with the times: bringing more leading employers, extensive opportunities, and greater ease-of-use to your career search. Speed up the process by visiting What's New?, take a corporate tour on-line through Employer Profiles, and enhance your employment outlook by posting your resume on-line to Resume City, our extensive database searched by leading employers worldwide.

Monster Momentum! The Monster Board now features 500 employers offering over 2,900 job listings. Progressive companies who have expanded their recruiting efforts through The Monster Board include Bay Networks, Compaq, Edgewater Technology, the good guys!, Hewlett-Packard

the high-technology and biotechnology industries, as well as employer profiles and resumes (for posting or browsing). Career Search is performed by location, industry, company, discipline, or keyword. The Cyberzone is designed for college students and recent graduates. HR NET offers human resources news, information, media suggestions, and recruitment services.

EXCERPT:
...Thousands of rewarding career opportunities literally at your fingertips....

Monty Python Page

http://alfred.u.washington.edu/~uffda/python.html

Python fans will have a good time at this page. There are some pictures and lots of scripts from Monty Python movies and sketches. Join the news group at alt.fan.monty-python.

Moon City

http://www.euro.net/5thworld/mooncity/moon.html

This site is an online guide to Amsterdam, including images, reviews, and

R ecently, the 66 books of the Bible were fed into a non-biased, objective system computer at a top-secret governmental research facility. The resulting analysis provided some frightening insights into the true character and personality of the figure we commonly refer to as "God". The report recommended that, if "God" was an actual member of our society, He should be prevented from pursuing any career in child care.

McChurch Home Page: http://mcchurch.org

directory information. From high-brow art links to low-brow sex establishments, the various links cover virtually all there is to see and do in Amsterdam. It offers an attractive site, embellished with photographs and full-color art work, cute graphics, and on-line street signs to point out directions. For nightlife and cultural diversions in Amsterdam, this is a terrific resource.

EXCERPT:

...Check out the action, from raves to art, from club hopping to coffee-shopping, from movies to meditation...

Most Fucked-Up Person Alive Tells All

http://www.digimark.net/mfu

Kay presents full-text fiction about an anti-hero's adventures in alienation. The story has many humorous links to other web sites and has its own share of sick humor. Among the linkages are the Cognitec/Third Force Home Page, the What SNOOz Page, and Hollywood's Coming (a movie review site).

EXCERPT:

I was born to hijack space shuttles and blackmail cities and start world neurologic wars...

Mothersongs

http://www.ucls.uchicago.edu/faculty-

This collection of poems about motherhood and memories of mother are presented in attractive pages. Here's a sample: Mommy said to stop throwing sand, Kevin/Or I'll make you take a timeout, /Her dark glasses glint meanly. Short streaked hair. /Fortyish.

Motive

http://granite.sentex.net:80/~motive

Motive is an electronic biweekly publication with a focus on "Media, Culture, Art, and Opinion" in its pages. Art and entertainment are the primary subjects, with a discernable Canadian bias. Though not good enough to be professional quality, the site shows good art design and a novel approach.

EXCERPT:

Cuttin' Edge? Nah. Just trying to keep a grip on things...

Mountain Travel - Sobek Adventures

http://synapse-group.com/mts

The company provides a postcard delivery service using online post cards with scenes from trips that Sobek has sponsored. Visitors can browse the gallery of outdoor scenes, select a card, and send it with a short message to anyone with an Internet mailing address. To receive the card, recipients must visit the home page. Though other sites offer a similar service, this site is distinguished by its outstanding selection of scenic photographs.

EXCERPT:

Welcome to the Postcard Rack. All 184 of the pictures were taken on Mountain Travel...

B ecause of the unwholesome and deleterious nature of the subject of the study, the computer recommended that a new religion be created… a religion that rejected outdated dogma and complicated liturgy, replacing these harmful and inefficient elements with a more functional and convenient religious ritual.

McChurch Home Page: http:mcchurch.org

MTV.com

http://www.mtv.com

It's not immediately clear why you'd want to log onto the MTV homepage instead of just turning on the cable TV channel. It's not like you can click on an icon to watch your favorite video on your CRT. On the plus side, if you want to see the MTV News, you don't have to sit through several agonizing zit cream and denim jean commercials to get caught up. You can also vote for the Video Music Award winners and participate in other MTV contests, but for now, MTV is not a particularly effective MWEB.

MUD Connection

http://www.magicnet.net/~cowana/mud.html

MUD Connection provides an interactive system for fantasy game players, allowing them to create personas for Multi-User Domain (or Dungeon) games. Use the live link to the Encyclopedia of MUDs Dictionary, listing over 181 available MUDs on the World Wide Web. Each entry provides a site, a description of the game, the code base used by the game, links to its web home page, and Telnet links to the MUDs themselves.

The MUD Connector is a complete online service designed to provide the most up-to-date listings of registered Multi-User Online Games.

Multimedia MOOs

http://www.peg.apc.org/~firehorse/mmm/mmm.html

This web site presents a director-based multimedia object-oriented dimension (MOO) using LambdaMOO, the most popular type of MOO software, written for Unix servers. The information includes full-text descriptions of MOO, LambdaMOO, Director Client indexes, CD-ROM programming, users, developers and wizards, virtual room creation techniques, character icons, and links to MOO telnet sites.

EXCERPT:

When I was first introduced to LambdaMOO, I was immediately captivated by this incredible ability to socialize on a global scale....

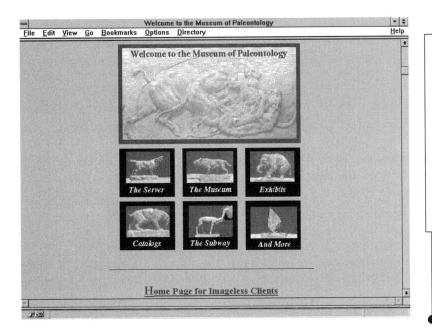

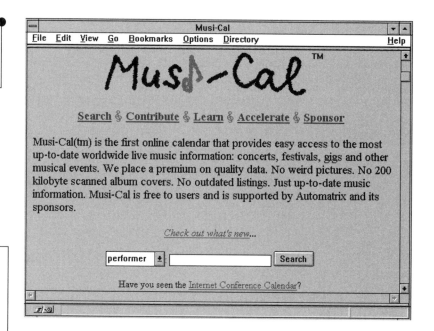

The Museum of Paleontolgy

http://ucmp1.berkeley.edu/welcome.html

Fossils galore with easily understandable text that explains paleontology and nice photos of exhibits. The Museum of Paleontology's enormous collections are ranked 4th in America in size and include protists, plants, invertebrates, and vertebrates. Take the time to explore.

EXCERPT:

UCMP is charged with the conservation of paleontological materials, collections development, and research and instructional support....

Musi-Cal!

http://www.automatrix.com/concerts

This musical-events database allows searching by performer, city, state, country, type of music, or date. Live links are provided to orchestra home pages, Folkbook, the Yahoo artist list, the Ultimate Band list, Ceolas Celtic music archive, Mammoth Music Meta-list, CDWorld online music store, Dirty Linen, Sony Music, and scores of related musical web sites. The information is kept remarkably current.

EXCERPT:

Musi-Cal! (tm) is the first online calendar database that provides up-to-date worldwide live music information...

My Brain Hurts

http://ayup.res.wpi.edu/~pogo

The editor of this web page presents some biographical details and sample pages of a 'zine he began before his work at Microsoft made him leave Worcester and his friends at WPI. The magazine—Data Control—is a compendium of punk-related reviews and information. Its value is almost exclusively historical, but there are some active links to other punk web sites.

EXCERPT:

I currently work at Microsoft...I do the Internet connectivity for MSN....In my free time off work I do normal punk things like going to shows....

My 3DO Page

http://tss.ca/~hans/3do/3do.html

This site is devoted to 3DO, an experimental technology that will either revolutionize communications or is a big myth. Its supporters envision a day, a couple years from now, when a box on your television will allow you to go online, interact with others, play extremely realistic video games, and more. This site samples some 3DO games and discusses 3DO technology and prices.

EXCERPT:

...The 3DO corporation...produces a multimedia specification that anyone is free to license and implement in hardware or software.

mystery
science
theater
3000 at
portnoy's
complaint

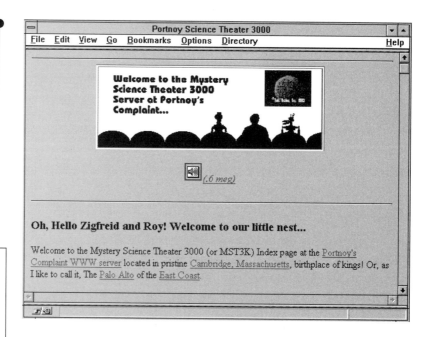

Portnoy Science Theater 3000

File Edit View Go Bookmarks Options Directory   Help

Welcome to the Mystery Science Theater 3000 Server at Portnoy's Complaint...

(.6 meg)

Oh, Hello Zigfreid and Roy! Welcome to our little nest...

Welcome to the Mystery Science Theater 3000 (or MST3K) Index page at the Portnoy's Complaint WWW server located in pristine Cambridge, Massachusetts, birthplace of kings! Or, as I like to call it, The Palo Alto of the East Coast.

Mystery Science Theater 3000 at Portnoy's Complaint

http://portnoy.tiac.net/mst3k/index.htm

Portnoy's Complaint is a busy network, but once you jump on, you can hit the Mystery Science Theater 3000 site run by Rob De Millo. Though there's a link for the newbie, most of the stuff on this home page is for the occasional if not the hardcore MST3K fan. There's a program schedule, news, an episode guide, links to other sites and Usenet groups, and all sorts of related distractions. There's even a Bill Holbrook cartoon with an MST3K reference: De Millo cares for his page. This web site's full of text and imagery; it takes a few minutes to load up, but it's well worth the wait.

EXCERPT:

Although Crow is a close, personal friend of mine, I'm just a conduit for 90% of the information in these WWW pages. Many, many strange and odd people donated hours of their time to providing this information across the Internet. My only task was to gobble it all up and plop it in one place. Their names are many and each MST3K page credits the original author(s).

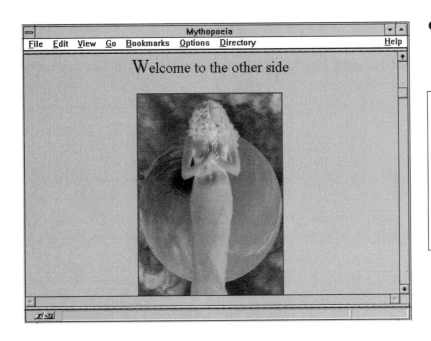

Mythopoeia

http://www.myth.com/mythopoeia/mythopoeia1.html

This amazing photographer presents in four parts a vision of mythology by using historical and mythological figures in stunning photographs and textual accompaniments. Several new creatures are presented in this fanciful and (literally) fantastic series of full-color pages. The site presents subtle navigational clues by means of buttons and other icons. The theme pages are beautiful and worthy of lengthy contemplation.

E X C E R P T :

My work is not about manifest reality, it is about fantasy....I am inspired by Fairytales, myths, vampires, gods and goddesses....

Mythtext

http://www.the-wire.com/culture/mythology/mythtext.html

If you need to name the Greek goddess of beauty or the Roman god of war,

Mythtext's list of gods, goddesses, and sundry immortals from around the world (somewhere between 3,000 and 4,000 at last count) can help. Entries vary considerably in length, ranging from single sentences to several paragraphs. Also included are full texts of several mythological works. For devotees there are FAQs about Mythology; Bibliographies; Large Mythological Works; Smaller Mythological Works; and Archives.

EXCERPT:

A list of gods, goddesses and sundry immortals...with brief biographies...

Nadia: The Secret of BlueWater

http://utd500.utdallas.edu/~hairston/nadiahp.html

This site has an amazingly developed digest of the plots, graphics, and music for the Nadia series of Japanese animated television shows. The series was (is) loosely based on the Jules Verne "20,000 Leagues Under the Sea" novel. Find out everything about Nadia with links to Synopsis of Series; Character Guide; Episode Guide; Production Credits; and more.

EXCERPT:

Nadia: The Secret of BlueWater is a 39 episode anima series and one of the most popular animated series ever done in Japan...

NandoNet Music Kitchen

http://www.nando.net/music/gm

This site presents a list of home pages that are officially sponsored by musical bands themselves. Included are press releases, discographies (most of which are complete), pictures, cover art, lyrics, audio files, software, and concert information for Beastie Boys; Redd Kross; Bonnie Raitt; Rock-It Comix; Grand Royal Records and Magazines; Breeders; Wild Colonials; and World Domination Records.

NASA Kennedy Space Center Home Page

http://www.ksc.nasa.gov/welcome.html

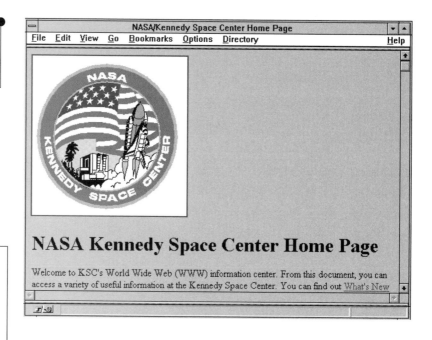

NASA Kennedy Space Center Home Page

Welcome to KSC's World Wide Web (WWW) information center. From this document, you can access a variety of useful information at the Kennedy Space Center. You can find out What's New

One small step for man.... The world of space can be accessed via NASA's web page. Learn about the Kennedy Space Center, check out the latest Shuttle information, and find out about all the neat programs and resources available from NASA. Follow the links to Recent NASA Missions; Space Station Launch Site Home Page; and Additional Space Related Services. 5-4-3-2-1 Blast Off!

The NASA Shuttle Web Archives

http://shuttle.nasa.gov/

Information galore about the United States space program. Images and audio clips from the Apollo 11 moon landing. It supplies comprehensive details of recent and upcoming Space Shuttle missions, question and answer sessions on scientific topics, and news releases and a photo gallery. If you are looking for a space guy to talk to, there's a schedule of astronaut speaking engagements.

EXCERPT:

This suite of pages is designed to give visitors the opportunity to experience a virtual Space Shuttle mission....

National Hockey Players Association Web Site

http://www.nhlpa.com

Center ice, even in the heat of summer. Very newsworthy professional hockey player profiles, draft analysis, interviews, trivia contests, updates on retired players, action photos. Links to Player of the Day; Hockey's Mad Masks; and Be A Player.

EXCERPT:

It's something every young hockey fan dreams of—standing at center ice, picking up the Stanley Cup and lifting it over your head...

National Schoolnet Atlas

http://www-nais.ccm.emr.ca/schoolnet/

An atlas from a kid's perspective. High school students across Canada input data about their home towns—everything from population statistics to the best fast food restaurants. Hop on the links to Atlas of Canadian

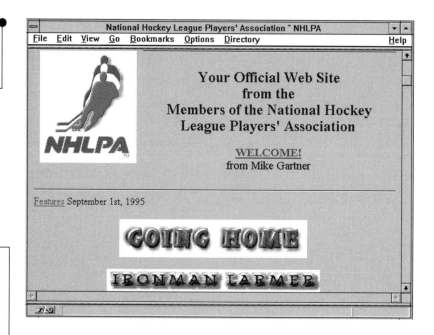

Communities; Create a Map; Find a Geographical Name; and the National Atlas of Canada.

EXCERPT:

...This digital atlas illustrates students' likes and dislikes about their communities, origins of place names, local history....

Nebraska Game and Parks Commission

http://ngp.ngps.ste.ne.us/gp.html

It's like having a cup of coffee in a Nebraska hunting and bait shop. Lists and maps of fishing spots and boating outlets, hunting and fishing guides and regulations, state parks and wildlife area maps, old photos, land resources data base, and phone numbers for state natural resources officials.

Necro Enema Amalgamated

http://www.phantom.com:80/~blam1/

Rebel without a cause? A site of pornography and protest. Writer Eric

Swenson seems to be worried that the twin Big Brothers of Corporate America and Governmental America will use the Internet to more closely watch over us.

EXCERPT:

...A Devil's Advocacy group and entrepreneurial innovator of manipulative software, subliminal semionics, and coercive advertising....

.net

http://www.futurenet.co.uk/netmag/net.html

This 'zine is all about the Net and has some original features, such as an exploration of how people are using the Net to deal with world problems (the Kobe earthquake, for example.) You'll also find articles on Internet commerce, security, and other related issues.

EXCERPT:

The new directory to the electronic world.

Net Day: This Week on *iWorld*

http://www.mecklerweb.com:80/netday/newsmenu.htm

Net Day is just what it claims to be—an outstanding way to begin a day of net surfing. There are all sorts of good, useful links designed to keep the sagacious surfer aware of what's what on the Internet. The "Take Note" link alone is worth the visit. It informs you about what's going on TODAY on the net. There are also articles, book reviews, stock quotes, and more. Hey, it's just a great site!

EXCERPT:

Net Day is *iWorld*'s daily Internet news and features area and the first place for users to stop on their tour through our site. Tune in each morning over your first cup of coffee, and make Net Day your first stop every day.

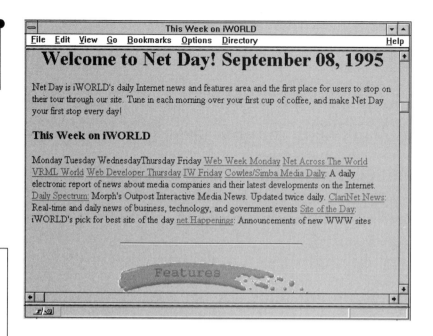

 is itself the browser window containing the following text:

Welcome to Net Day! September 08, 1995

Net Day is iWORLD's daily Internet news and features area and the first place for users to stop on their tour through our site. Tune in each morning over your first cup of coffee, and make Net Day your first stop every day!

This Week on iWORLD

Monday Tuesday WednesdayThursday Friday Web Week Monday Net Across The World VRML World Web Developer Thursday IW Friday Cowles/Simba Media Daily: A daily electronic report of news about media companies and their latest developments on the Internet. Daily Spectrum: Morph's Outpost Interactive Media News. Updated twice daily. ClariNet News: Real-time and daily news of business, technology, and government events Site of the Day: iWORLD's pick for best site of the day net.Happenings: Announcements of new WWW sites

Net in Arcadia

http://www.parnasse.com/net.in.arcadia.html

A trip to the art gallery. As the page says, it's a "virtual museum dedicated to contemporary classicism." The site features the paintings and drawings of Alfred Russell, Andree Descharmes, their colleagues and students, and other guest appearances. All the artists share a humanistic and a temporal vision unique in the postwar world of modernist art.

Netboy.com — Choice of an Online Generation

http://www.intelli.com/netboy/

A news wire for Internet techies. Daily news updates about computers, the net, and new media. You can link to Netboy.com; Oooooo News; The Daily Broadcast; and The Weekly Broadcast. You'll keep up with all net happenings here.

The Monkees phenomena remains a major event of 60's pop culture. Many argue that it began the idea of music video as promotion, and the marketing of TV show products to pre-teen audiences, as well as opening the door to multi-media.

Some still revile the music of the Monkees as "manu-factured," others remember it as a fond memory of their childhood. The Monkees were a real working band in every sense of the word, and provided quality music and comedy in a format that had never been tried before, and were wildly successful at it.

...At exactly the same time Star Trek was beginning to amass its small but rather loyal following, the Monkees were exploding onto TV sets all over the country. These imitation Beatles quickly became something of a national phenomenon, and the Monkees' TV show was a sensation. For these reasons, Gene zeroed in on the lucrative bubble-gum crowd and conjured up the character of Pavel Chekov as a consciously designed, rather close approximation of Monkees front man Davy Jones.

The Monkees Home Page:
http://www.primenet.com/-flex/monkees.html

The NetGram Snailmail Postal Proxy

http://www.netgram.com/

Forget the stationery. Here's a way to send greeting cards, letters and other documents, via e-mail, to folks not yet on the Internet. The NetGram memo is a one-page, text-only document and delivery options include first-class mail, overnight mail, and fax. Nice way to stay in touch with non-techie types.

EXCERPT:

...The NetGram memo is a one-page, text-only document....We are also going to support...First Class mail, overnight mail and fax.

NetGuide Home Page

http://techweb.cmp.com/ng/current/

Though it claims to be updated daily, it's hard to figure out what has been added to the *NetGuide* site each day just by looking at the home page. In fact, there's almost no text on the page at all. Instead there are several net links. But what are these links? You won't know until you're four or five more links deep into the system. Right now, the print magazine still offers a lot more at a glance than this online version.

NetJohn's Gallery

http://www.presentmoment.com/Nets_Gallery

If you can't make it out to the museum on your lunch break, you can always cruise the Net for some art. Here at NetJohn's Gallery, you can see examples of John Harvey's graphic arts, photography, and multimedia work. John also does digital consulting, and you can read all about it here.

Netsam

http://www-bioc.rice.edu/~clarage/netsam.html

An offbeat 'zine with short stories, poetry, and photos of colored hair. Link to titles like Immerse Yourself in a Bawdy Tale; Dye Your Hair So It Looks Like It's on Fire; Catch the Chicken Pox (a funny story about an adult with chicken pox); and 17 more.

EXCERPT:

...The digits on the clock radio make me squint. 6:25 a.m. It's not even light out yet. And tiny dynamo wants to play....

Netscape Server Galleria

http://home.mcom.com/home

Netscape promotes and indexes its own products and the Internet itself at this site that is an extensive offering of software for downloading, product descriptions, and information about the company. Try the link to Exploring the Net (Best of the Net, Netscape Galleria, Search and Beyond, Internet Directory, What's New, What's Cool, Virtual Tourist, Search Engines) and Reference Material Index for loads of useful Internet info.

Netsurfer Digest

http://www.netsurf.com/nsd

An on-line 'zine offering access to new software and other computer equipment, how-to articles for the Internet, and articles about emerging cyberspace issues. This is a valuable resource for all surfers; don't forget to check out the links to What's New; What's Available; and Netsurfer Digest Back Issues.

E X C E R P T :

Our Objective: More signal, less noise....We're a free e-mail-delivered e-zine bringing cyberspace directly to your mailbox.

Nettweb

http://www/wimsey.com/nettwerk/

Artist profiles, catalogs, and other news from this independent record company located in Vancouver, British Columbia. Some of the artists you can read about are Sarah McLachlan, Mystery Machine, the Rose Chronicles, Ginger, and Single Gun Theory.

E X C E R P T :

Nettwerk Productions is...home to Sarah McLachlan, Mystery Machine, the Rose Chronicles, Ginger, Single Gun Theory and much more.

Pavel Curtis, a Xerox researcher who runs a fascinating Multi-User Dimension (or MUD)—a kind of a "virtual world" within the Internet with its own simulated geography, characters and interactions—reports that a significant portion of people logging into his system switch genders for the identities they assume. Most common are young men who portray themselves a women; indeed, it's become a rule of thumb that any sexually aggressive female on this MUD is really a man.

Gary Chapman, in *The New Republic*

Network.23

http://net.23.com/

Go back a decade in pop culture. Here you can find everything you ever wanted to know about Max Headroom. In addition to stories of Max, this site includes sounds, writings, images, and some full-motion video clips. You can also learn more about Network.23 and browse through Quotes of the Day.

New York Web

http://nyweb.com/

A magazine covering New York City. Main topics include Citylife, Nightlife, and media. Also home to the New York Web Internet services company, a catalog of hard-to-find computer products, a directory of lawyers, a lawyer-locator service, and access to an online radio show.

EXCERPT:

Our mission is to empower organizations to participate effectively in the ongoing communications revolution....

The New Zealand Symphony Orchestra Home Page

http://www.actrix.gen.nz/users/dgold/nzso.html

Besides concert schedules and news about the New Zealand Symphony Orchestra, this is a mother lode of resources for classical music aficionados and performers. E-mail lists for musicians, orchestral mailing lists, and music archives are just a few of the more than four dozen offerings. Music buffs will want to explore the link to Some Pointers to Classical Music on the WWW.

EXCERPT:

The New Zealand Symphony Orchestra is the first symphony orchestra in the world on the World Wide Web!...

NeWWW: A Magazine for and by Internet Explorers

http://grafton.dartmouth.edu:802

The Internet version of a college newspaper with features and reviews of Internet resources written by Dartmouth College students and staff. The mission of NeWWW is to keep the Dartmouth community informed about new Internet developments. Some links that might be of general interest are WWWhat's NeWWW?; Review of New Internet Resources; and Letters to the Editor.

The Nexus Gate

http://frank.mtsu.edu/~troy/home.html

The personal 'zine of a Middle Tennessee University student. Includes moderately funny, Lettermanesque Top 10 lists, sound clips from a hard progressive rock band called "The Mayonnaise Farmers," and links to some of Troy's favorite web pages like the Unsigned Underground.

EXCERPT:

Knowing the Internet is a vast resource, it's understandable how one can really get sucked into cyberspace and lose track of time in the conventional world.

The Nicholson Wall of Beer

http://www.halcyon.com/shummer/wall.html

A tribute to suds. Brent Nicholson's southern California garage is walled with more than 750 beer bottles from around the globe. View the Wall and read the list of Nicholson's beers. The site includes beer ratings and access to other web sites dealing with beer. 750 bottles of beer on the wall....

EXCERPT:

Brent solicits no help in emptying a bottle, consequently please do not mail him your empties.

The Nine Planets:
A Multimedia Tour of the Solar System

http://seds.lpl.arizona.edu/nineplanes/nineplanets/nineplanets.ht

A cool and comprehensive tour through space for multimedia users. Better than *Star Trek*! A universe of information, sights and sounds from our solar

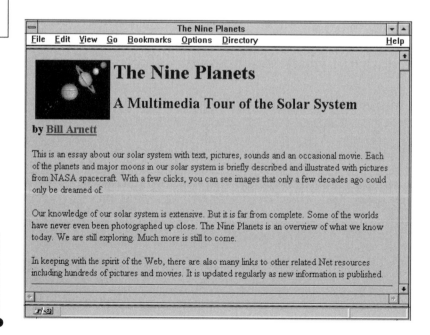

Stripped of the external trappings of wealth, power, beauty and social status, people tend to be judged in the cyberspace of the Internet only by their ideas and their ability to get them across in terse, vigorous prose. On the Internet, as the famous New Yorker cartoon put it, nobody knows you're a dog.

Philip Elmer-DeWitt, in *Time*

system with a very extensive table of contents to its links. Pictures from NASA illustrate each of the planets and major moons in our solar system.

911 Gallery

http://www.iquest.net/911/iq_911.html

911 Gallery features changing exhibitions of digital fine art—emphasis on the FINE, not the weird stuff you find in some electronic art galleries. Try out the links to other exhibits: Current Show; Previous Shows; Traveling Exhibits; Video; and Call For Entries.

EXCERPT:

911 Gallery...specializes in digital art: computer graphics, video, and electronic music. Our mission is to promote awareness of electronic media as a fine art.

1990 U.S. Census LOOKUP

http://cedr.lbl.gov/cdrom/doc/lookup_doc.html

LOOKUP is an experimental WWW server for retrieving data from 1990 U.S. Census summary tape files stored on CD-ROM. You can look up the population of Providence, RI (160,728; go on, amaze your friends), and nearly anything else you'd care to know about America in the '90s. Includes troubleshooting tips and a list of alternate sites.

EXCERPT:

On 6/21/95, LOOKUP was chosen as Cool Site of the Day by Glenn Davis of InfiNet. On that day the number of users and the number of LOOKUP sessions were 20 times greater than normal

1994 California Election Home Page

http://www.election.ca.gov

The information from 1994 is a little outdated, but this home page is an excellent example of how election returns and voter information can be made accessible to voters and taxpayers. Includes results from all statewide races, judicial races, and propositions, the Final Official Canvas, voter returns by county, campaign finance data, and links to nonpartisan election information.

EXCERPT:

This service provides voter information and election returns for the 1994 California general election via the World Wide Web...

'95 Global

http://www.mech.gla.ac.uk/~gsapd/sig.htm

'95 Global is a preview of gadgets we might be using in the 21st century. This site has lots of great images (and descriptions) of projects entered in Glasgow School of Art's 1995 Product Design Degree Show. If you're on a slow connection, be patient—it's worth the wait. Try the links to Furniture, Packaging, Objects, Systems, Concepts, Urban Design, Designs for children, and CAD.

The 1995 Pulitzer Prize Winners

http://www.pulitzer.org/

A place to sample the best and brightest of prize-winning American writing journalism, letters, drama, and music. Find out who won the awards for feature writing, newspaper investigations, plays, and compositions in 1995. Get more details with cool links to Winners, History, Board and Juries, and Entry Forms.

NJOnline Weather

http://www.nj.com/weather/index.html

Nationwide, five-day weather forecasts, daily tidbits from the Farmer's Almanac, and the Ultimate Summer Guide to seasonal fun in New Jersey. Not a bad site for finding out whether to take the beach umbrella and suntan lotion along on your trip to the shore.

nj's Web Strands

http://http.cs.berkeley.edu/~nj/

The autobiography of a Berkeley graduate student—his musical interests, writings, and favorite web pages. The author introduces himself as a dilettante who has many interests but few real accomplishments. Is this someone you want to spend time with?

EXCERPT:

I am interested in a lot of things, but suffer from the unfortunate disease of having not gotten good at any of them.

Nomadic Research Labs

http://microship.ucsd.edu/

The trials, tribulations and other tales of a technomad as he cruises around the country on a scientific bicycle. Roberts has been a technomad for the last 11 years, and he has traveled over 17,000 miles around the country on a vehicle he calls Behemoth. You can bike to links for the Latest Update and his Adventures and Bikelab Reports.

Today 30 million to 40 million people in more than 160 countries have at least E-mail access to the Internet; in Japan, New Zealand and parts of Europe the number of Net users has grown more than 1,000% during the past three years.

Philip Elmer-DeWitt, in *Time*

EXCERPT:

...A small enterprise devoted to the pursuit of nomadness... created by Steven K. Roberts....

Nothingness.Org

http://www.nothingness.org/

Run by an anonymous MacIntosh programmer who goes by the nickname "Spud," this site offers an extensive list of connections to other web sites on many topics, including computers, politics, culture, literature, and more. Site also links to the Situationist International Archives.

EXCERPT:

Nothingness.org is not what it is and is what it is not...

Nutscape

http://thule.mt.cs.cmu.edu:8001/tools/nutscape/

Nutscape, a web site of Stupid Netscape Tricks, is a cyberplace where experienced World Wide Web users can test their knowledge of how the HTML protocol effects Netscape-viewed web pages. This home page is okay or surfers who want to learn more about designing web sites, but there's nothing here to inspire infotainment-seekers.

EXCERPT:

I firmly believe that all mankind should be able to benefit from the inspired extensions to HTML promoted by the nice folks at Netscape Communications Inc. Unfortunately, many web information providers are not using these extensions to their fullest potential....

NWHQ

http://www.knosso.com/NWHQ/

A literature and art magazine with nifty photographs of the Vancouver region, photo essays, illustrations, and short stories. The contributors describe themselves as independent artists. You can check the Current Issue; Listing of Authors; and Future Projects.

EXCERPT:

NWHQ is a publication devoted to free expression and the distribution of artistic ideas....

Nye Labs

http://www.seanet.com/Vendors/billnye/nyelabs.html

This bright home page is an extension of Bill Nye's science program for

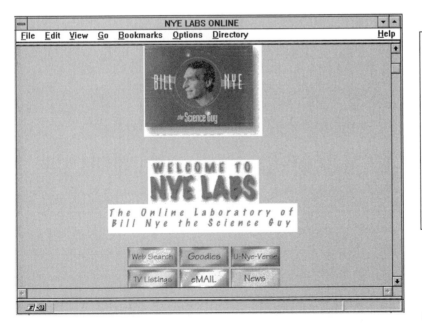

young people. The science guy answers kids questions and provides links to a variety of scientific and educational sources (Bill Nye's Top 20) that include PBS, Headbone Interactive (hip games for kids), NASA's Space Calendar, Le Web Louvre, ION Science, The Nine Planets, Frog Dissection Online, The Smithsonian Institution, Franklin Institute Science Museum, Web Elements (the elements from A to Z), and Honolulu C.C. Dinosaur Exhibit.

EXCERPT:

Navigate the Internet with Adventure Bill! This is your way cool access to finding science online....Happy hunting!

NYNEX Interactive Yellow Pages

Imagine having access to every business phone number and address in New England, without having to rummage around for a phone book or hoof it to the library reference desk. You can do a Business Name Search; Business Category Search; Top 25 Headings Search; or call the Hot Sites.

EXCERPT:

With our interactive Yellow Pages, you can get business listings for the entire northeastern United States....

NYU Center For Digital Multimedia

http://found.cs.nyu.edu

This site is basically an advertisement for this New York University Program, which provides access to laboratory and library resources, creates networking opportunities, and offers semester-long classes and shorter seminars to help small businesses and nonprofit groups learn how to use the Internet.

EXCERPT:

We assist individuals and small multimedia developers by sharing information [and] providing access to laboratory and library resources....

Of Man, Mind and Machine

http://www.dataspace.com/WWW/documents/consciousness.html

Are we creating computers that someday will think independently? Can minds exist in media other than the human brain? This dry, academic paper by the host of a weekly Internet radio program raises the possibility.

EXCERPT:

...If one accepts a materialist, meme-based theory of mind, then one will be forced to consider the potential for minds to exist in media other than the human brain.

O.J. Central

http://www.pathfinder.com/@@wICQozFtcwMAQLa4/pathfinder/feature

The trial that went on forever has its own place on the Net to help you keep up. Pathfinder, the Time, Inc. web site gives you O.J. Central. You can get articles from *Time*, *People*, *Vibe*, *Sports Illustrated*, and Court TV, along

The Albuquerque Tribune and St. Louis Post-Dispatch, for instance, offer electronic editions containing national and international wire stories not published in the newspapers....

Michael Meyer, in *Newsweek*

with transcripts from the courtroom. If you can't get enough, there's always more. You are required to register and have an active e-mail box before browsing the site

EXCERPT:

Pathfinder's O.J. Simpson site is intended to illuminate the different angles of the man and the crimes he is accused of.

100 cc

http://www.iuma.com/~co

You'll find numerous images here, but none of them make sense. There's also a keyword searchable index to the Usenet alt. * hierarchy, organized in the form of a typewriter keyboard. This also doesn't make sense. Unfortunately, there's nothing in the way of a "Hi, welcome to our site, this is who we are and what we're trying to do." Rather than waste your valuable surfing time here, go up a level or two to the Internet Underground Music Archive (http://www.iuma.com/) instead. This site is just plain weird.

Open Virtual Reality Testbed

http://nemo.ncsl.nist.gov/~sressler/projects/nav/surr/navSurr.html

Virtual Reality fans stop here for several MPEG movies that highlight the work at the Open Virtual Reality Testbed and links to other sites and documents related to virtual reality. There's a cool demo of surrogate travel that integrates web browsers (Mosaic and Netscape) with virtual environments. Try it!

EXCERPT:

Mission: To facilitate the development of standard interfaces and testing methodologies to the many novel types of human interface devices which when integrated form a Virtual Reality system.

Operative Term Is Stimulate (OTIS)

http://sunsite.unc.edu/otis/otis.html

The OTIS site is primarily original art works, submitted by the artists. It also provides some links to other art-related sites. The Artchives has thousands of images, dozens of categories, hundreds of artists, Synergy exhibits collaboration projects of the past, present and future, and Artists is a complete directory of the OTISts.

EXCERPT:

OTIS, at it's most basic interpretation and intention, is a place for image-makers and image-lovers to exchange ideas, collaborate and, in a loose sense of the word, meet....

Orange Coast Online

http://orangecoast.com

An online version of the established monthly magazine of Orange County. Doesn't contain as much as the print version, but the site has good archives and guides to Orange County life, the Best of Orange County, Dining and Entertainment, and good photos. You can get the contents of the current print issue and read the feature story as well.

EXCERPT:

With our new electronic edition, Orange Coast Online, the magazine's storied blend of clear-eyed journalism and upscale advertising is more dynamic than ever.

Organ Eversion Utility

http://cspmserver.gold.ac.uk/tongues/tongues.html

A site that'll have your tongue wagging, particularly if it's photogenic. The anonymous host of Organ Eversion likes to get pictures of your tongue and will be happy to send you a copy for your computer files. Hmm...makes you wonder about how some people spend their time.

I will take the residue of the act of your tongue Xeroxing....

Oscarnet

http://bazaar.com:80/Oscarnet/

Lists all nominations for the Oscars, odds on who will win, Oscars history, and a chance for fans to pick their own winners in an online forum. Try the links to News&Stats; Enter the Contest; Your Choice Awards; About Oscarnet. Enjoy Oscar night every night at Oscarnet.

...An unofficial WWW site for the 67th Academy Awards, benefitting AIDS Project Los Angeles and the A-T Children's Foundation.

The Outrageous Online Uncle Al

http://vvv.com/adsint/freehand/uncleal/

Guppies, asparagus, homosexual armies, freeway engineering and other thoughts, musings, and ramblings from an anonymous group or person known only as Uncle Al. Needless to say all the words are fiction, and some may be offensive to some surfers.

...There is no attempt made nor desire extant to libel or otherwise cause malicious damage, loss, public contempt, defamation, blasphemy, treason, sedition, or ridicule....

Pac-Man

http://www4.ncsu.edu/eos/users/m/msstow/WWW/Pac-Man/pac-man.html

Wocka, Wocka, Wocka. Remember the original video game? Pac-Man is alive and well at this site, your guide to many computer versions of everyone's favorite hungry little yellow guy. Also includes cool graphics like Pac-Man wind-surfing in shark-infested waters. The links sound cool: Clones on the Internet; Graphics; Sounds; and Strategy & Tricks.

EXCERPT:

Need a breather? Just park yourself in the spot immediately to the right of where you start and make sure that no monsters are looking at you when you do it....

Page-0-Bizarro

http://www.best.com/~johnp/bizarro.html

You can sample newsgroup chatter at this web site that is about—you guessed it—a newsgroup. The users of talk.bizarre think they are so interesting that they advertise via this web site. Check it out and listen in—maybe even get a chuckle. One of the best offerings is the Nixon poems listed under "John's Best t.b. posts."

EXCERPT:

Talk.bizarre is a newsgroup...funnier than rec.humor, more artistic than rec.arts, and more sensible than any President or Congress.

"Cyberspace is the land of knowledge," proclaimed an information age Magna Carta issued in his name [Newt Gingrich]. "And the exploration of that land can be a civilization's truest, highest calling."

Philip Elmer-DeWitt, in *Time*

Paintings by Eu-Huang (Christina) Chung

http://www.cs.mu.oz.au/~ljk/exhibit.html

If you're just interested in seeing Chung's paintings of landscapes and flowers, you'll be satisfied with the quick-loading, mini-inline graphics of her work from a show she had at the Australian Chinese Museum in Melbourne, Australia. But the page could have shown more about Chung the artist and better explained the whys and wherefores of her work and its place in the Far Eastern art world.

EXCERPT:

Taiwan-born artist Christina Chung's work fuses classical Chinese traditions and western use of color and light to create a new way of depicting the classic Chinese subjects of landscape and flowers.

Paintings of Vermeer

http://www.ccsf.caltech.edu/~roy/vermeer/

Web junkies like Roy Chickery are what's good about the web. This Cal-Tech webmaster presents the art work of Dutch artist Jan Vermeer on a page that's very informative and a nice visiting spot for the curious. The page features imagery, links to Vermeer history, and helps you Find Your Closest Vermeer.

EXCERPT:

Jan Vermeer created luscious canvases of limited scope: generally women

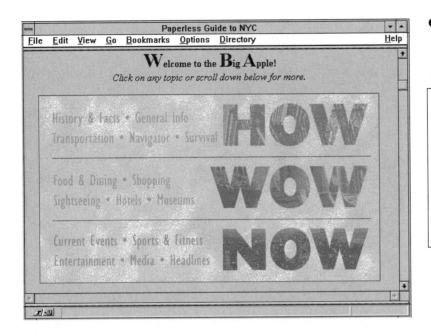

and men in Seventeenth-Century rooms, but also occasional outdoor scenes, allegory, and religious themes....

The Paperless Guide to New York City

http://www.cs.columbia.edu/nyc/

Get to the core of the Big Apple fast: history and facts about NYC, tourist information, transportation guides, navigation aids, entertainment schedules, news headlines, and guide to media outlets. The New York links say it all: How; Wow; Now; and Marketplace. And that's it in a New York minute.

E X C E R P T :

...Provides a resource for visitors and denizens alike to capture the essence of the metropolis through cyberspace.

Paris Pages

http://www.paris.org/

Gay Paris—the City of Light—aglow in all its Internet splendor. More

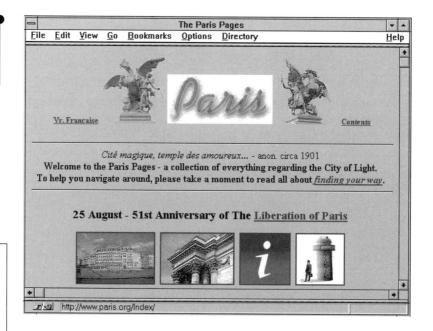

details than you could ever stuff in your suitcase with guides to cafes, schools, monuments, museums, an interactive map, etc. Don't skip the links to The City; Its Culture; Tourist Information; Paris Kiosque; and many more. A perfect stop for cyberspace surfers and Concorde passengers.

ParkBench Project

http://found.cs.nyu.edu/CAT/projects/parkbench/parkbench.html

An advertisement for kiosks in New York City that provide public Internet access and guides to community and cultural information. It's a new form of phone booth. (Clark Kent, are you ready?) You can link to big, online flea market called Barterama or to the Videophones.

EXCERPT:

A public access network of kiosks for the people of New York City....

Pathfinder

http://www.timeinc.com/pathfinder/Greet.html

Mainstream media's slick entry into cyberspace. An online amalgamation

of Time Warner's publishing empire, featuring daily news articles, features from *Time*, *People*, and other publications, photos, and a plethora of special interest topics and chat groups on Money&Business; Technology; Sports; Arts&Entertainment; Kidstuff; and much more.

Pat Paulsen for President

http://www.amdest.com/Pat/pat.html

Comic relief on the campaign trail. Paulsen, the comedian and perennial presidential candidate, offers his platform and amendments to the Constitution. Pat's all ready for election day with links to Words to Iowa Voters; Amendments to the Constitution; Biography/Pat Paulsen on the Issues; and Campaign Volunteers Needed.

EXCERPT:

From his hillside home in California, Paulsen will...answer "relevant" questions from prospective constituents...by way of E-mail, which he calls "yesterday's onramp to the information superhighway and tomorrow's Post Its."

The Penguin Page

http://sas.upenn.edu/~kwelch/penguin.html

Aptly named, this web site contains 38 nested pages of facts, images, and links related to spheniscidae (penguins) and related species. The site can serve as an introduction to the basic biology and behavior of penguins and as an advanced information source for researchers. Review all 18 species of penguins in Species Information; learn the prehistory of penguins in Fossil Penguins; and discover the behavioral aspects of penguins in Penguin Ethology.

PhoNETic

http://www.soc.qc.edu:80/phonetic/

PhoNETic will convert a telephone number into all combinations of the associated telephone keypad letters. This is an easy way to figure out if your phone number spells out any neat words—and to decode the phonetic phone numbers into digits. (Do you know what number to touch for R?)

Photon

http://www.scotborders.co.uk/photon/

Here's a monthly magazine of great portfolios and technical articles on the art of photography. Snap to links for Current Edition; Archive; Permanent Contents; Model Agency; Photographer Pholios; and International Photo Store. Content will appeal to weekend enthusiasts and professionals.

EXCERPT:

...A monthly [photo] magazine for the working enthusiast, freelance, and professional aimed at the creative solo operator.

The Pickup Truck Home Page

http://www.rtd.com/~mlevine/pickup.html

Bubba's dream web site. Trucks, trucks, and more trucks—a tailgate full of photos, model specs, reviews, debate, racing statistics, and news reports. You'll love the links to Reader Pickup of the Week; The Latest News; Pickup Truck Profiles; Off Road Racing; Factory Sport Trucks; Custom Sport Trucks; and NASCAR. Welcome truckers!

Ping datascape

http://www.artcom.de/ping/mapper

A net site to help you expand your artistic horizons and participate in artistic anarchy. Hundreds of individual images entered by everyday web surfers. The site changes constantly and seems to be limited only by human imagination. You can find more datascapes in links to Map; View; and Story.

Debating the trial in cyberspace has become so popular that people even log on to the O.J. forums to express their contempt for people who log on to the O.J. forums.

Peter Lewis, in *The New York Times*

EXCERPT:

Let it render, constitute an object to the ping landscape. It will subsequently show up as a new icon on the map of the ping landscape.

Pink Pages

http://www.euro.net/5thworld/pink/pink.html

A gay and lesbian guide to Amsterdam and homosexual web sites around the globe. Find out about dating clubs, leather shops, magazine articles, AIDS research, and check the Amsterdam entertainment guide. Follow more pink links to Kinky Pinky; Mr. BU's WWW; Rainbow Magazine; Fight for Life; and Safe Sex.

EXCERPT:

...Unique gay & lesbian information on our great city and the rest of the world not found anywhere else on the Web!

Pixel Pushers

http:www.wimsey.com/Pixel_Pushers/

The 21st Century Art museum that displays computer-generated artwork from all over North America. Rev up your modem—even at 28,800 baud, it takes a while to draw these complex images. Also check the link to About the Artists and About the Gallery.

EXCERPT:

Pixel Pushers Gallery was formed in 1994 to bring the work of North America's premiere digital artists to a new worldwide audience.

pixelMotion

http://aton.hypercomp.ns.ca/pix_dragon_gal.html

Computer graphics of TV spaceships, computer-generated architecture, and other neat computer animation from this multimedia firm. Beyond the images, this site is an advertisement for the company and exhibits samples of work done for clients.

Plan 10 From Outer Space

http://mcchurch.org/plan10

All the details about a controversial film that spoofs Utah history and Mormon ideology. A gallery of production shots, an interview with the film maker Trent Harris, and an online store of Plan 10 merchandise. Needless to say, this site is not for the traditionalist.

EXCERPT:

Mormons, sex and aliens! Plan 10 is a whacked out interpretation of Utah history and Mormon ideology....

The Plastic Princess Collector's Page

http://deepthought.armory.com/~zenugirl/barbie.html

The life and times of beautiful, blonde Barbie. An exhaustive list of magazines, clubs, gossip, price guides, tips, trading posts and just plain accolades for the plastic babe of the nuclear age. With original Barbies selling for big bucks, collecting Barbies isn't a hobby just for kids.

EXCERPT:

Now there are lots of people out there who will ask why one bothers to collect dolls..... Because it's something to do that's fun and can be challenging.

PM Zone

http://popularmechanics.com/

PM Zone is the cyberversion of *Popular Mechanics* magazine. Get out of the garage long enough to turn on this Web page and you just might learn something about those power tools. Actually, we're talking about much more than power tools here: software guides; daily technology updates; specs and evaluations of hundreds of vehicles; and a home computing forum. This site has more than 1000 links!

EXCERPT:

Here *Popular Mechanics*, a magazine that for 93 years has documented the dreams and deeds of those who believe technology will transform the world for the better, is itself transformed.

Point — The Top Sites of the Web

http://www.pointcom.com

The Point reviews and rates thousands of the Web's top sites. There's also

Like talk radio programs, Internet discussion groups have the ability to galvanize public opinion in a matter of minutes. The Internet played a role in rallying disapproval of Time magazine's altered O.J. Simpson cover...

Suzan Revah, *American Journalism Review*, March, 1995.

an escort service for web pedestrians. Opinions abound—contributed by the web public. Links to Survey Web Previews; New and Noteworthy; and more.

E X C E R P T :

Point reviews and rates thousands of the Web's top sites.

Postmodern Culture

http://jefferson.village.virginia.edu/pmc/

The electronic *Journal of Interdisciplinary Culture*, an academic journal dealing with all aspects of postmodern culture. Check the current issue, search back issues, and delve into special collections.

The Practice Hall

http://www.nesc.kiz.ar.us/ph_stuff/ph.html

An electronic companion to *Tooth&Claw*, the newsletter of myth and martial training. You'll find thoughtful writings about martial disciplines and their role in self-improvement as well as links to What is Mythic Combat?; Tooth&Claw; Oikiasuchou School; and The Human Blade.

E X C E R P T :

...The essays and stories here recount humanity's link to the fighter/warrior as icon archetype, and as a source of courage and bravery for men and women.

Primordial Shmooze

http://shmooze.net/pwcasual

Every grungy guitar player's online guide to alternative music and college bands, from web magazines to worldwide show listings, record labels, music charts from stations all over the place, online comics, print-based music magazines, etc.

EXCERPT:

...A forum for bands, record labels, comic artists and print-based music magazines.

Project Mind Foundation

http://www.webscope.com/project_mind/project_mind.html

The aim of this foundation is to get scientists to recognize the spiritual nature of their vocation. This site contains essays and other thoughts aimed at encouraging scientists to become more ethical and spiritual and to use their mind power to more rapidly solve global crises. Many links to related sources.

EXCERPT:

...We believe science to be the greatest spiritual undertaking ever, but that scientists have yet to recognize the spiritual nature of their vocation.

Psycho-Babel

http://www.mc5.net/~stvlange/http/psycho_babel.html

One helpful guy's list of sites on the web he thinks you should see. Includes Worthy Wastes of Time (Steve's list of favorite sites), literary links, poetry pages, and a lot of information on Chicago.

Public.com.personals

http://www.public.com/personals/

Everyone loves the personal ads—whether you're just looking or doing some serious scouting for companionship. You might call this site the Love Web. Would you believe more than 17,000 online personal ads for every imaginable kind of lifestyle? Many of the listings are broken down according to geographic regions.

EXCERPT:

This is a sanctuary, a gathering place, a sun-drenched meadow soaked with sounds and smells of springtime, forever youth, giddy and often unbridled expectation....

Pulp Fiction

http://turbo.kean.edu/%7 Elisajoy/PulpFiction/

It's no big surprise that someone was inspired to create a *Pulp Fiction* web page. After all, the movie has been a hot ticket since its release. Run by

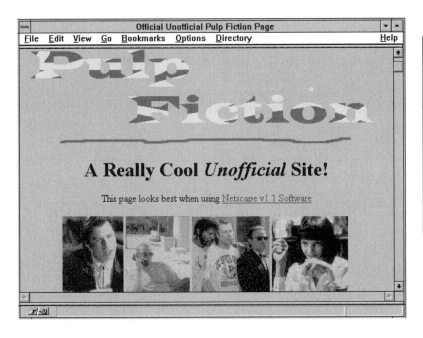

PC/LAN analysis student Lisajoy Jaclin Germinario, this online homage to *Pulp Fiction* offers a myriad of source materials and "cool" stuff for flick-o-philes ultra-keen on Quentin Tarantino's 1994 hit movie. Check out such intriguing links as Quentin Tarantino's Home Page, FAQ, *Pulp Fiction* Gallery, Sounds of Pulp Fiction, Tarantinoverse, and more. Well done!

EXCERPT:

Pulp Fiction is a group of stories revolving around a gangster boss. Tarantino's story [centers] around four different tales about a group of people, and the hardships and deaths that they encounter.

Pure Sheng

http://www.york.ac.uk/~rydh1/db.html

A page created by some roughs from the British city of York who describe themselves as a collective of undesirables. The site tells about their four-year history of parties, occasional run-ins with police, and provides the text of interviews some of their favorite musicians.

EXCERPT:

A collective of undesirables from York who have been throwing parties large and small since 1991.

Putrid Afterthought

http://bazaar.com/Art/mendoza.html

The site proclaims to be "art on the edge of piracy." Everything in these pages was once someone else's copyright. The stuff includes off-beat digital artwork, glorification of serial killers, pornography, and links to other putrid sites like Celebrate Anathema; Generation Hex; and Latex World.

EXCERPT:

Putrid Afterthought is what is seen at the end of the double-barreled shot gunned cesspool of hyperreality. View at your own risk....

Question of the Day

http://www/ptown.com:80/qod/

How many diseases are discovered each year? What is the capital of Malaysia? Little brain teasers like this every day make this site a virtual Q and A, a source for daily trivia. You can also check yesterday or today's usage statistics, and submit your own questions. Will you come back? Did you enjoy the questions? Why are you leaving?

EXCERPT:

It's all in the name of Net Fun, so have a good time and check out the question tomorrow.

Ranjit's HTTP Playground

http://oz.sas.upenn.edu/

Occasional dispatches and favorite places to play on the web from a WWW electronic publishing consultant. There are loads of links and Ranjit's resume is available for anyone who might be interested in hiring him.

EXCERPT:

My resume is available for those of you who for some reason want to hire me.

Rant of the Week

http://www.chaco.com/~stev0/rant.html

Rant of the Week selects (arbitrarily, one presumes) a subject for its weekly "rant" and delivers a page full of opinions every week on the subject. This web site is unapologetic and minces no words. The webmaster covers a wide range of topics such as Why I hate Christmas, Why I hated 1994, Why I hate sports, Why I hate Valentine's Day, Why I hate Boston, and other rants.

The Rat Pack Home Page

http://www.primenet.com/~drbmbay/

A bit of Vegas nostalgia. Remembering the golden years of Frank Sinatra,

The first issue of *Playboy*, featuring Marilyn Monroe on the cover, was undated so it could remain on the newsstands as long as possible because there was no certainty of a second issue.

The first "Playboy Interview," in which a budding journalist named Alex Haley interviewed jazz great Miles Davis, appeared September 1962.

Before it became a best-seller, before it was a movie with Robert Redford and Dustin Hoffman—*All The President's Men* was serialized in *Playboy*.

Playboy **Magazine: http://www.playboy.com/**

Sammy Davis Jr., and Dean Martin out in the desert before Vegas became a theme park. It's a cool site, especially for those who like to remember the good old days.

The Real Beer Page

http://and.com:80/realbeer/

A guide to the many small breweries popping up all around the country and plenty of barroom conversation about beer: tours; how to build your own brewery; advice from expert brewers; beer news; and beer games. It will keep your busy for awhile.

EXCERPT:

...Brew tours, like surfing, are perfect for the Web.

Real Life

http://www-leland.stanford.edu/~dove/

Poetry, prose and essays from a pretty regular guy in California. Don't skip the links to Electric Prose; Magnetic Poetry; The Suicide Letters; and Kilroy Wuz Here!

The Realist Wonder Society

http://www.rrnet.com/~nakamura

A well-designed 'zine of original fables, fairy tales and screenplays. It's a safe site for kids, who will love the illustrations. Try Mole and Owl; Screenplays and Film; Fables and Fairy Tales; Art and Poetry; and Feedback and News.

EXCERPT:

A whistle-stop of imagination between way stations of reality.

The ReBoot Home Page

http://uts.cc.utexas.edu/~ifex534/main.html

Saturday morning cartoons come to the Net. ReBoot, the first TV series produced entirely with computer graphics, has an older following than your usual Saturday morning cartoon crowd thanks to its astounding computer graphics and pop culture references. You can learn more about ReBoot here, and link up to other ReBoot sites like Episode Guide and Press Releases.

EXCERPT:

The show is well written, filled with fast action, and contains dozens of computer puns, in-jokes, and pop culture references.

Recent Global Events

http://www/civeng.carleton.ca/cgi-bin/quakes

This site takes responsibility for reporting on earthquakes round the world. When the "big one" hits, all the details will be here. Technical, up-to-the-minute details and maps for earthquake activity worldwide with lots of links to earthquake topics.

EXCERPT:

...Responsible for reporting on moderate to large earthquakes throughout the U.S. and large earthquakes worldwide.

Recipes for Traditional Food in Slovenia

http://www.ijs.si/slo-recipes

Just the Slovenian food facts, ma'am. No fancy graphics. No bells and whistles. Hey, one of those check-out aisle cooking magazines might look nicer, but where else are you going to find exotic recipes like "young goat with wine" and "carp with onions"?

Reinventing Government Toolkit

http://www.npr.gov/

More than 800 documents (sound like red tape?) on the Clinton administration's ongoing plans to reform everything from the federal budget to the Pentagon. Here's your starting point to participate in what the providers call "this historic change."

Reiveland

http://www.phantom.com/~reive

A 'zine from a recent Washington, D.C., journalism school graduate. You can sample poetry, fiction and creative nonfiction, an interesting column called Rant of the Week, or link to the Sexual Politics Resource List.

The Relief Goddess Office Home Page

http://www.hsr.no/~geir-f/amg.html

An online, mythological soap opera? Maybe, but it's kind of hard to figure

Playboy is logging 620,000 visits a day to its World Wide Web location and the numbers are growing, said Eileen Kent, the magazine's director of new media. That means Playboy is 1 of the 10 most-visited sites on the Web, Ms. Kent said. *Penthouse Magazine*, *Playboy's* longtime rival, is doing even better. On March 1, its first day on the Internet, *Penthouse* recorded 802,000 visits, said Kathy Keeton, president of *Penthouse's* parent company, General Media International.

The New York Times

out just who's who and what's what and who's doing what to whom, but, then again, you can't just tune into the *Guiding Light* one day and immediately figure out all the subplots.

Resort Sports Network

ttp://www.resortsportsnet.com/biz/rsn/

Is it snowing in Aspen? Is the sun shining at Pebble Beach? Get weather reports for resorts all over the country, sports action photos, and video links to other adventure-sports web sites, link to Awesome Videos; Play Per View; Surf-N-Win; Chateau Relaxeau; and Sport Trips. You'll enjoy the exercise.

EXCERPT:

From mountain sports to water sports, it is our goal to provide information and instill inspiration into your resort sports experience....

Restroom Utilization Measurement Project

http://entity.vuse.vanderbilt.edu/project

An anonymous spoof on academia. The writers claim to have installed motion and pressure sensors and methane meters in Vanderbilt University bathrooms in the name of sewage progress. Complete with bibliography of faux academic studies on the topic.

EXCERPT:

The goal of RUMP is to...improve the quality of human waste management.

The Resume of Mark-Jason Dominus

http://www.cis.upen.edu/~mjd/

Mark-Jason Dominus was a senior planner and programmer for Pathfinder, Time-Warner's WWW project and main Internet service. Now his resume is on the web for everyone to see. You have to give this guy an A for ambition, but frankly, few web surfers really care. Anyway, hope he gets the job he wants.

EXCERPT:

...I developed Web applications, planned technical infrastructure, administered the UNIX systems....

Adam Rifkin

http://www.cs.caltech.edu/~adam/adam.html

With 13,321 hits on his page as of 8/95, Adam Rifkin is one very popular guy. His page is a testimonial to himself, who he is, and what he likes and deserves a stop if only as a guidebook to constructing your own personal-dossier web page that gives the world a comprehensive peek at your own warped, computer-geekedly obsessive mania. Adam's page sports more links than a 100-foot chain! Good work!

EXCERPT:

Adam Rifkin...is also known as foghead, hitlistee, the Spot addict, Angels fan, Cult Director (Not!)...netsurfer (cowabunga), and Candyman.

Ritual of Abandonment

http://www.art.net/Studios/Visual/Fenster/ritofab_Home/fenster.ht

Words and pictures—with Dada and Surrealist tints—from a prolific virtual artist. Look for more inspiration at Inspiration and Images & Stories; Web Stories; Symbolism; and The Creative Process. The artist says he uses silicon chips as the tool to transform electrical patterns into art.

EXCERPT:

My art is a combination of myth, spirit, science, and technology.

Rocktropolis

http://underground.net/Rocktropolis/

An awesome Rock-N-Roll Web site. Great graphics. The site is a rock cityscape, with separate buildings for Jim Morrison, Sting, IRS Records, groups, concert information, sheet music, and lots of other good stuff. Pop cultures greatest musicians and cult heros all live here.

Major movies now virtually require a web site, and it's rare to find a popular album or TV show without a home page.

Bruce Haring, *USA Today*, July 20, 1995

EXCERPT:

Welcome to Rocktropolis, a Rock-N-Roll fantasy theme park, a surreal city landscape inhabited by some of pop culture's greatest musicians...

Rockweb (tm) Interactive

http://www.rock.net/

Rockweb claims to be state-of-the-art, but you wouldn't know it from looking at its web page. There's an attractive, BIG inline graphic, but it throws off the text on the page when it loads up. Nevertheless, there are lots of great links here for rock enthusiasts who are looking for all sorts of stuff about bands, various musical organizations, and Usenet groups. Rockweb's main links include: What Critics Think, Features, Bands, Listeners, Organizations, and Rockweb.

EXCERPT:

This is state-of-the-art web technology in the hands of some really creative artists, writers, and musicians who sometimes alone and sometimes together come up with some really cool things.

S

Sailing the Abnormalcy

http://www.indirect.com/user/warren/index.html

Sailing the Abnormalcy is a personal home page. it's not very interesting, except for the Flag Burning page, where there is plenty of debate and tracking of current legislation. This web site also provides links to The Spinning Jenny Home Page and Breakfast Surreal.

EXCERPT:

Welcome to my home page. It will be cooler later.

St. Petersburg Press Home Page

http://www.spb.su/sppress

This online version of the Russian newspaper is an excellent source of information about activities, news, and developments in the former Soviet Union. Though it lacks a key word index, it provides a weekly chronicle of life in Russia, with historical archives to July 1994. Looking for a job? Check the classifieds.

EXCERPT:

...Readers wishing to read the complete *St. Petersburg Press* can subscribe to the printed version.

St. Petersburg Times Interactive Media

http://ww.times.st-pete.fl.us/

This colorful site provides interesting news and commentary, stunning photography and images, and visitor information related to the Tampa Bay area. The images seem to outweigh the textual content, but there is enough of both to keep most people occupied. Links include Florida Travel, Congressional Quarterly, Governing, and Community Smart Books (all products of the Times Publishing Company), and a visit to the Florida Aquarium.

EXCERPT:

Welcome to the experimental Web site of the *St. Petersburg Times* Interactive Media Department. Don't miss the new Florida Aquarium virtual visit....

Salmo-Trutta: Fine Art Online Gallery

http://gn2.getnet.com:80/salmoart/

An online art gallery of the paintings of Stephen J. Cullen, an artist living in Arizona who specializes in "piscatorial and organic watercolors," or fish and nature art. Surfers can view and purchase paintings such as "Camel and Three Trout" and "Hi-Lo Trout Club." You might like to check links to Portraits and Photographs of the Artist and Buena Vistas along the Infobaun.

EXCERPT:

...I have endeavored through my paintings to encapsulate the spirit and beauty of the mountains, highlands, and riparian regions of the western landscape, especially those found in Arizona.

San Francisco Examiner Home Page

http://cyber.sfgate.com/examiner/

The *Electric Examiner* is one of the best online newspapers around, with an

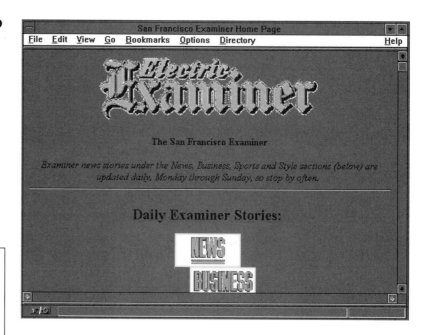

edge to be expected from the city by the bay. No smattering of articles here—instead, you get daily doses of dozens of discourses. Daily stories are found in four sections: news, business, sports, and style. Article archives can be searched back to the beginning of 1995, but they will eventually extend back to 1988.

EXCERPT:

The EE has been an experiment-in-progress since June 1994....Our aim is to try new things and listen carefully to your response as we shape a new service in a new medium.

San Francisco Free Press

http://www.ccnet.com/SF_Free_Press/welcome.html

The *San Francisco Free Press* was an online newspaper that lasted only as long as the strike that spawned it—11 days to be exact. It was produced by the striking employees of the *San Francisco Chronicle*, the *San Francisco Examiner*, and the San Francisco Newspaper Agency. You may still want to visit...especially if you have an interest in recent newspaper strikes.

EXCERPT:
Editing, producing, and delivering a newspaper...under strike conditions was both exhilarating and exhausting....

Today's *San Jose Mercury News*

http://www.sjmercury.com/today.htm

The *San Jose Mercury News*, like few other online newspapers, is a harbinger of the electronic newspaper of the future. It's an attractive, well-designed web site from one of California's best-run and most forward-thinking news sources. The *Mercury News* has more links to explore than many online newspapers, and much of it is free. However, the really good stuff is available to subscribers only, but at $.95 a month it's not a bad deal. Check out the following links (which may or may not be free): Front Page, International, National, Local & State, Editorials & Commentary, Business, Sports, Living, Entertainment, and Comics.

EXCERPT:

The *San Jose Mercury News* is the daily newspaper of San Jose and the Sili-

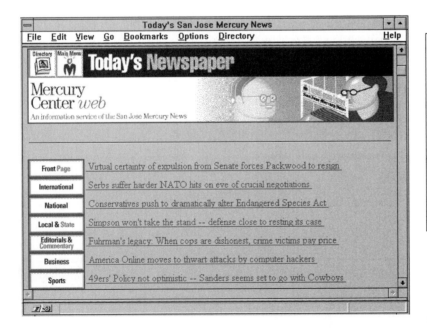

> Rollercoasters afford a rare opportunity. We, as civilized members of society, are allowed, even expected, to scream our throats raw in a very public way....This outburst is an important catharsis. How many times have you wanted to just let go with an ear-piercing shriek standing by the water cooler at work? Or waiting on line at the post office? Or sitting politely at a family dinner? But you didn't, wisely, because it would have gotten you fired, arrested or disowned. Probably all three.
>
> **Rollercoaster!**
> **http://mosaic.echonyc.com/~dne/Rollercoaster!/**

con Valley in northern California...weekday circulation is 280,000 and Sunday circulation tops 340,000. The editorial staff numbers over 300...The full text of the Mercury News is available on the Internet and American Online.

Sandra's Clip Art Server

http://www.cs.yale.edu/homes/sjl/clipart.html

An excellent starting point for clip art scavengers. Site includes lots of clip art images in tar compressed format collected from several large collections. The images can be viewed and/or downloaded. Also includes handy links to the original sites of the collections plus pointers to generic picture archives.

Sarabande.com: Digital Communication Services

http://www.sarabande.com/default.html

This advertising site describes the various offerings of a digital communication services company called Sarabande. Unless you need an Iris Proof or Repro paper (or know what such things are), there is no need to visit this site—other than to see Sarabande's photos of the intersection of Houston and Broadway in New York City taken from a camera at a car wash at the corner.

EXCERPT:

We are relatively normal people who try hard to do great work.

The Saturn Site: For Owners, Shoppers, Team Members, and the Curious

http://www.saturncars.com/

If you're annoyed by Saturn commercials, then stay away from this site—it exudes Saturn's "We Are Family" attitude. Saturn workers, interested owners, and potential owners, however, might find this site worthwhile, perhaps for its photos of the current models or the directory of Saturn retailers or the possibility of ordering a brochure without leaving the keyboard.

EXCERPT:

The Saturn Site...[is] one more way that we can keep in touch with everyone and anyone who's interested in Saturn.

Science Fiction and Anime Page

http://www.best.com/~sirlou/scifi_anime.html

This site contains links to a variety of science fiction (mostly TV and movies) and anime (Japanese animation) web sites. Of the science fiction, there is lots on *Star Trek* and *Star Wars*, with a smattering of sites for such sci-fi classics as the *Twilight Zone*, *Quantum Leap*, and *Battlestar Gallactica*. The Anime links include one for classic *Speed Racer* animated series.

EXCERPT:

Anime...is visually stunning and themes range from dark (Akira) to absolutely silly (Ranma _).

Scoop! The CyberSpace Tip Sheet

http://www.cais.com/makulow/scoop.html

The apparent purpose of Scoop! is to tip off journalists to potential stories. The tidbits uncovered at this site were found by the editors of Scoop! while surfing the Internet. An example of the "scoops" provided here: a contract with a Russian institute to build a critical component of the U.S. Star Wars project. Journalists, use your judgment.

EXCERPT:

Scoop! The CyberSpace Tip Sheet presents comments on items uncovered or stumbled upon while navigating the Internet.

Screensavers for Windows

http://optimum.optimum.nf.ca/savers/savers.htm

Tired of your current screen saver? Check this site out for links to places where a variety of screensavers can be downloaded. It's an eclectic mix— Camaro, Canadian Football League, cats in motion, cheese, chick (eggs thrown at cartoon characters, including Barney), Coca Cola products, cows, craters, CRT spray (featuring flying hippos). And those are only the names of screen savers that start with "C." Look for lots of good helps and hints, too.

Secret E-Mail Addresses and Home Pages

http://www.islandnet.com/~lureee/fanmail.html

Here's a way to pester or worship the beautiful people. This site lists e-mail and home page addresses for dozens of famous actors, singers, comedians, models, politicians, and magicians. You can send e-mail to Jimmy Buffet or Janet Jackson, Meg Ryan or Hugh Grant, Guy la Horn, the prime minister of Hungary, or King Bhumibal Adulyadej of Thailand.

Although hundreds of companies are flooding the Web with goods for sale—everything from flowers to cars—shopping online is still in its infancy. According to Forrester Research, last year American consumers spent more than $1.5 trillion in retail stores and a mere $200 million online. It's only the smartly targeted niche campaigns that have enjoyed success online.

PC Computing, July, 1995.

EXCERPT:

Some of the pages are actually maintained by the celebrity listed, some are excellent examples of well maintained fan pages....

Sedona On-Line

http://www.sedona.net/sedona.html

Everything from soup to nuts about the classy resort town of Sedona, Arizona: Where to Stay; What to Do; Where to Eat; and Shopping & Souvenirs. Sedona is located about halfway between Phoenix and the Grand Canyon; and in the words of a booster, its "world class amenities are enhanced by a spectacular setting, a rich creative atmosphere, and a location central to northern Arizona's major attractions."

EXCERPT:

...Sedona is a visitor destination of unparalleled richness, offering a variety of cultural experiences and a chance to enjoy nature at her finest.

See the USA in Your Virtual Chevrolet

http://www.std.com/NE/usatour.html

Travel the U.S.A. from A to Z with entertaining dialogue along the way. This site lists links to online tourist information for many states. Go to

Florida for a guide to Walt Disney World; go to and check out the guide to Chicago's restaurants; or go to Oregon and get the latest hunting and fishing information. One weakness: not every state is listed.

EXCERPT:

A cybertour of the U.S. from Everybody's Internet Update, No. 4 (July, 1994). You can find past Update issues via the Electronic Frontier Foundation.

The Seed: U.K. Alternative Information

http://web.cs.city.ac.uk/homes/louise/seed2.html

Anarchy in the U.K.! The Seed's host, Louise Schuller, edits and organizes the home pages of several U.K.-based alternative organizations such as Squall, the London Psychogeographical Association, and Class War. The page also features links to other radical Internet sites around the world.

EXCERPT:

A year and one car door later, I still cycle fearlessly and recklessly round London (Turnpike Lane to Piccadilly Circus in 25 mins.) and I continue to drink far too much Cider. . . . Stay cool, Stay happy!

The Sega Web

http://www.segaoa.com/

Sega addicts will revel in the variety of information available at this official site of Sega of America. Accompanied by terrific graphics, users will find lots of information about Sega video games and other products, including press releases, game hints and cheats, screen shots, and new release notices.

EXCERPT:

The Sega Web has been established to provide public information about Sega and its products and services. This server contains tons of text and image files....

Seinfeld

http://www.engr.wisc.edu/~heinj/seinfeld.html

Seinfeld, that cool TV comedy, has this fan-based web page. What can you expect here? Same old, same old, not that there is anything wrong with that. Trivia, pictures, and links to The Stars; Seinfeld Fun Stuff; Seinfeld Episode List; and The Seinfeld Page FAQ. Fans, enjoy!

EXCERPT:

I put it together as somewhat of a learning experience and it has turned into what it is today.

SETI Institute Home Page

http://www.seti-inst.edu/

The SETI Institute conducts and supports research into life in the universe, popularly known as the search for extraterrestrial intelligence (SETI). The Institute's field of interest includes all science and technology aspects of astronomy and the planetary sciences, chemical evolution, the origin of life, biological evolution, and cultural evolution. If you're interested in alien activity, check it out.

EXCERPT:

The SETI Institute serves as an institutional home for scientific and educational projects relevant to the nature, distribution, and prevalence of life in the universe....

SHOT Gallery

http://www.pavilion.co.uk/PIG//Shot/shot.htm

Part of the Pavilion Internet Gallery, the SHOT Gallery displays the work of some of England's female photographers and especially showcases their photographs of seminude women. SHOT tries hard to be provocative—describes itself as "a shooting gallery—for adults only." Art and provocation are in the eye of the beholder.

The future, Prodigy has found, lies with communication rather than transactions. People want to talk to one another, says Kurnit. More than 100,000 messages are posted on Prodigy's "bulletin boards" every day, linking on-line users into hundreds of digital "salons" specifically interesting to them.

Scott Kurnit, executive vice president for Prodigy, *Newsweek*

EXCERPT:

SHOT... is cool, vertical, and part of the Festival of Women Photographers. A series of scattered images through the sights of your PC. Like the streets this gallery is open 24 hours.

SiamWEB

http://www.eskimo.com/~putt/siam

This site is a good example of the creation of a cyberculture. SiamWEB presents a variety of ways for those interested in the country of Thailand and its people to interact: photo archives, news summaries, information on travel opportunities and meetings, even a romance connection. This site's offerings are rounded out by links to sites about Thailand and to educational institutions.

EXCERPT:

SiamWEB is where a group of people who have interests in Thailand and its people joined up via WWW, and eventually formed into this friendly, lively, Cyber environment.

David Siegel's Home Page

http://www.best.com:80/~dsiegel/home.html

You saw the movie, now read the web page. Yes, Dave Siegel, of *Pulp Fic-*

tion fame, has his own web page. He's here to give you some tips in website design and teach you how to tell more realistic stories to today's demanding audiences.

EXCERPT:

This web page actually kills the germs that cause dandruff!

SIGArch

http://www.acm.uiuc.edu/sigarch/

From the Special Interest Group for Computer Architecture (SIGArch), the student chapter of ACM at the University of Illinois, comes this site that describes student proposed, designed, and built projects. Among the projects described here—perhaps soon to be coming to a CompUSA near you—are the ultimate phone device, bit-mapped chase lights, and digital name tags.

Silicon Studio: Technology for Entertainment

http://www.studio.sgi.com/

This is the web site for Silicon Studio, Inc., a technology specialist that provides services for the entertainment industry. It's a good site for pros and future innovators to visit because the studio posts its current job openings. While you're there, don't forget to check out the links to Publishing; Interactive Entertainment; Collaborative Support; Avenue of the Stars; Training; Partners; Coming Attractions; and more.

EXCERPT:

In the past, technology was driven by defense. Today, it's driven by entertainment.

Silly Little Troll Publications

http://pobox.com/slt/

The site for an electronic publisher of a continuously updated online magazine called "Sam Johnson's Electronic Revenge," manuscripts not available in book form (such as Working Girls: Interviews with 22 Prostitutes by D. L. Logan), and "reprints" of titles in the public domain (such as Evolution and Occultism by Annie Besant, first published in 1913). The manuscripts and reprints can be purchased in HTML format. The publisher of the future? You decide.

EXCERPT:

Silly Little Troll Publications is an electronic publishing enterprise dedicated to the reemergence of provocative writing in the information age....

Sinatra

http://www.io.org/~buff/sinatra.html

Fans of Ol' Blue Eyes will find much to sing about at this site. The musical career of Frank Sinatra is the focus here through song lyrics, album covers, interviews and articles, photos, a filmography and discography, and links to other Sinatra sites. You'll even find Frank's thoughts on rock music and his recipe for spaghetti sauce. This is a site strictly for fans of the musician, not those searching for dirty laundry.

EXCERPT:

If you are a Sinatra fan, and have anything you'd like to add, please let me know. I'm doing this my way, but may I say, not in a shy way, that if you'd like to contribute you'd be welcome.

Sinister Connections

http://www.webcom.com:80/~conspire/links.html

The mother of all tangled webs, Sinister Connections offers access to a full range of sites relating to conspiracies and conspiracy theories. All the usual suspects are here—government coverups of UFO landings, JFK, the Illuminati, the John Birch Society—plus a host of other, more obscure plots and cabals from the paranoid around the world. Also linked are "subversive" sites and a few sites of the government organizations that figure so prominently in many of these theories. Enjoy cyberparanoia.

I was the top student in my class. But to be fair, that was not what you'd call a competitive environment. I never once took a book home to study. The other 30-odd students (and I do mean odd) were mostly destined for careers in the custodial arts. Only my arch nemesis Gina...was a threat to my rightful place as Valedictorian. Tragically, Gina opted for a challenging Physics course in her senior year instead of the typing course that I took. I don't know how often Gina has to calculate velocity these days, but I'm typing right now. And my "A" in typing helped make me Valedictorian.

The Dilbert Zone—Scott Adams: Unmasked! http://www.unitedme-dia.com/comics/dilbert

EXCERPT:

Weaselly Disclaimer: We don't necessarily endorse all of these links; some may contain idiotic, racist, or otherwise nutty opinions.

sKATEBOARD.com

http://tumyeto.com/tydu/skatebrd/skate.htm

For skateboarders and skateboarders only—no coverage of snowboarding or inline skating here. sKATEBOARD.com includes competitions and contests, fiction, photos, articles, events, 'zines, companies, organizations, and other WWW sites, all relating to skateboarding. Special features include a worldwide skate park directory.

EXCERPT:

Yeah, you're here. It's sKATEBOARD.com. The "premiere" digital skateboarding information source.

skew

http://www.ot.com/skew/

Skew is a monthly e-zine but very hard to describe. It appears to be concerned with the general area of culture and sometimes covers the Lehigh Valley area from which it originates. Examples of items in the first eight issues may help you figure out skew's mission: places to eat in the Lehigh Valley, a review of *Miss Saigon*, feature on the Pennsylvania Dutch, "thoughts on bowling," and a brief overview of urban legends. Any suggestions?

Ski Web

http://diamond.sierra.net/SkiWeb/

Maintained by Sierra-Net, an Internet access provider in northern Nevada, Ski Web aims to cover the whole world of snow sports for downhill skiers and snowboarders (cross-country skiing is not emphasized here). The resorts that participate in this site describe themselves and report on current ski conditions, number of lifts, difficulty of runs, length of runs, and provide other ski information. (The exact information included varies from resort to resort.) Of special interest are a couple of Quicktime movies of a Sierra Nevada run taken from a helmet camera.

Skywings on the Web

http://test.ebrd.com/Skywings/home.html

Skywings on the Web is an abridged version of the monthly magazine on hang gliding and paragliding from England. Bimonthly issues cover various competitions, news, profiles of pilots, and feature articles. For flying enthusiasts in the United Kingdom, the site also features a lists of U.K.-based flying clubs and schools for learning how to hang glide or paraglide.

EXCERPT:

Skywings brings you all the hot news of national and international competition, keeps you up to date on the latest flying equipment, and reviews what's happening in the hang gliding and paragliding world.

SLED: Four11 White Page Directory

http://www.Four11.com/

A well-built Web site that's become a popular way to locate other Internet users. Four11 claims 1.1 million listings of people who use the Net. Sign on and you register your own e-mail address. Then you can punch in a name to get an e-mail address for a long-lost friend. One drawback: there are still plenty of online users who aren't registered here.

EXCERPT:

The Four11 White Page Directory is...where Internet users can register their Internet addresses (e-mail and Web) and look for other Internet users. Free basic access....

The Slipper of the Future

http://slipper.mit.edu/

Slipper of the Future reports "research" on the future development of the slipper and includes a bulletin board for discussions on slippers and links to sites with info on slippers and feet. By the way, MIT students run this site, and more than 100 people connect to it each day. Decide for yourself if this exercise has any value or exemplifies how to waste the Internet's precious resources.

EXCERPT:

Each day we actively seek out more information about slippers, foot care, other types of foot gear, and foot related sites in general to add to our stockpile of information about slippers.

Smitty's UFO Page

http://www.schmitzware.com/ufo.html

Maintained by Dave Schmitz, a researcher at the NASA Ames Research

SEARCH PHRASE: Love. Results of search for love: Four matching items—alt.pub.cloven-shield (a bulletin board filled with rambling stories set in the Middle Ages), aol.neighborhood.nation.slovenia, soc.culture.slovenia (sample posting; what are your favorite Slovenian albums?) and ont.sf-lovers. (Ont.sf-lovers turned out to be a bulletin board for Ontario science fiction lovers, not single female lovers.)

SEARCH PHRASE: Relationship. Computer response: No matches were found for this search. Please try a less restrictive search phrase.

Daniel Pearl, *Wall Street Journal*, February 13, 1995.

Center, the focus of Smitty's UFO Page is the secret government air base known as Groom Lake in Nevada. Schmitz describes two trips he took to the vicinity of Groom Lake in 1994 and provides 3-D rendered images of the area and links to the Internet UFO Group (IUFOG) web site, which contains a broader range of UFO-related information.

EXCERPT:

What is proof of extraterrestrial life? Some say the government already has it. Others say God will provide it. Others need a saucer to land in their own backyard....

Smurfs

http://www.umich.edu/~starchild/hannabarbera/smurfs/

A lame site that is probably of little interest even to Smurf heads. This site contains only nine animation stills (such as "Gargamel about to Net a Smurf") and two Quicktime movies.

EXCERPT:

Where everyone must be smurfy.

Snake Oil: Your Guide to Kooky Kontemporary Kristian Kulture

http://fender.onramp.net/~analyst/snake/Snakeoil.html

Keep an eye on the fundamentalist far right via this site. It's an electronic preview of Snake Oil, a 'zine dedicated to uncovering and commenting on the continuing exploits of televangelists and other evangelical Christians including Robert Tilton, Bob Larson, and Tammy Faye Bakker. Content includes news items, descriptions of the evangelicals' crusades, and ordering information for items for sale from the Snake Oil Home Shopping and Prayer Network (such as Robert Tilton trading cards).

EXCERPT:

"They know not the depth of their sacrilege." — Robert Tilton, commenting on Snake Oil.

The Snow Page

http://rmd-www.mr.ic.ac.uk/snow/snowpage.html

Although other sites may be better organized, the Snow Page covers an incredible range of information on downhill skiing, cross-country skiing, and snowboarding. Included here or via the numerous links are trail maps, photos, travel services, weather, maps, resort information, and loads of other useful snow-related data. This is a good first stop for skiers and snowboarders.

The Social Cafe

http://www.social.com/social/index.html

The Social Cafe intends to be the online equivalent of a coffee shop with news updated daily from USENET newsgroups, discussion groups through which users can "converse," and such amusements as comics, sports information, and games. The site also features resources for women that can found on the Internet.

The Social Cafe is a place to relax and enjoy a cup of the best roasted brew around. You'll find people enjoying some games, discussing the latest news and getting to know each other....

The Sofasphere II Project

http://ftp.std.com/homepages/stevec/SSII/intro.html

A takeoff on the Biosphere II Project, the Sofasphere II Project takes a humorous look at how humankind can absorb the oft-predicted 500 channels of cable. It proposes such creative solutions as an ergonomic sofa/toilet/access station, plants photosynthesized through the light from televisions, and the National Information Sewer Network.

EXCERPT:

Man and nature shall watch TV in symbiotic harmony.

SonicNet

http://www.sonicnet.com/

This "alternative online site" features special chat lines with guest "artists, punks, musicians, writers, and freaks," such as Timothy Leary, Thomas Dolby, and Henry Rollins of Black Flag; online-only singles from alternative bands; coverage of the Macintosh New York Music Fest held in July 1995; discussion groups about sex and dating; links to songs available on the Internet; and links to other alternative sites.

Sound Bytes: The WWW TV Themes Home Page

http://ai.eecs.umich.edu/people/kennyp/sounds.html

Sound Bytes archives a host of TV themes from the 1950s through the 1990s. The audio files, which range from 10KB to 900KB, are in .au format. So tune into Theme of the Week; Comedy Shows; Drama Shows; Action/Adventure; Action/Sci-Fi; Daytime Soaps; Network Intros; TV

"I think security is a big red herring. I have not seen one documented case about someone actually stealing and misusing a person's credit card number."

Dave Taylor, coauthor of *The Internet Business Guide*

Magazines; Misc. Shows; Children's Shows; Other Fun Things; and Some TV Commercials.

Soundprint Media Center

http://soundprint.org/

Soundprint produces documentaries that are aired on public radio stations. Available for downloading are a selection of full-length documentaries and shorter excerpts in .au format. Also included is a list of stations that carry the Soundprint programs, brief audio clips, program summaries, and reading and resource lists.

EXCERPT:

The primary purpose of SMCI is...the development and dissemination of audio, video, and multimedia programs and ancillary print educational materials; and research, editorial, and production support services.

Sounds from Movies

http://www.netaxs.com/~dgresh/snddir.html

A neat site for movie fans, Sounds from Movies provides a rotating selection of audio clips from about 20 movies. Most of the sequences are sections of dialogue from the movies, such as the meeting on the pitcher's mound from *Bull Durham*. Many of the clips are in .wav format, but other formats are also represented. The site also has links to other sites where movie fans can hear more movie sounds.

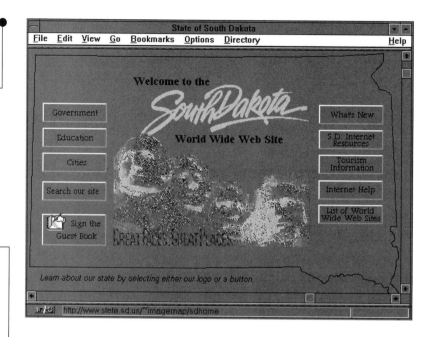

South Dakota World Wide Web Site

http://www.state.sd.us/

Travelers, researchers, geography buffs, students, and everyone interested in South Dakota should visit this official site. For example, the travel information includes accommodations, calendar of events, cities, fun facts, group tour planning guide, maps, national and state parks, outdoor recreation, and travel tips. Users can leave online requests for additional information to be mailed to them. Another really nice additional feature is an Internet help page, which could help Internet novices get up to speed on the web.

The South Florida Dive Journal

http://www.florida.net/scuba/dive/

Divers and scuba enthusiasts will love this gorgeous display of scuba diving pictures and downloadable videos. There are some minor problems with display-line lengths, but the difficulty seems to be browser dependant.

Sovereign's WWW Content Page

http://www.primenet.com/~lion/

Welcome to Paranoia Central. Sovereign's WWW Content Page is a veritable clearinghouse for conspiracy theorists. If you think that the United Nations is planning to take over the world, or that the AIDS virus was invented by the U.S. government, this is the place for you. And if you don't believe any of these theories, here's a good way to find out about those who do.

Space Age Bachelor Pad Music

http://www.interport.net/~joholmes/index.html

Space Age Bachelor Pad Music is a site for enthusiasts of Space Age Pop: the instrumental music of such artists as Henry Mancini, Martin Denny, and Juan Garcia Esquivel popular from 1954 to 1964 and enjoying a revival in the 1990s. Featured here are sound samples in .aiff format, album covers, photographs of the artists, bibliographies, discographies, and news about upcoming releases. Mix a martini and enjoy the retro ambience.

The Space Between New & Used Books

http://www.tagsys.com/Ads/SpaceBetween/

This is the online site for a bookstore called The Space Between, which spe-

Freudian Analysis of *Cat in the Hat*. By Joshua LeBeau.

The *Cat in the Hat* is a hard-hitting novel of prose and poetry in which the author re-examines the dynamic rhyming schemes and bold imagery of some of his earlier works, most notably Green Eggs and Ham, If I Ran the Zoo, and Why Can't I Shower With Mommy? In this novel, Theodore Geisel, writing under the pseudonym Dr. Seuss, pays homage to the great Dr. Sigmund Freud in a nightmarish fantasy of a renegade feline helping two young children understand their own frustrated sexuality.

The Dr. Seuss Page: http://klinzhai.iuma.com/-drseuss/seuss/seuss.home.html

cializes in such fringe topics as UFOs, conspiracy theories, secret societies, survival, esoteric wisdom, and the occult. Interested readers can check the listings of new, used, and signed titles and browse the list of titles the store is looking to purchase.

EXCERPT:

We pride ourselves on being a source of information not readily available through other outlets. No publisher is too small, no topic taboo.

Spacecoast Hidden Mickeys at Walt Disney World

http://iu.net/tshaw/trs/HiddenMickey.html

First there was Waldo. This site is dedicated to uncovering and reporting "hidden Mickeys," which are "images of Mickey Mouse concealed in the design of a Disney attraction." There are apparently lots of them at Walt Disney World in Florida. Listed here are reported sightings of hidden Mickeys in rides, at the resorts, in the parking lots, on the golf courses, and in the souvenirs. They're everywhere! Users are urged to report their own sightings immediately.

Sparky's Ads in Cyberspace

http://cyberzine.org

The best thing about advertising on the Web is you don't have to read it unless you really want to. Sparky's Ads is a home page devoted to providing advertising space to businesses. You can read the ads from a wide range of vendors from chocolate sellers to tax consultants. By the way, the charge for ads starts at $15 a month.

Spatula City

http://www.wam.umd.edu/~twoflowr/index.html

Spatula City is a humorous site that features a catalog of spatulas not really for sale, such as the X-GF Spatula of Death, the SXS Stealth Spatula, and the Dolby Surround Spatula. Surfers will also find fiction published on the Internet; a fun area with puzzles, games, and the like; and fun things for downloading. Try the Kitchenware 'n' Candybars aisle or the Silly Zone and Black Light Specials.

EXCERPT:

All who resist Spatula City suffer painfully humiliating deaths in front of large television audiences on Donohue. Do not taunt Spatula City.

Species

http://www.digiplanet.com/species/index.html

Species is the promotional site from MGM for the 1995 film of the same name. Visitors will find information about the cast and the film makers (including the special effects crew), the story of the making of the "Sil" creature, and Quicktime format video clips from the movie and trailers. The site also features an online adventure game called the Web Adventure. There's an original title for you.

EXCERPT:

The Web Adventure transports you into a world where alien and human psychology go to war inside your mind....Your goal is to escape, survive, and discover your true identity—before you're captured and terminated.

SpeedNet

http://www.starnews.com/speednet/

If you follow auto racing, you'll enjoy this web site which is managed by the daily newspapers in Indianapolis. SpeedNet contains all of the latest racing news from the Associated Press, complete with photos. The design of the homepage is particularly good—very attractive and full of color, yet easy to download.

EXCERPT:

The SpeedNet World Wide Web site is an automobile-racing information service provided free to Internet users by *The Indianapolis Star* and *The Indianapolis News*. Its purpose is to provide complete coverage and interactive features related to IndyCar, Indy Racing League, NASCAR/Winston Cup, USAC, NHRA and Formula One auto racing.

Speleology Information Server

http://speleology.cs.yale.edu/

Caving fanatics will unearth a wealth of information at the Speleology Information Server. Featured here is a directory of caving societies, a calendar of events, an archive of caving information, pictures in GIF format, clip art and cartoons, cave surveying software programs, a list of newsletters and periodicals, and links to other cave sites.

Sphinx Productions

http://www.io.org:80/sphinx

Sphinx maintains an entertainment magazine and catalog at this site, emphasizing the company's own work and highlighting Canadian entertain-

A reporter for *Computer Life* magazine posed on the Internet as a 15-year-old cheerleader and got more than thirty e-mail messages of a sexual nature, including requests for her panties and her telephone number.

Gary Chapman, in *The New Republic*

ment and media. Lots of links to try: Comics; Dance; Drugs; Education; Food; Jazz; Movies; Painting; Photography; Poetry; Radio; and Small Press.

SpinnWebe

http://www.thoughtport.com/spinnwebe

SpinWebbe presents an eccentric assortment of images, quotes, interactive games and software, stories, and links to other web sites. The site is a "Group 19" site, which are WWW outposts of innovative and iconoclastic home pages. Links to some bizarre-sounding sites like The Zweblo Underground Fan Cult Online Catalog (offering custom t-shirts and bumper stickers); Realtime/Interactive (with a "Mystic 9-Ball" link); Dysfunctional Family Circus; and 1-900-ZWEBLO7.

EXCERPT:

The last update markers currently show you the last time a thing was updated down to tenths of days (I could have made it days and hours, but I think tenths is kinda cool in a geeky way)....

The Spot

http://www.thespot.com

The Spot follows the adventures and real lives (apparently) of a small group of people living in the same Hollywood-area house, including aspiring actors and actresses, and a movie director. Each housemate maintains a running diary with photographs, answers his/her own mail, and participates more or less in the site's construction. The site maintains its own relay chat node for live discussions with one or more housemates or fans.

EXCERPT:

So you want to discover for yourself if the Spot is everything people say it is....Some like to do it everyday. Others want to do it less frequently and indulge in long, luxurious Spot sessions....

Sprawl Home Page

http://sensemedia.net:80/sprawl

An incredibly complex, stunning visual display supports a virtual game site on the web with sounds, graphics, imaginary worlds and characters, and total interactivity. Based on the WOO (Webbed MOO) Transaction Protocol, the "game" (it's much more than that) enables users to create objects that interact with web objects (programs, audio clips, etc.) to create gadgets, places, and things for others to encounter in the Sprawl.

EXCERPT:

...The Sprawl is a virtual community where all users are given the ability to

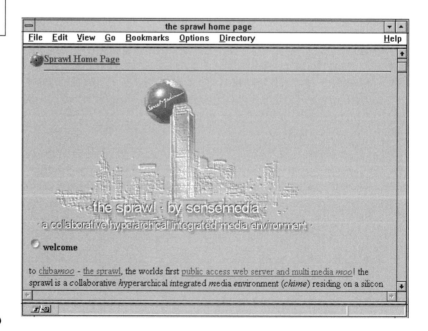

Has the Internet become a seedy neighborhood where perverts post lewd photographs on lampposts and phone poles, where children roam adult bookstores and XXX-rated video arcades? How seamy is the Net?

The proportion of raunchy material is small, but it exists. If you want to avoid sex on-line, that's fairly easy. But if you know where it is, you can get it.

Leslie Miller, in *USA Today*

extend the cyberspace in an unrestricted manner, creating a huge and sprawling virtual reality.

Spud's Unpredentious Proclamation

http://www.access.digex/net/~spud

Another in the never-ending line of eclectic home pages, this one features links to alternative cultures like animal rights home pages, the antiprison movement, and anarchy. Of course, you will find plenty of poetry and some semidecent digital art.

EXCERPT:

As the World Wide Web expands exponentially, we are unfortunately forced to submit ourselves to a mass of terrible design, duplicated information, confusing layouts and poorly-written copy—JUST LIKE THE REAL WORLD!

Spunk Press

http://www.cwi.nl/cwi/people/Jack.Jansen/spunk/Spunk_Home.html

This site is a researcher's dream if the topic is anarchist writing. The site maintains an extensive bibliography (the Spunk Press Catalog) with subject and numeric indexes and links to online publications by a variety of anarchist and political writers including, but not limited to, Mikhail Bakunin, Alexander Berkman, Hakim Bey, Bob Black, Noam Chomsky, Sam Dolgoff, Guy Debord, William Godwin, Emma Goldman, Abbie Hoffman, Peter Kropotkin, Malatesta, George Orwell, Alexander Tarasov, Henry David Thoreau, Oscar Wilde, and Zapatismo.

EXCERPT:

Welcome to the Spunk Press home page. Spunk Press collects and distributes literature in electronic format, with an emphasis on anarchism and related issues....

Squashed Bug Zoo

http://www.roundabout.org/~matthew/zoo/zoo.html

This rather weird home page presents photographs (a tad grainy) and brief descriptions of just what the title suggests: squashed bugs. There are only six such images currently, but two recent additions hint at a new direction for the page: small vertebrates. The comments of visitors to the page—from sick humor to shocked outrage—are presented in a linked page.

Squid Page

http://www.algorithm.com/squid/squid.html

The Squid Page presents a hodge-podge of materials, recipes, and links to anything remotely related to squids (including people with "squid nicknames"). Researchers will have to sort through a lot of irrelevant materials to find genuine information about squids, but browsers may enjoy the site's lack of coherence. Among the links: Squid Museums (one); Popular Cartoons with Squid Themes; People Who Have Squid Nicknames; Literary Squid (Moby Dick); and Squid and Music.

EXCERPT:

For some years, some biologists have argued that there was a 7th day of creation, during which God thought about his prototypes and finally made the crowning glory of his creation here on Earth: the giant squid....

Stanford Computer Graphics

http://www-graphics.standord.edu

This site is an excellent starting point for anyone seeking information on computer graphics. It offers links to graphics demonstrations, morphing demonstrations, movies, software, rendering competition winners, and a wealth of information about computer graphics techniques. Take a break and link to the Weekly Graphics Lunches and Cool Demos.

Star Trek: The Next Generation

http://cruciform.cid.com/~werdna/sttng

A fan's site more than a novice's introductory source, this site presents a huge amount of information, images, sound files, video clips, and commentary about *Star Trek: The Next Generation*. It lists Emmy awards, episodes in which almost anything searchable happened, trivia notes, and humor along with links to related web sites.

EXCERPT:

Barclay: "May I? Checkmate in nine moves."
Troi: "I didn't know you played chess."
Barclay: "I don't."
— "The Nth Degree", Stardate 44721.9

Star Trek: Voyager

http://voyager.paramount.com/VoyagerIntro.html

This multimedia entertainment site presents huge, complex color photographs of the Voyager spacecraft, crew backgrounds, and a multitude of facts and trivia about Paramount's newest *Star Trek* series and accesses schedules, GIF files, audio and video files, mission details, and technology notes in a tastefully designed series of graphics pages.

EXCERPT:

...Your knowledge of this information is vitally important to the success of our

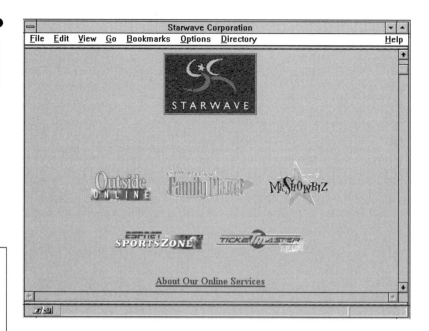

mission. When you feel confident in your knowledge, select the Evaluation button. The doctor will determine if you're ready to return to active duty.

Starship Design Home Page

http://sunsite.unc.edu/lunar/starship.html

This site provides an absorbing accumulation of data and facts related to starship science and engineering. Design projects, engineering advice on rocket and engine classes, paradoxes related to relativity and other physics problems, bibliographies, references, online contests, downloadable software, online membership forms, and a wealth of physics information.

EXCERPT:

Established in 2032, the Lunar Institute of Technology occupies a sprawling campus in the eastern half of Crater Copernicus....

Starwave Corporation

http://starwave.com/

An impressive conglomeration of current entertainment, sports, and educa-

The computer medium turns traditional big-brand advertising on its head. No longer is it enough to deliver a simple message that appeals to everyone—to say in sweeping terms to a mass audience, "Buy this car [or beer, or soap, or airline ticket] and get this life." On-line consumers talk back. They demand instant information. The moment they lose interest, one click of the computer mouse, and they are gone. There is no lingering until the show comes back on.

Janice Castro, *in Time*

tion titles with multimedia resources, this site is one of the richest and deepest on the web. It includes information services in areas like sports, adventure travel, families, and entertainment news, each of which offers full-motion video and animation, audio clips, images, photographs, and programming tools.

StatiC DesignS

http://192.96.7.160/~kon/index.html

This site discusses and displays animations and 3-D images that have been produced with Autodesk's 3D Studio, Photoshop, and/or Fractal Design Painter. You might try some of the cool-sounding links to places like Digital Asylum; Surf City; Picture Grabbag; Guestbook; and Music Disk.

EXCERPT:

...If you're bored with looking at those dull POV fractals or KPT Bryce dime-a-dozen landscapes then you're at the right place!

Stellar Crisis

http://www.lenox.com/games/sc

This interactive multiplayer space-battle game has the standard space-battle goal: conquer the known universe. There are actually several games available, ranging in play time from five minutes to long term, with updates twice a day to keep players informed about other players' moves.

EXCERPT:

...If you are new to Stellar Crisis, it's a complete multi-player space opera strategy game in which players compete to build huge galactic empires, and fight pitched battles in far away star systems....

Strange Interactions

http://amanda.physics.wisc.edu/show.html

The artist displays Strange Interactions as a series of scanned paintings, drawings, etchings, and woodcuts. Brief descriptions of each work are available, and GIF image files may be downloaded for personal use only.

EXCERPT:

...My work is representational but surreal, perhaps best described as an attempt to cast intense, personal dream-states into visual form.

Strawberry Pop-Tart Blow-Torches

http://cbi.tamucc.edu/~pmichaud/toast

Check this out: a tongue-in-cheek scientific study (complete with abstract, introduction, materials, experimental procedures, etc.) to verify Dave Barry's assertion that Kellogg's Strawberry Pop Tarts can emit flames "like a blow torch" if left in a toaster too long. Photographs of the experiment's steps (including the burning toaster) are included. His recommendations and follow-up comments are hilarious.

EXCERPT:

Strawberry Pop Tarts may be a cheap and inexpensive source of incendiary devices. Toasters which fail to eject Pop Tarts cause the Pop Tarts to emit flames 10-18 inches in height.

Street Cents Online

http://www.screen.com/streetcents.html

This is a web version of a popular Canadian consumer awareness program for children with transcripts from the television shows, links to further consumer information, and buying tips. Interesting links to technical details about the show's production, the show's history. Hair; Food; Part-Time Work; School; Whining; Body; Snow; Habits; Stox and Investing; and Green Careers.

EXCERPT:

Street Cents Online is about your money—how to get it and how not to get ripped off when you spend it....

Studio X

http://www.nets.com

This "experimental media company" deals with, among other things, the establishment of the "Santa Fe Archive," a web server for the Santa Fe area. The links take on the sound of the southwest: Dewey Trading Company (Native American blankets); Santa Fe Photographic Workshops; Santa Fe Marketspace; Dead Can Dance; Santa Fe Opera; Monastery of Christ in the Desert; Known World (whitewater rafting and wilderness adventures); Ski New Mexico; Virtual Los Alamos; and RoadRunner Tracks.

Stupid Homepage

http://metro.turnpike.net/S/spatula/

"Spatula" and his sock puppet Macauley present a collection of "stupid files" (mostly culled from other web sites and newsgroups) and strange songs. Their only unifying theme is their inherent vapidity.

EXCERPT:

Welcome to the New Stupid Homepage....I've added these HUMONGOUS new icons and merged several files and...and now we've got the new Bacon Sandwiches pages here! Life is good.

Sumeria

http://www.lablinks.com/sumeria/

Alternative and new age approaches to life are extensively discussed here, with links to similar web sites. Conspiracy theories abound, as do alternative health methodologies, herbal information, and fringe science discussions and resources. Though this is a jumble of information, researchers will find much to keep them occupied.

Sunrayce 95

http://www.nrel.gov/sunrayce/

This site chronicles the biennial intercollegiate solar car race, Sunrayce. The race took place June 20-29, 1995; check here for all the results, a description of the race, and photographs and information about the race and the 40 teams that competed in the event.

EXCERPT:

If you are interested in finding the results of Sunrayce 95, then you have come to the right place....

Suns'n'Roses

http://www.stars.com/roses

This site boasts a heap of images and quotations loosely related to cosmology and metaphysics from sources that include Taki Kogoma, Joge Luis Borges, Roger Penrose, Paul Davies, Benjamin Woolley, William Gibson, Fred Hoyle, Timothy Ferris, and Carl Sagan. While the quotes and images are provocative, researchers may have trouble sorting through the tangle of Mathematics; Computation; Simulation; Virtual Reality; Cyberspace; Cosmology; Metaphysics; and Fiction.

Somewhere out there on the Internet, there is a translation of "Hamlet" into Klingon. There is information on the upcoming International Paperweight Festival, an Osmond family site and a message from a man in Norway that begins, "Hello to all you hot girls...."

David Colker, *Los Angeles Times*, May 19, 1995.

EXCERPT:

Images of the Universe; mathematical and computational models; speculations on the nature of reality....WARNING: Reality under construction; just a little heavier on graphics than on the mind.

Superbowl XXIX Host Committee Page

http://www.imll.com:80/superbowl/

Now that the game has been played, this page has limited historical interest. Diehard fans might still want to check out Super Bowl Merchandise; San Diego Chargers Memorabilia; and Super Bowl Gourmet. The URL for Super Bowl XXX has been announced as http://www.superbowlxxx.com, but as of this printing was still being developed at http://www.superbowl.asu.edu.

EXCERPT:

Great Super Bowl Merchandise is Still Available....

SuperChurch

http://clarksville.mc.utexas.edu/~jess/superchurch.html

An idolatrous and satirical attack on religion, this site is the home of Reverend Jess and his followers. Follow the "heavenly" links to The SuperChurch FAQ; Intro to the SuperChurch; SuperChurch Hierarchy; Revelations; Benign All; Buzzwords; The Big Rules; and Make a Spiritual Donation to the SuperChurch.

E X C E R P T :

The sweet sounds of salvation are whispering right outside...."Give in," they say, "experience the Benign All."

Surreal Make-Over Gallery

http://marshall.edu/~jtoney/facepage.html

This web site solicits scanned portraits of people or pets in order to make them over with surreal graphical art. The webmaster then posts "before" and "after" graphics on his home page. As they say in advertising land, seeing is believing.

E X C E R P T :

This gallery is in perpetual flux. If you don't like today's picture, come back tomorrow for a brand new beautification!

Surrealist Compliment Generator

http://pharmdec.wustl.edu/cgi-bin/jardin_scripts/SCG

"Compliments" are the entire content of this site, and are generated randomly each time a visitor arrives or reloads the page. A Latin version of instructions appears when the user deigns to add his or her own comments. The source of the compliments is said to be "Jardin Mecanisme" and a Surrealism Server.

Michael Swartzbeck, Sinkers@his.com

http://www.clark.net/pub/sinkers/home.html

This site offers the digital art work of Michael Swartzbeck, a political satirist and cartoonist. Also provided are links to the Deadheads Web Page, the OTIS Project, and the Internet Love-Fest as well as links to Vaguely Shakespearean (digital paintings); Human-generated (year-by-year index of Swartzbeck's exhibits and art works); "The Sinkers" (cartoon comic strip); and Political Cartoon Pages.

Currently publishing "The Sinkers" Deadhead comics online on the Deadheads' Web Page...

System Zero

http://www.slip.net/syszero/syszero.html

System Zero is an independent organization of writers, artists, and other creative people devoted to the creation and public dispersal of unique art, literature, and texts. Membership is free and the submission policy is very indulgent.

System Zero is, among other things, a gathering place for the collaborative exploration of creative experiment—especially those of exotic or controversial nature....

Tabatha's Days at Work

http://www-white.media.mit.edu/~martin/snaps/

Tabatha, a free spirit, musician, and web consultant, is photographed at her workplace, and the photos are presented in a variety of formats (notable MPEG). Sadly, Tabatha has changed workplaces, with a consequent loss in the quality of some of the photography.

EXCERPT:

Welcome to the automagical Tabatha MPEG movie maker. She has a camera pointed at her which snaps a photo every five minutes....

Taglines Galore

http://www.brandonu.ca/~ennsnr/Tags/

Each tagline in this large collection of taglines (53,424) from unknown (or unidentified) sources points to a familiar celebrity, historical event or person, television show, or other quotable source. The file is divided (by letter) into 26 individual files that may be separately downloaded.

EXCERPT:

Well, here it is folks. Taglines, more taglines and even more taglines...There are currently 53,424 taglines in this collection.

...**M**ost Web-based consumer marketing efforts are doomed. They will be no more successful than those of a man who opens a hot dog stand in his alley. He figures that because the alley connects to Main Street, which connects to the state highway and finally to the interstate highway, he is putting his business in a position to successfully sell to every one of the 200 million-plus individuals who motor around the U.S.

Jeffrey C. Frost, *Computer World*, August 7, 1995.

Talker

http://www.infi.net/talker

Talker presents an Internet relay chat site tailored to fit the World Wide Web. After selecting a name and graphical image (animal, cartoon character, or texture), visitors join in an interactive conversation with others. The site is extremely popular, and therefore encounters frequent connection timeouts and server errors during heavy Internet traffic.

EXCERPT:

Talker allows users to select an animal, cartoon character, or "bizarre texture" to appear alongside their messages....

Tank Girl

http://www.dcs.qmk.ac.uk/~bob/stuff/tg/index.html

Her head is shaved, except for some long, hacked-up orange stuff on her forehead. She proudly wears combat boots, carries a baseball bat with a nail stuck through it, and is the antithesis of all those sweet, smiling, submissive gals in the *Archie* comics. This site is a punker's guide to *Tank Girl* comics and where to find *Tank Girl* philosophy, merchandise, and the new *Tank Girl* movie.

EXCERPT:

...It's hard to explain what Tank Girl is if you don't know already....She's a punkster girl that takes no shit."

Tarot

http://cad.ucls.edu/repository/useful/tarotceltic/tarotceltic.html

This virtual Tarot reading site interprets the cards that are graphically presented on the screen. You can request simple three-card readings and a Keltic Cross reading. For more, try the links to Tarot FAQ sites and Katz's I-Ching and Biorhythm sites.

EXCERPT:

Do you fear your future... Take control of your life today... How will your money/love/power change...

Taz-Mania

http://www.realtime.net/~lthumper/taz-mania/index.html

For researchers of the Taz-Mania television show, this site has a sizable collection of resources including opening song lyrics, merchandise links, images, episode details, links to sites discussing Tazmanian Devils, images, and animation links.

EXCERPT:

Taz-Mania is a Warner Brothers Animation TV show. The main character is Taz, apparently the same Tazmanian Devil that appeared in the old Bugs Bunny cartoons...

TeleCircus San Francisco

http:www.we.com/www/tcircus

An off-beat guide to Bay Area entertainment, art, and digital art, what they call the artso-digital world. The magic of the circus links to Flathead; Cobra Lounge; Burning Man; Cyberlab 7; Joe's Digital Diner; and Anon Salon.

EXCERPT:

...We will attempt to build a choice selection of some of the more interesting eruptions taking place inside the artso-digital world of San Francisco.

Tele-Garden

http://www.usc.edu/dept/garden/

The Tele-Garden is located at the University of Southern California and is open for public viewing. Members (anyone with a valid e-mail address can register) may also plant, water, and monitor the growth of the seedlings in the garden. An industrial robot does the actual planting and watering, while cameras supply color photograph feedback to site visitors. The viewing is best with a Netscape browser.

Karen TenEyck's Scenic Design Studio

http://www.inch.com/user/kteneyck/

Karen TenEyck's site draws the user into the world of a theater designer. You

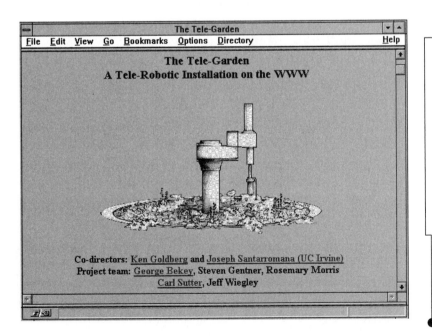

299

P ity the couch potato. Even in the world of 500-channel television, he will probably have only a few dozen sports programmes to pick from at any one time. The computer-minded sports fan, on the other hand, has an entire electronic universe to delve into.

The Economist, April 22, 1995.

can view play and opera sets, works in progress, and even read about what exactly a designer does. The graphics are truly awesome in this behind-the-scenes look at New York theater. Ms. TenEyck has provided separate links for Netscape and Mosaic users—the Netscape-enhanced pages have image maps, while the Mosaic pages paint .gif images and separate links.

Tennis Country

http://www.tenniscountry.com

Everything you ever wanted to know about hard courts, clay courts, and grass courts. Find out where you can play tennis while you are traveling in Bali or Cap D'Agde and take a free tennis lesson. Tennis information galore, from biographies and news about pros to polls about tennis issues and tips as well as an online pro shop.

EXCERPT:

...Follow all the latest tennis news, scores, tournament info...even purchase your favorite tennis racket or tennis outfit...

Terra IncogNeta

http:www.vpm.com/tti

Another road map for the web. Lists and descriptions of sites on many topics with live links to The Stick; Dynamite Site of the Nite; Poems for People Who Hate Poetry; Pure Stupidity; and Celebrity Endorsements.

EXCERPT:

A pantload of fun and links a'plenty!

Tezuka's "Jungle King" and Disney's "Lion King"

http://bronze.ucs.indiana.edu/~tanaka/Tezuka_Disney/Tezua_Disney

There is some debate as to whether the Disney movie, *The Lion King*, is based on a Tanaka Tezuka's Japanese production, *Jungle King*. This site is the archive of various newsgroups discussing this possibility. There are also images of the two lions.

The Thai Heritage Page

http://emailhost.ait.ac.th/Thailand/wutt.html

A tour guide to Thailand culture. You can meet His Majesty and Her Royal Highness, travel on the royal barges of Siam, visit the temple of the Emerald Buddha, and learn the history and prehistory of the country.

EXCERPT:

This page contributes historical and cultural of Thailand or Siam to the world....

Thee Computer Animation Index

http://skynet.oir.ucf.edu/~suzan/companim/companm2.shtml

Catering mostly to computer animation buffs, Thee Computer Animation Index provides a comprehensive collection of links to the myriad Internet resources on computer animation. Apart from the links themselves, there's nothing particularly original at this web site, but it's a good watering hole for graphic artists.

EXCERPT:

As well as providing a list of relevant Web and ftp sites related to computer animation and imaging, I intend to put up information on schooling, practical how-to-advice for animators and related technical issues, other information sources, etc...

Theodore Tugboat

http://www.cochran.com/tt.html

A great site for kids. Theodore Tugboat is a cheerful tugboat who likes to be friends with everyone and a popular icon from Canadian television. This site also offers links to more than 100 other web sites for kids and resources for teachers, parents, and children's television professionals.

Thomas: Legislative Information on the Internet

http://thomas.loc.gov/

A must for online politicos. Full text of Congressional legislation and the Congressional Record, a C-Span program listings guide, e-mail directory to Congress, and much more.

EXCERPT:

Thomas is named for Thomas Jefferson and is sponsored by the Library of Congress. It's official!

Tic-Tac-Toe

http://www.bu.edu/Games/tictactoe

In case you get bored with all the really cool stuff on the web, here's an age-old way to pass the time of day. Play Tic-Tac-Toe against a Boston University Computer. The game was created by the staff of the Scientific Computing and Visualization Group at Boston University.

Lamar Alexander, the former Governor of Tennessee, broke the news that he was running for President on an on-line talk show. Greg Louganis recently discussed AIDS and his diving career with a computer audience. And Joan Rivers, serving as dishy host of an Oscar post-mortem, quipped, "I thought Diane Keaton looked good in the hat that covered her bald spot."...A list of recent guests includes big names like Garth Brooks, Alan Dershowitz and Jimmy Page of Led Zeppelin, who, when asked for an autograph, typed "Best Wishes, Jimmy Page."

Trip Gabriel, *The New York Times*

Ticketmaster Online

http://www.ticketmaster.com/

Ticketmaster Online is good because it's functional. If you want to purchase tickets to a concert, sift through the schedules of events at the venues near you, or just visit Clubland, then TM Online is a worthwhile stop on the WWW. But TM's not about to make it easy on you. In fact, you might have to hit six or more links to find the lists you want. Sure, there's a lot of information here, but TM could have set up a better information management system on the homepage directory. TM's main links include: Events, Connections, Back Stage, Spotlight, About TM, the TM Store, and Clubland.

The Time Machine

http://webmart.interaccess.com/timelaps/

Computer images that change right before your eyes. The web in motion. Some interesting stuff and great special effects from a computer graphics firm with lots of national work under its belt.

303

EXCERPT:

Take a ride on the Time-Machine! An adventure in special-effects. Experience our world on fast forward.

Time Out

http://www.timeout.co.uk/

Travel guides to favorite tourist cities like Amsterdam, Berlin, London, Madrid, Paris, and Prague in Europe, with New York City thrown in just for fun. Lots of details—we really mean details—with maps, interactive postcards, events listings, and city guides.

Tiny Vine Organization

http://www.interport.net/~marinaz

A colorful, but rather incoherent amalgamation of images from an artist who specializes in art for music videos, albums, and documentaries.

Tips For Web Spinners

http://gagme.wwa.com/~boba/tips.html

Learn the fine point of nettiquette and how to create your own online newspaper, find templates for home pages and tons of tips from a page builder and Internet celebrity who wants to share his insights. There are many links in this book-length, technical document.

EXCERPT:

That's right fellow weavers, it's time to repent of our ignorant ways. My first rule is: do what you want to do....

Today's Computer Cartoon

http://zeb.nysaes.cornell.edu/ctoons.cgi/l-english

The Today's Computer Cartoon home page is brought to you by a computer programmer who moonlights as gag writer. Web-surfers can view a new comic every day. While these are mildly entertaining gag cartoons, they're not of the same caliber as, say, a Scott Adams *Dilbert* comic strip.

EXCERPT:

After years as an invisible unnamed gag writer (for many top strips) it's nice to see my name on something. Who knows, maybe some day somebody will offer me a book deal, or a CD-Rom deal or a calendar deal??? (I'm a Mets fan so I'm a born optimist.)

Tom's World Home Page

http://turnpike.net/metro/L/LastStop/index.html

The diverse home page of a 35-year-old married hairdresser from Indianapolis. Check in on Tom's Electric Salon and catch up on the ongoing saga or link to The Sanctuary or the Tour Bus. Tom also has games and links to other home pages.

Tool User Comics

http:www.armory.com/comics/

The 1990s version of reading the funnies. Many comics and online artists, but there's a small charge for some subscriptions. While you're there find out what's hot, what's new and check the weekly special and comics index.

EXCERPT:

It's Easy! Find a comic, read it, and if you like it, order a subscription!...

Top Ten What?

http://www.southwind.net:80/~rjones/top10.html

America's fascination with the top-ten anything continues. Here, you can view other folk's version of the top-ten cheap domestic wines, the top-ten men's fragrances, the top-ten performances by actors with very small parts, etc., etc. This is an OK place to waste time, which is really all you do here. It's all words, no graphics.

EXCERPT:

Everyone has an opinion, huh? This is a list of the top ten of whatever comes along....

Toronto International Film Festival

http://www.bell.ca/toronto/filmfest/

The Toronto International Film Festival Site is a directory to the 20th anniversary of the Festival, Sept. 7-16, 1995. It is alive with color and sights and sounds! There are guides to events, information for the traveler, including restaurants and accommodations and access to the Film Reference Library. The images are colorful, a delight to the eye...but load s-l-o-w-l- y.

EXCERPT:

Experience sight, sound and motion with cine-bytes, film schedules, reviews and ticket info. Browse the poster gallery, and sneak backstage for paparazzi stardust....

Total New York

http://totalny.com/

Arts, politics, fashion, food and other fun in this 'zine about New York City, written by top-notch freelancers. Follow links to Daily Dose; Calendar; Substance; Voices; Source; and Texture and you won't miss a thing about what's doing in the big city.

The Toups Zone

http://www.tyrell.net/~robtoups/index.html

If you haven't heard about this page already, this is one of the most talked about home pages on the web, mostly because Mr. Toups has assembled a Babes on the Web section featuring many attractive, intelligent women and their home pages. Beyond that, Toups comes up will all kinds of things to keep you interested, from a page full of his Passport stamps from Asia to Capitalism Zone, a page about Internet commerce.

EXCERPT:

...If you came here expecting the highest in culture, sophistication and grace, its just time to hit that BACK button...If you are expecting this site to be COOL, you are in luck....

Tracespace

http://www.tracespace.com/

Lots of cool computer graphics—raytraced imagery, actually—but be warned, they take a long time to load.

Welcome to Tracespace, a gallery of raytraced imagery. A personal collection of images created with the superb freeware raytracer POVRAY.

Trahison des Clercs (Betray Your Intellect)

http://metro.turnpike.net/L/Lorenzo/Index.html

Some pretty snarky and snappy writing on books, politics, sex, and weird topics like the worst way to die and "what to do with that trashy lingerie your man bought you for Valentines Day." A nifty 'zine by anonymous publishers. Go for it: sUds ...SeX ...sINs ...SEcrEts ...Capital Comic ...Interactive Haiku

As professional writers—tired of churning out boring corporate crap—and perfectionists—tired of getting everything right—we decided to put out our own totally imperfect crap....

Transeform

http://hyperreal.com/transeform/

Click around this page long enough and you might figure out that it's about rave parties and their associated music, but mediocre graphics and music charts that haven't been updated for eight months make this site a loser. Dedicated ravers may find some worthwhile biographical material on popular rave disc jockeys in Europe.

This summer, I spent two months travelling in Europe and raving like a maniac. I ended up spending a lot of time in Norway with my friend, DJ applepie, and I got to spin at 3 raves.

Travels With Samantha

http://www-swiss.ai.mit.edu/samantha/travels-with-samantha.html

Following a theme stolen from John Steinbeck's *Travels With Charlie*, this online memoir recounts the travels of an MIT grad student who embarks on a summer trip across North America to help him get over the death of his dog. He's a good writer and a decent photographer, and you meet bored youths in the Midwest, North Dakota Harley riders, and struggling single mothers in the Yukon. But after you read a little, it seems like watching someone's vacation slides.

Tribal Voice

http://www.tribal.com/

Visitors to this Native American web page will find guides to Native American events, as well as discussions of Indian issues and spirituality.

EXCERPT:

A part of the intent of Tribal Voice is to be an uncensored, blunt and direct outlet for the Native American heart.

Tripod

http:www.tripod.com/

All those lectures Dad always gave about money and responsibility can be found here, along with a travel guide to help you get away from it all. Inexplicably, the site administrators demand that you apply for membership. The sign-up process is extremely annoying, especially given that so many more interesting web sites are available without such a country club protocol.

EXCERPT:

Tripod provides Tools for Life....It's about getting people to think about investing wisely in their own futures and the future of their communities.

In a *TIME*/CNN poll of 800 Americans conducted in January by Yankelovich Partners, 57% didn't know what cyberspace meant, yet 85% were certain that information technology had made their life better. They may not know where it is, but they want desperately to get there.

Philip Elmer-DeWitt, in *Time*

The Troll Hole

http://www.mmedia.com/clients/trollhole/

An online version of Dungeons & Dragons? Nice graphics from an engineer with a lot of science fiction imagination. But if you are into online games, this doesn't seem to have much action.

EXCERPT:

I have played several versions of Role-Playing games since my high school days some 10+ years ago. I have tried to produce a virtual world I call "The Troll Hole."

Turtle Trax—A Marine Turtle Page

http://www.io.org/~bunrab/

Created by a pair of sport scuba divers from Ontario, this page is devoted to Hawaiian sea turtles and their plight. Enjoy the really nice photos and some easy-to-read environmental writing. The work of these two divers shows both the beauty and troubled plight of the turtles.

EXCERPT:

Turtle Trax was conceived with these purposes in mind: To provide a web site that gave people a chance to become familiar with the wonder and beauty of the marine turtle....

TV Net

http://tvnet.com/TVnet.html

If they can tear themselves away from the tube long enough, TV freaks will find lots of good information here: e-mail addresses and links to every network and local station home page, polls on recent TV shows and issues, previews of new shows—AND NO COMMERCIAL BREAKS.

EXCERPT:

TV Net is designed for retrieving information, and for providing web homes for television and cable stations throughout the U.S. and the World.

Twilight Zone

http://www.mcs.net/~xanax/

Find out what's happening in this twilight zone. The amalgamation of sounds and graphics at this site are available via anonymous FTP, but only to computers that contain the Gravis Ultrasound card.

EXCERPT:

Twilight Zone...is a group of coders, musicians and artists who try to push the limits of the IBMPC...

U

The Ugly Contest

http://www.gatech.edu/steve/ugly

What a waste of web space! A bunch of guys with names like Daffy, Butter-fly, and Eggo decided to launch a net-wide contest to determine which of the eight of them is the ugliest. They posted their pictures (all are quite ugly) but never post the results of the poll. Dumb...dumb.

EXCERPT:

It all started a long time ago when one guy asked for an account on another guy's machine. The machine owner granted the account, but named the person "Ugly."

The Ultimate Band List

http://american.recordings.com/wwwofmusic/ubl.html

A great resource that will only get better as more musicians find out about the web. This is the ultimate giant list of musicians and bands of all genres, from classical to jazz to rock to rap. Information on each band/individual includes mailing lists, fan clubs, and places on the net to find their lyrics and music.

EXCERPT:

Welcome to the web's largest interactive list of music links where you the visitor can add the latest music links for your favorite bands....

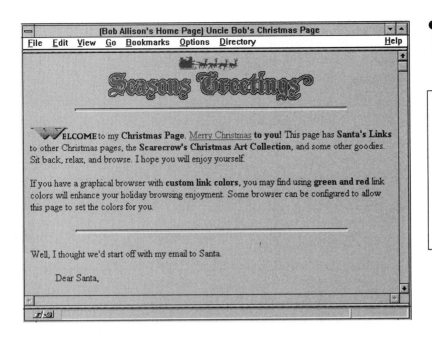

Uncle Bob's Christmas Page

http://gagme.wwa.com/~boba/christmas.html

Online holiday cheer from a master web builder. Bob Allison brings us Christmas carols rewritten in government-speak, links to dozens of other holiday web sites (including Scarecrow's Christmas Art Collection), poetry, short stories, and, of course, Christmas decorations.

E X C E R P T :

Welcome to my Christmas Page. Merry Christmas to you! This page has Santa's Links to other Christmas pages...

Uncle Bob's Kids Page

http://gagme.wwa.com/~boba/kids.html

A masterpiece from one of the most prolific page designers with links to Legos, SeaWorld, the Muppets, Mountain Bikes and many, many more chil-

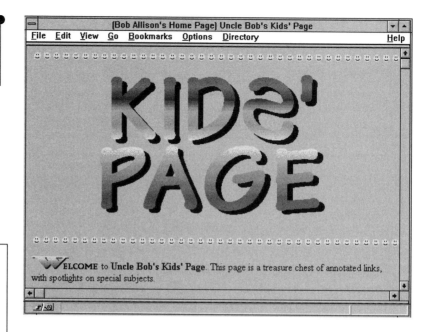

dren's sites. There is enough stuff here to keep kids busy for hours. But, as Uncle Bob warns, kids should be supervised when using the Net because a few missteps with the mouse can lead a child just about anywhere, including pages intended for adults only.

EXCERPT:

This page is a treasure chest of annotated links, with spotlights on special subjects.

Under Puget Sound:
Underwater Photography by Scott Freeman

http:.//weber.u.washington.edu:80/~scotfree/

These colorful underwater photos were taken on location in Puget Sound and beautifully depict the icy waters of the great Pacific Northwest. However, the page would be more engrossing if the photographer described the photos and explained how he acquired them.

The top 10 anagrams for "Information Superhighway" are:

10. Enormous, hairy pig with fan.

9. Hey, ignoramus—win profit? Ha!

8. Oh-oh, wiring snafu: empty air.

7. When forming, utopia's hairy.

6. A rough whimper of insanity.

5. Oh, wormy infuriating phase.

4. Inspire humanity, who go far.

3. Waiting for any promise, huh?

2. Hi-ho! Yow! I'm surfing Arpanet!

And the No. 1 anagram for "Information Superhighway" is: New utopia? Horrifying sham.

Peter Lewis, *The New York Times*, 1995

Universal Access Inc. Blackjack Server

http://www.ua.com/blackjack/bj.html

Step up to the gaming tables and try your luck at Blackjack! Start with $1000 of virtual money, and see how you do. The entertaining game proceeds quickly and even keeps track of the top players.

EXCERPT:

Note: This is a game for amusement only. There is no money involved....Any wins or losses in this game are simply for fun, and no real money is changing hands.

Universal cHANnEL

http://www.mca.com/tv/

Universal cHANnEL has great graphics, some fun stuff like the "Zappers Lounge" online game show, and some informative stuff like behind-the-scenes details of how television shows are produced. In large part though, this is an advertisement for the Fox Network.

EXCERPT:

Universal cHANnEL is the official 'net home for some of the most popular television shows in the world....

University of Art and Design Helsinki

http://www.uiah.fi/

At first glance, this web site appears to be nothing more than an online version of a typical campus catalog. It features a comprehensive list of programs and faculty available at the University of Art and Design in Helsinki. But beyond the promotional material, a web surfer will find a useful Internet guide with an exhaustive list of Internet servers around the globe and the university's Art2 online magazine.

The University of California Museum of Paleontology

http://ucmp1.berkeley.edu/exhibittext/entrance.html

The UC Museum of Paleontology provides a good, no-nonsense web site for students of geology and evolution. By reading the clear, lucid prose files, you can learn how scientists study such topics as the age of the Earth and the origin of species. Overall, the home page design is clever and clean. However, there are a lot of missing links here—and not just on the evolutionary scale. A major overhaul would make this site even better.

EXCERPT:

The theory of evolution, formalized by Charles Darwin, is as much theory as is the theory of gravity, or the theory of relativity...Evolution is the binding force of all biological research. It is the unifying theme.

University of Tennessee Canoe & Hiking Club

http://feeder.oac.utk.edu/utchx.html

Need a well-designed guide to canoeing and hiking in the eastern Tennessee region? It's right here with links to chat groups, satellite photos, up-to-date weather information (including river levels), and clubby stuff like war stories from canoeing adventures. An extremely useful web page for canoeists in Tennessee.

The Unofficial Cyberpunk Home Page

http://rohan.sdsu.edu/home/vanzoest/www/cyberpunk/

Cyberpunk is a literary genre that combines gritty urban adventure with high technology. The films *Johnny Mnemonic* and *Blade Runner* are examples of cyberpunk. If you're looking for imagination with an edge, you've found the right place. The home page is a bit of a mess, so try downloading the text-only version of the site for best results. From there, you'll find links to cyberpunk resources throughout the Internet.

EXCERPT:

...In any cultural system, there are always those who live on its margins, on "the Edge," criminals, outcasts, visionaries, or those who simply want freedom for its own sake. Cyberpunk literature focuses on these people, and often on how they turn the system's technological tools to their own ends. This is the "punk" aspect of cyberpunk.

Unofficial Elvis Home Page

The http://sunsite.unc.edu/elvis/elvishom.html

Even on the web you're not safe from Elvis sightings. Although this is an unofficial page, there is plenty of information, official and otherwise on The

> **A**lmost a dozen states have put their official travel guides on the Internet, giving business travelers and vacationers immediate access to information about hotels, destinations and even the weather.
>
> Edwin McDowell, *The New York Times*

King. You can link over to the Graceland Tour, read Elvis' Last Will and Testament, find an Elvis Pen-Pal, or shop from the Elvis Souvenir Collection. Don't forget to sign the Guest Book and take a look at the Space Elvis Chronicles.

EXCERPT:

Is Elvis about to come out of hiding this summer in Ontario? Get the scoop from the Elvis Pages' own Deep Throat.

The Unofficial Moira Kelly Home Page

http://www.sirius.com/~eaquino/Moira.html

A decent tribute to this rising actress with a nice photo gallery from Kelly's movies, including *Chaplin* and *With Honors*. But the biographical section is too brief and the fan page has only two recent entries. (Maybe she isn't rising so fast after all, if this page is any indication.)

Urban Desires

http://desires.com/

This 'zine is packed with things to make your life in the big city more manageable and more hip. Articles in a recent issue included "Confessions of a Flea Market Junkee" (an essay on New York's version of hunting), a devilish little how-to article on barbecuing in the city without ticking off your neighbors, and features on topics ranging from fly fishing in the West to

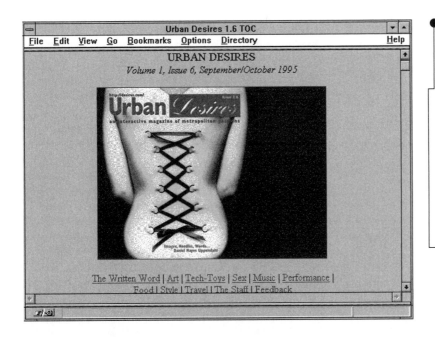

photographers. All of it comes with strong graphics. A really good 'zine for New Yorkers.

The URL-minder

http://www.netmind.com/URL-minder/URL-minder.html

Make this site your own personal WWW librarian. It's always ready to tell you about changes in your favorite reading material. First you register your favorite site(s) with a company called NetMind (via e-mail). NetMind monitors your site and e-mails you when anything in it changes. Could be a time saver.

EXCERPT:

Your Own Personal Web Robot!

URouLette

http://kuhttp.cc.ukans.edu/cwis/organizations/kucia/uroulette/uroulette.html

So, you're sick of the same old sites in your bookmarks, and you're too lazy

319

to trek all over the Net looking for new stuff. Here's the answer. The University of Kansas roulette wheel spins you off to a new site every few seconds. We're talking about millions of random possibilities here. It's pretty cool.

EXCERPT:

URouLette is one of the newest ways to travel the World Wide Web. Most times it'll work, sometimes it won't....We hope you enjoy your ride.

The Used Software Exchange

http://www.hyperion.com/usx

Easy-to-use, online classified ads that bring together buyers and sellers of used software. A couple of warnings: the service frowns on sales of pirated software and the participants must work out their own payment systems and resolve their own disputes. The service provides exchange rates for many currencies so that it can be used by people all over the world.

EXCERPT:

... A marketplace for buying and selling used software of all kinds.

Useless WWW Pages

http://www.primus.com/staff/paulp/useless.html

Get ready to seek revenge on the seems-like-a-million narcissistic page builders who think other surfers actually care what they nicknamed their car and how they spent their summer vacation. But this whole concept begs the question: With so many good sites out there, why hang out here and dwell on the bad?

EXCERPT:

We at the Useless WWW Pages make fun of other pages with sarcasm and cynicism....If you see a page and think "Good God, WHO CARES?" you have found a likely submission.

The UTNE Lens

http://www.utne.com/

"The Best From the Alternative Press" goes online with a well-designed, graphically pleasing electronic version of its popular *UTNE Reader*. Recent articles include a critique of O.J. Simpson media coverage from black journalists, an examination of declining membership in Christian churches, and a look at same-sex marriages.

Vampyres Only

http://www.vampyre.wis.net/vampyre/index.html

This is vampire central where you one can learn virtually anything about vampires, from their powers and limitations to their biology and pregnancy. You can also take tests to determine if you, indeed, are a vampire or are vulnerable to vamp attack. Or, you can just enjoy the gallery of vampire photos. Who has time to put this stuff together, anyway?

EXCERPT:

You have joined the other Creatures Of The Night on the Vorld Vide Veb. Welcome!

The Virtual Baguette

http://www.mmania.com/

A hangout for Francophiles, this site offers off-beat photos, essays, and poetry about France. You can link to Listen; See; Touch; Taste; Speak; and the French Connection, but you could probably fly to Paris in the time it takes to load these pages. Sad to say the content isn't very well organized and isn't really worth the wait.

EXCERPT:

It was a beautiful Sunday afternoon in May and I did not know what to do, so I just followed the French proverb "In May, do whatever you want."

Here's the great thing about postcards: They're cheap, they're quick, you write 'em, you send 'em, and you forget about 'em. Your friend is psyched, and it only cost you five minutes and 50 cents.

Here's the bad thing about postcards: They're great souvenirs of your trip, and you'll never see 'em again. Don't kid yourself. Mom puts it on the fridge for a few days, and then it's gone. At best, in the attic. At worst, in the trash.

The small gesture of words hastily scribbled may be the only meaningful record of an incredible experience. If only there were a way to keep those gems for yourself and still share them with the world. That's why we think that when you come up with a good one, you should put it where you can see it. And everyone else can see it as well.

That's what Tripod Travel Postcards is all about. Members will have the opportunity to post their travel photos, with postcard-length messages, for all the world to see.

Tripod Travel Services: www.tripod.com/travel/travel.html

Virtual Irish Pub

http://www.misty.com/ulysses/vip/index.html

Have a pint and enjoy a chat on topics ranging from Irish sports to job searches to lost loves. Complete with handsome bartender, this site launches you, beer-in-hand, into a wide range of discussion groups, including a live chat line. Feeling introverted? You can also go on a lone journey to pages on Irish travel, literature, and music.

EXCERPT:

This is the internet's only authentic Irish Pub. Come in, sit down, and have a pint....

The Virtual Mirror

http://wwa.com/mirror

An eclectic online magazine with specialties in gardening, books, and software reviews. Interestingly, this Washington, D.C.-based publication seems to shy away from politics. There is no regular production schedule, but the site is updated often.

EXCERPT:

We at the Virtual Mirror hope to break new ground in electronic communications. We aren't just trying to create a magazine that's available online, but rather a new medium entirely.

The Virtual Multimedia Interactive Mystery Theater

http://www.cris.com/~bumm/intro.html

The Virtual Multimedia Interactive Mystery Theater, sponsored by a Florida stereo store chain, is supposed to let you tag along as a fictional detective solves a terrible crime. But the site is riddled with design problems. Some clues are embedded in pictures that take far too long to download. Worse yet, on a recent visit, the site was riddled with missing links that made solving the mystery impossible.

EXCERPT:

I'm Detective Hotlead with the Boonietown, Maryland, police force. Some consider me the best detective on the entire force. I can't say I disagree. However, it often gets lonely when you're the only cop on the force, so I study my enforcement manuals (spelling: cheesy spy novels).

Virtual Nashville

http://virtualnashville.com/

Click around the city of Nashville with your mouse in search of a wide variety of items—sort of a Nashville scavenger hunt. The goal? Find enough items to win a recording contract—what else do people in

DID YOU KNOW?

...That Denise Crosby originally tried out for the role of Counselor Troi and Marina Sirtis tried out for the role of Security Chief Tasha Yar?

...That Gene Roddenberry's full name is Eugene Wesley Roddenberry, thus, in creating Wesley Crusher, Gene used his own middle name and based the character on what he wanted to be like when he was young?

...[Stephen] Hawking was on the Paramount lot for the video release of the film *A Brief History of Time*. He was given a tour of the set, and when they reached the bridge set, he began tapping out something he wanted to say through his voice synthesizer. After about a minute, it said "Could you take me out of my chair and put me in the captain's chair?" Now, Hawking "never" asks to be taken out of his chair, so this was clearly a very big deal.

Star Trek: The Next Generation:
http://cruciform.cid.com/~werdna/sttng

Nashville seek? The graphics are fine, but as games go, this is nothing special.

EXCERPT:
Virtual Nashville is an on-line game that takes place in Nashville, TN. The game pushes web browsers to the limits of their abilities.

The Virtual Pub

http://lager.geo.brown.edu:8080/virtual-pub/index.html

More beer than you can drink along with discussions among brewers, results from beer festivals and, most importantly, guides to beer drinking in

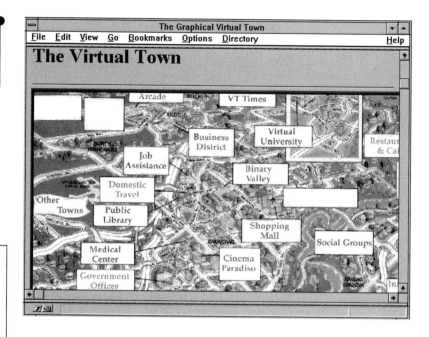

cities and countries around the world. Lot's of good stuff here for barley and hops fans.

EXCERPT:

This is a WWW server which is intended to be a place for network beer aficionados to gather information, about themselves and about other things related to the enjoyment of drinking beer (in moderation, of course).

The Virtual Town

http://www.cs.ucdavis.edu/virt-town/welcome.html

What a great concept! These master surfers from the University of California at Davis view the entire web as a town full of many neighborhoods and districts that flow together. Go to Government Buildings for links to the Library of Congress, the House of Representatives, and other federal entities. Swing into the Arcade for games aplenty. And turn into the Business District for the latest stock and other financial information. Well done!

EXCERPT:

Hello! Welcome to the Virtual Town. I am the mayor, Vik Varma. I have tried to assemble various links on the web into a form that resembles what you and I would find in a typical town. There are stores, public offices, and much more!

Virtual Vacation

http://www.neosoft.com/sbanks/vacation/vacation.html

This guy was so obsessed with the web that he downloaded images from Disney World, late at night, in the middle of his vacation. It's just like watching somebody else's vacation slide show in almost real time. The author acknowledges that he doesn't know why anyone would care about his family vacation—it's just an experiment, he says. Don't bother.

EXCERPT:

...Why in the world would you want to watch me having fun at Disney World while you slave away at work or school or whatever? Beats me....

Virtual Vegas Online

http://www.virtualvegas.com/

The prototype of the future—as soon as lawyers figure out a way to make online gambling legal—this site includes chat lounges, a beauty contest with online contestants, and a variety of interactive casino games. Warning: You'll find better odds in a real casino, and the games, especially blackjack, take a while to load. Currently, the casino is just for fun (no real wagering) but it looks ready to go whenever lawyers give the word.

EXCERPT:

There has been a lot of noise going around about gambling on the Web. Well sure, it's going to happen, but at Virtual Vegas we're not interested in being quasi-legal or quasi-secure, we're interested in having a good time....

VirtualFlylab

http://vflylab.ca.statela.edu/edesktop/VirtApps/VflyLab/IntroVflyLab.html

Who knows what kind of viruses you're putting in your computer by play-

> According to the Annual Report on Trends in Brand Names, applications in 1994 for the word "Internet" leaped 172%, to 87. "Multi-media" climbed 123% to 96. "Virtual" jumped 92% to 226, "cyber" was up 83% to 199 and "Interactive" increased 66% to 199.
>
> **Jennifer DeCoursey, *Advertising Age*, June 26, 1995.**

ing this little game? (Just kidding.) Some folks at California State have developed this site to help you learn about genetics, and it's really more fun than it sounds. Your job is to mate different types of ugly little fruit flies. It's kinda fun, but don't try to mate the purple-eyed, yellow-bodied male with the purple-eyed, black-bodied female; it doesn't work.

EXCERPT:

...Imagine yourself as scientist trying to discover the rules of genetic inheritance. Your research model is a species of common insect called a fruit fly (Drosophila melanogaster)....

Virtually Reality

http://www.onramp.net/~scroger/vreality.html

Virtually Reality brings hip technology to the comic strip. You'll find a large group of moderately funny comics and nice graphics that load quite quickly. Some of the comics are in 3-D if you have the right software.

EXCERPT:

Welcome to Virtually Reality, a 3-D rendered cyberspace comic created by yours truly, Eric Scroger. I've taken the single panel comic and given it a new twist using 3-D modeled and rendered imaging....

Virus

http://198.147.111.

A magazine of lampoon—"God Sues Michael Jackson for Sexual Molestation"—sexual content—"The Slut in Purple"— and a variety of other poetry, stories, and, in the producers' words, "chicken scratches." All in all, it's not very interesting stuff. But it is democratic journalism. The publishers are constantly asking you, the slightly warped web audience, for contributions.

EXCERPT:

Help us corrupt Middle America. Send us your contributions now. We're looking for...features, short stories, poems, interviews, drawings, paintings, chicken scratches, butt scans, photos, videos, recordings.

The Void

http://www.phantom.com:80/~voidmstr/

If you like a senseless riddle, this might be your place. Otherwise, steer clear of this stupid web page. Some anonymous person who goes by the name "Void Meister" thought it would be interesting to take surfers through two pages of useless graphics only to arrive at a third page of graphics where you must click on icons like chairs and blue balls to get to any information. What a waste of time.

VRML from HELL

http://www.well.com/user/caferace/vrml.html

A page all about Virtual Reality Modeling Language, the tool programmers and page builders are experimenting with to bring 3-D to the web. If you are a web pedestrian who just likes to stroll around with your mouse, this page won't be very interesting to you. If you are a web spinner, you might want to check it out. The site includes information on software, current VRML sites and details of how to build them.

VRTower

http://www.biddeford.com:80/~questor/VRTower.html

Another in the increasing list of online villages, this Cybertown takes on the

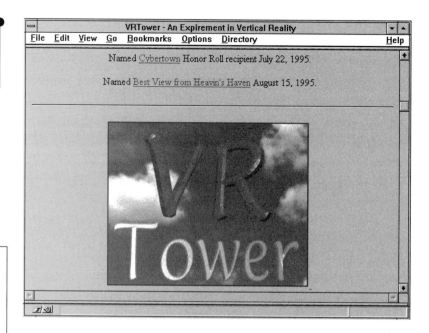

form of a big-city apartment tower. Check out the second floor, where you can find businesses including travel, employment, and adoption agencies. Further up you'll find everything from the police to toy stores, churches and e-zines, pubs, coffee shops, and penthouses where you can park your home page for a month or so.

EXCERPT:

VRTower is an experiment in Vertical Reality. It is a CyberTower with all the luxuries of AnyCity, USA. It contains a Mall, Post Office, Gift Shop, Newspaper, Arcade and much more....

Wall O' Shame

http://www.milk.com/wall-o-shame

An amazing collection of wacky and bizarre tales from news reports, lawsuits, and other electronic information sources hang on the wall o'shame. Check out all kinds of stuff illustrating just how weird things can be.

EXCERPT:

This is my attempt to characterize the erosion of our world by displaying true stories and tidbits that are just too nonlinear.

The Andy Warhol Museum Home Page

http://www.warhol.org/warhol

The Andy Warhol page is a great tool for those who want to take a tour of this Pittsburgh museum or check schedules and descriptions of the exhibits. Mini-inline graphics and a zippy connection to USA OnRamp help load the art samples quickly. It's not the flashiest home page, and it doesn't sport as many links as some museum pages, but then Warhol was just one guy, one artist. There aren't many museums devoted to just one artist, and this one is worth a look.

EXCERPT:

...The Andy Warhol Museum is essential to the understanding of the most influential American artist of the second half of the 20th century....

People ask what the difference is between the web and the [Internet]. The web is the space of all information accessible over networks. The net is made of cables. When you explore the net, you find computers. When you explore the web, you find information.

[Tim Berners-Lee, the Web's inventor], Sasha Cavender, *Los Angeles Times*, **May 31, 1995.**

Washingtonian Magazine Online

http://www.infi.net/washmag/

The online version of *The Washingtonian*, an established monthly leisure magazine in Washington, D.C., includes a good entertainment-events calendar and a restaurant directory. A nice break from the intensity of the government-dominated, Washington journalism mainstream.

Marius Watz's WWW Site

http://www.uio.no/~matz

Watz presents a diverse selection of links to other web sites, with no apparent underlying theme other than his own fondness for these sites, including Architecture; Hakim Bey; Bolo, the Multiplayer Tank Game; Computer-Generated Writing; Cybermind List; Computer Art; Fiction-of-Philosophy List; and Future Culture List.

EXCERPT:

I truly love the web, and see in it the implementation of a global information distribution system...

WaxWeb

http://bug.village.virginia.edu/

The online version of the 1991 independent movie *Wax*, which was about bees, television, and death (a strange combination). If you have a CD-ROM, you can actually view a version of the movie. Everyone else can follow a well-organized narrative, with still shots scattered throughout.

Wayne Manor

http://www.books.com/batman/batman1.htm

Wayne Manor is an eerie castle devoted to Batman. Its filled with computer images from Batman comics and images and music from the *Batman* movies. The Guest Rooms contain links to many other Batman pages. The graphics in here are well done, but they take forever to load, even with a really fast modem. Try looking through a Batman comic book instead.

Wearable Wireless Webcam

http://www-white.media.mit.edu/~steve/netcam.html

One MIT graduate student's vision—literally, what he sees—and his desire to transmit it worldwide via the Web. Original, but not very interesting. But it's worth a visit just to get a glimpse of the contraption this guy wears on his head! Find out if It's Fun Being A CyBorg? and get the lowdown on Applications of Visual Filter and NetCam.

EXCERPT:

Science fiction writers have wondered what it would be like if we could tap into the visual path from eye to brain, routing the visual information else-where....

Q: People say there's too much on the Net to be able to find things. A: There's a lot of paper out there too! There's a lot of junk in each medium. In each case, there are ways of finding quality things. It's an information street. You have to be streetwise. *Caveat lector.*

[Tim Berners-Lee, the Web's inventor], Sasha Cavender, *Los Angeles Times,* **May 31, 1995.**

Web Advanced Research Project Home Page

http://www.hia.com/hia/pcr/

Isaac Newton would hang out here for a while. Lectures and essays on physics, a few short stories, research and physics reviews. Take a trip to the future space beyond space time.

EXCERPT:

You have just fallen into and out of a webhole. Don't be alarmed. You will not be harmed....

Web Autopilot

http://www.netgen.com/~mkgray/autopilot.html

O.K...So you like the web, but you are really a television addict and can't pull away from the boob tube long enough to navigate through cyberspace. Well, Web Autopilot is to television junkies what nicotine gum is to smokers. With Web Autopilot, you just sit back and watch. Every 12 seconds a new page pops up on your screen. There are 8,000 separate pages, so it will be a while before you hit reruns.

EXCERPT:

Autopilot tells your browser to reload a new specially selected random homepage every 12 seconds, allowing you to sit back and watch the web go by....

The Web Developer's Virtual Library

http://WWW.Stars.com/

Chilton's publishes books to guide amateurs through car repairs. Well, consider this web site to be like a Chilton's manual for beginning web page builders. It explains protocols, providers, WAIS, and lots of other under-the-hood terms and is loaded with expert advice from web masters. It's all here to learn. Good luck!

The Web Nebulae

http://seds.lpl.arizona.edu/billa/twn/top.html

You don't need a clear night to see these stars. Wonderful images from space created with cameras and telescopes and entered on the web by a guy who really understands and loves space. Bill Arnett puts together top-notch web pages dealing with space topics. In this one, he offers color images and technical, scientific details of a couple dozen nebulae. Nice work.

EXCERPT:

If you look up at the night sky with your naked eye all you see is a black void with a few points of white light. But with a camera and a telescope an entirely different view unfolds in brilliant color and amazing detail....

Web Pick of the Day

http://www.mecklerweb.com:80/netday/pick.html

Web Pick features a new site each day. In its first four months, the service selected everything from games to online newspapers to the Peace Corps. The site provides a three paragraph review of its site of the day, along with the address, and a list of all previous picks. This site is a lot like this book; its a good overview of the territory ahead.

> **T**o be overloaded by the existence of so much on the Web is like being overloaded by the mass of beautiful countryside. You don't have to visit it, but it's nice to know it's there.
>
> **[Tim Berners-Lee, the Web's inventor], Sasha Cavender,** *Los Angeles Times,* **May 31, 1995.**

Web Puzzler

http://imagiware.com/imagiware.cgi

Imagiware loads its home page with games, including Nowwwhere, a game of exploration, to advertise its Internet web production services. The company's vision is to create web pages that are fun, useful, visually appealing, and fast loading; this page shows it all.

EXCERPT:

We create cutting-edge games and applications for the World Wide Web. We can do this for you, or teach you how to do it, or both....

Web Queen

http://www.mtnlake.com/holtz.html

A pretty excellent home page from a professional page builder. Tabatha maintains the swift page of the National Hockey League Players Association, among others, and she brings lots of expertise to her own page. And does she ever get around! Watch as Tabatha battles beside Kevin Costner in *Waterworld* and then tries out for the Toronto Ballet. And be sure to check out her favorite web sites in the Stay Pretty, Die Young section.

Web Travel Review

http://www-swiss.ai.mit.edu/webtravel/

The Travel Review prints dispatches from a about a dozen global travel destinations (organized by continent), including Prague, the Cayman Islands, New York, Disneyland, Costa Rica. The site specializes in photography (over 2,000 photos) and narrative writing (600 pages of text) and features the works of celebrated Internet travel writer Philip Greenspun.

Web Wide World of Music

http://american.recordings.com/wwwofmusic/

Tons-o-music. Anybody who loves music has got to see this site. The Ultimate Band List has web page and e-mail information for all kinds of artists in virtually every category: jazz, classical, rock, rap—you name it. The Online Charts section allows you to track artists and their current hits. You can also find lists of music 'zines, music polls, forums for discussion of musical topics, and just about anything else dealing with tunes.

EXCERPT:

Your interactive guide through thousands of band web pages, music and lyrics servers, and more.

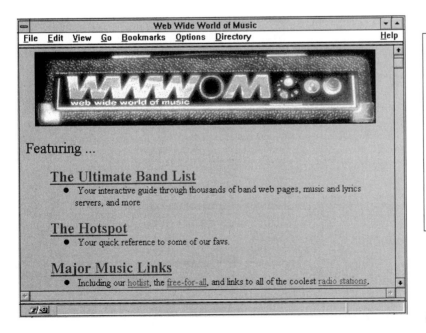

Webaholics Home Page

http://www.ohiou.edu/~rbarrett/webaholics/ver2/

The most interesting feature of this page is the long list of true confessions from web addicts. "Please help me, I'm an addict. My entire social life exists in the virtual world. I recently spent ten hours on the web alone, then I had E-mail to answer. Somebody shoot me or give me money to pay for my habit!"

EXCERPT:

Remember: Admitting that you have an addiction is the first step to finding more and more really cool web pages!

WebChat Broadcasting System

http://www.irsociety.com/wbs.html

Another spot for all you big mouths out there. This chat line has many different topics. The What's Hot section allows you to see the most active conversations, just in case you can't help being trendy, and a search engine enables you to find talk topics of your choice.

EXCERPT:

The WebChat Broadcasting System is open to everyone who enjoys live chatting—come explore the dial and talk with people around the world....

WebComics

http://www.cyberzine.com/webcomics/

Designed to be an organized site where the average web-surfer can go to find a link to their favorite comic strip, this home page is well-conceived, but not very well-executed. As it promises, WebComics contains numerous pointers to good comics on the web, but the pages are designed so that you have to download comics you don't want to see, as well as the one you want. These extra steps lead to a lot of wasted online time—a delicate matter if you're paying by the hour to surf the web.

Top Ten Signs Your WWW Home Page Is Not Cool:

10. Hotlist is only lukewarm

9. Links to your page keep using the adjective "fetid"

8. Disney wants to buy the rights to use in Mighty Ducks III

7. On Adam Curry's list of neat home pages

6. WWW Worm got bored and left

5. Condemned by the housing authority

4. Word "cool" is in the title

3. Nancy Kerrigan says it's the corniest page she's ever seen

2. Geek Code replaced by Geek C++ Code

And the number one sign your home page is not cool...

1. Access log shows tons of visits by Al Gore

The Websurfer's Handbook

EXCERPT:

WebComics was created by David de Vitry so that normal netizans like you and me could easily find most all the comics on the net. Before, one had jump from one site to another....Now, I maintain this site in hopes that all comics artists out there will submit their work.

WebCrawler

http://webcrawler.com/

America Online users will be very familiar with this page; this is AOL's effective and convenient search engine. It displays a standard 25 hits per

search. There's also a list of the 25 most requested sites; check them out—
that many people can't be wrong.

WebNexus

http://sunsite.unc.edu/lunarbin/webnexus.cgi

The creator's purpose is not entirely clear, but there are links from all over
the world on a wide variety of topics. Actually as links lists go, this one is
pretty bland. You can do better.

WebSite Central

http://website.ora.com/

This commercial page from a computer publishing company gives you
access to web-building software and many of the computer books published
by the company. Warning: make sure you check the system requirements
before you get too excited.

Weird Science

http://www.eskimo.com/~billb/weird.html

If you like science, it's worthwhile to latch onto this web veteran for a
while. It's not a pretty page, but it's full of substance. Offbeat science is the
specialty—with topics like cold fusion, science fiction, and gravity. And
check out the all the crazy inventions.

EXCERPT:
ENERGY, GRAVITY, "CRAZY" INVENTIONS.

The Weird Zone

http://mistral.enst.fr/~pioch/weird/

The weirdest thing about the Weird Zone is that this very poorly organized site doesn't seem to have a point. There's no central theme or easy-to-find explanation of what this is all about. The site is basically a monthly list of e-mail deliveries. There are better places to spend your time.

Western Vogue

http://mack.rt66.com/nmmarket/western.htm

A good, down-home Western 'zine that runs against a backdrop of snappy art. You'll find lots of stuff to connect with the big open country. Fashion pages have tips on Western home decoration and clothes. Check the crafts section for how-to advice on topics such as creating Apache baskets. There's also a folklore section loaded with Indian myths and legends.

WETFUN

http://www.wetfun.com/

Not bad, as personal home pages go. The highlights include exhaustive lists of links to online erotica and scuba diving resources. Speed is the major drawback here. The pages take a really long time to load, mostly because of their complex, blue background that adds very little to the site.

What Sn00z?

http://www.digimark.net/mfu/whasn00z.html

If you want to get an idea of how big the web is and how fast it is growing, check this out. Updated several times an hour, this page introduces the public to thousands of debut sites. Its just about the coolest way to stay on top of web trends and find out about the newest sites before they make someone's site-of-the-day list.

EXCERPT:

This page contains a list of links to the hundreds of thousands of new web pages that have been created and announced in the last 10 minutes....

THE LITIGIOUS SOCIETY

Etta Stephens filed a lawsuit against Barnett Bank in Tampa, Fla., in May, seeking damages for the heart attack she suffered. She was stricken after opening her monthly statement to find, due to bank error, that her $20,000 money market account was empty. [*USA Today*, 5-24-95]

News of the Weird: http://www.nine.org/notw/notw.html

What They Meant To Say Was...

http://www.netaxs.com/people/drmcomm/Meant2.html

Here's some moderately funny social commentary from a public relations firm. A sample: "Militia groups are all the talk lately. Groups with members who feel a strong distrust for government and authority. So what's a perfect name for a group that disavows a hierarchal system? Why, 'Unorganized Citizens Militia of Oklahoma,' of course. Optional attendance at meetings is mandatory. And that's unofficial!"

EXCERPT:

If you're frustrated by communications which misquote, misspeak, or otherwise mislead, we hope you will check out our new "column."

What's Miles Watching on TV

http://www.csua.berkeley.edu/~milesm/ontv.html

So...a UC Berkeley freshman uses his souped-up Macintosh to display images from the TV shows he is currently watching. The question is, why would anyone care what a 19-year-old in Berkeley is watching on the boob tube? While the technology is admirable, this site is dumb.

EXCERPT:

I'm a fan of the little guy who is just starting out on the web and needs

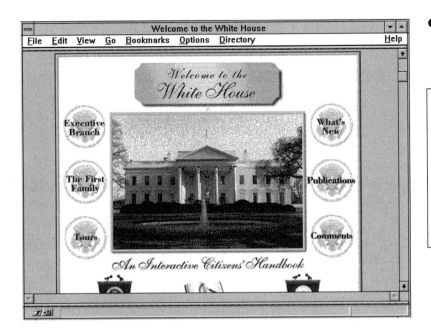

some links....If you have a page that is really hot (and you're just starting out), I'll give you a link.

The White House

http://whitehouse.gov

No matter what your political leanings, this is a wonderful resource for everyone interested in the workings of the federal government. Start out by reading the president's welcome message. Tourists can take virtual tours of the White House. Government wonks can find a mother lode of information from an online copy of the Constitution to presidential speeches, the federal budget, and links to nearly every executive agency. Don't forget to send e-mail Hillary and sign the guest book.

White Noise

http://www.artsci.wustl.edu/~rudolmc/why.html

This page may still be under construction. It's shaping up as yet another narcissistic home page full of inane, slow-to-load graphics. The most useful thing in here is a fairly exhaustive list of bands and their home pages.

Walt Whitman Home Page

http://rs6.loc.gov/wwhome.html

Walt Whitman scholars take note of this great online source of information about one of America's greatest poets and essayists. This site includes details on Whitman materials that disappeared from the Library of Congress more than 50 years ago but were recovered earlier this year, as well as a list of other Whitman resources.

EXCERPT:

This collection offers access to the four Walt Whitman notebooks and cardboard butterfly that disappeared from the Library of Congress in 1942. They were returned on February 24, 1995.

Who's Cool in America Project

http://www.getcool.com/~getcool/

Need some verification of your coolness? This is the place. Write a 100-word essay on what makes you cool, and some anonymous board of hipsters takes a couple days to evaluate whether you are, indeed, authentically cool. Seems like kind of a waste of time, but if you really need to bolster that self-image, think hard, pound out your best self-promotion, and hope for the stamp of approval.

EXCERPT:

Are you COOL? To be officially COOL, someone ELSE must determine this for you. This is why the CoolBoard exists....

Why Ask Why?

http://www.traveller.com/~rudy/why.html

What is another word for "thesaurus"? If 75% of all accidents happen

Big whales have had their own world-wide communication network for 70 million years. Only recently have homo sapiens reached the same level. Whales welcome you to join the world-wide communication network. Greetings from Whale.

Whale Watching: http://www.physics.helsinki.fi/whale/

within 5 miles of home, why not move 10 miles away? Hee-Hee. This site is a great, five-minute stop to pick up a little Gallagher-style humor. There are dozens of these one-liners for you to copy and paste into your e-mail messages.

EXCERPT:

Here are some facts of life that sometimes you just have to ask—WHY? Some people call them Gallagherisms....

The Wile E. Coyote Question

http://www.duke.edu/~rutabaga/wile.html

"Is Wile E. Coyote in fact, an example of the tragic hero, like Oedipus or Macbeth? What is the tragic flaw for which the forces of the universe have punished him (For instance, why are laws of nature suspended in the Road-runner's favor)?" Ponder such questions as these and read what others have opined in this site. It's no surprise that the person who came up with this site is an English major.

EXCERPT:

Wile E. Coyote. Yes, the most important cultural icon of our times. What is his significance? What does he symbolize?

Windows Rag

http://www.eskimo.com/~scrufcat/wr.html

A magazine for the average person out there in web land who can't afford to spend a fortune on computer equipment. The authors test software on three, low-end computers, the most hefty of which has only 8 mg of RAM and let you know what runs on an average machine. Some interesting stuff here about Windows95.

EXCERPT:

Welcome to WR, the on-line computer magazine for the rest of us. This magazine is for the on-line user who can't afford the biggest and best of computer equipment.

Wine.com

http://www.wine.com/wine/

Wine lovers of the web world stop here to find out how wine is made, learn about various wine awards, and get travel directions to many wineries around the world. The site also includes links to wine-loving resources such as Decanter Magazine, wine research sites, and the history of wine making.

EXCERPT:

Connecting the Worldwide Wine Community Together.

Wingspread

http://www.wingspread.com/

A very colorful and well-designed guide to 30 different kinds of Southwestern art, Wingspread includes links to the galleries of more than 300 artists and specific guides to art fairs in Taos, Santa Fe, and Albuquerque.

EXCERPT:

Use our pages to help prepare for your next visit—real or armchair—to the art of New Mexico.

The Winner's Circle

http://www.dakota.net/~pwinn/

Winner's Circle is a web experiment in publishing. For instance, *Winn's*

Consider, if you will, the following demographic profile of denizens of the World Wide Web, the Internet's most popular and fastest growing region. 90 percent of users are men. More than half are between 21 and 30 years old. 87 percent are white. According to the Georgia Institute of Technology, which released the study data earlier this year, the typical user is also unmarried and spends about 40 hours a week at his computer.

Fran Maier, in *The Washington Post*

World Wide Web Weakly weekly takes a somewhat humorous look at the move from big city to small town. *A Basic Citizen's Definitive Electronic Freedom Guide* takes a look at politics in America, and *Brainiac Digest* is devoted to trivia. It's all decent stuff.

EXCERPT:

The Winner's Circle is an ongoing experiment in publishing on the World Wide Web. This site is updated daily, so be sure to check back often....

Wood & Wire

http://www.ether.com.au/woodwire/

You'll find lots of music without all the big-label hype at this good-looking site. There are links to more than 100 independent bands from Australia, Europe, and the United States and to a wide variety of 'zines.

The Woodstock '94 Internet Multimedia Center

http://www.well.com/woodstock/

O.K., if you still can't get over the Sixties (or the '90s version of the '60s), you probably ought to check out this site. Revel in some 300 home pages created in a tent at Woodstock '94. They provide a unique perspective of the concert from the people who were there. But we gotta say, this site isn't as good as that movie about the first Woodstock.

EXCERPT:

From August 12-14, 1994, the WELL had a tent available on site at Woodstock '94 from which concert goers could share their experiences with the world of the Internet....

World Art Treasures

http://sgwww.epfl.ch/BERGER/intro.html

Good photos and in-depth descriptions make you feel like you are touring this art gallery with a knowledgeable curator who speaks both French and English. Take this rare opportunity to view photos of some ancient Egyptian artifacts, with special emphasis on the old holy city of Arbydos, as well as ancient sculptures from India.

EXCERPT:

The principal purpose of World Art Treasures is to promulgate the discovery and love of art....

World of Audio

http://www.magicnet.net/rz/world_of_audio/woa.html

A good resource for music techies with many site links to record labels and radio stations and discussions about synthesizers and other instruments. There is also a database of online music engineers. After all that, if you aren't satiated, there is a search engine specifically geared to the technical details of music.

EXCERPT:

The World of Audio strives to collect resources of interest to the professional audio community...

World of Interest

http://woi.com/woi/

There are tons of hot lists and favorite web sites all over the web, and here's another one. But this one promises to be brief and discriminating and to list only the best of the best on topics such as publications, kids pages, volunteer organizations, and art. Still, it's not really that brief, and you'll still find enough sites here to make your head spin.

EXCERPT:

This may be the most selective site index on the Net — making it the easiest to use successfully! Here you'll find only the top Internet sites listed in each category....

World 3

http://la.commerce.com/world3/

If you are sometimes perplexed about the philosophical implications of this carnival called cyberspace, you might want to debate the problems of online copyright or ponder the emergence of corporate America in formerly pristine cyberspace. World 3 is an OK site if you like deep thought about the Internet, but skip it if you would just rather enjoy your new toy.

EXCERPT:

World 3 is about many things but, fundamentally, it is a space about how to use space to communicate....

World Transformation

http://newciv.org/worldtrans/

Cynics beware....this site is full of positive vibes. How to make the world a better place; philosophy about "whole systems" and new ways of looking at the planet; how to make yourself a better person. It's all a little much, frankly, but it's good that somebody's thinking about the future on the web.

EXCERPT:

The overall theme here is to make the world a better place, to see things in a positive light, to stand up for one's rights, to pursue self-improvement...

World Wide Cats

http://www.xs4all.nl/~dmuller/wwc.html

As if it's not enough to ask of you to wade through the inane details of an individual's home page, some contributors want you to visit their cats, too. The site features "Cat of the Week" and "Cat Hall of Fame" sections. The photos are small, and computer-reproduced photos of cats just don't seem to make them come alive. There are very few resources here, other than page after page of cats that only their owners can love.

EXCERPT:

Your jumpstation to World Wide Web cat pages.

The World Wide Quilting Page

http://ttsw.com/MainQuiltingPage.html

Quilt show guides, quilt chat groups, quilting pointers, quilts and computers, fabrics, the history of quilting. You get the point. This page is a fairly exhaustive list of online resources about quilting. Too bad the graphics aren't as intricate as some of the quilts that are described.

The World Wide Web Dating Game

http://www.cid.cin/cid/date/

Esoterica comes to the Internet. This is very similar to the TV schlock. The date seeker asks questions of three contestants via public e-mail, the contestants answer, the viewing public sees all the answer and votes for a contestant, the date seeker makes his/her pick, goes on the date (paid for by the site sponsors, whose logos are plastered all over the site), then comes back and tells all. Who cares?

Although conventional wisdom has long put the ratio of men to women on-line at 9 to 1, a survey out last month from Matrix Information & Directory Services, Austin, Texas, suggests a ratio closer to 2 to 1.

Another survey, out this month from the Georgia Institute of Technology, Atlanta, also finds the number of women rising, but puts the ratio at about 5 to 1.

The real figures may be in between. But what's clear is that the presence of women on the Net is increasing. And the growing number of female-focused sites reflects that.

Leslie Miller, in *USA Today*

EXCERPT:

The World Wide Web Dating Game and its creators cannot be held responsible for any unpleasant dates....

World Wide Web Tennis Server

http://arganet.tenagra.com/Racquet_Workshop/Tennis.html

In this commercialized site, there is lots of tennis stuff, and what you can't find here, you can get through links to other tennis sites. Highlights include monthly tennis tips and a column about pro tennis from David Higdon who is a senior writer for *Tennis Magazine*.

EXCERPT:

Encouraging tennis players everywhere to GO TO THE 'NET for tennis information and equipment.

WorldCam

http://www.ovd.com/

Someday (hopefully soon) when everyone has tremendously fast modems and processors, the concept of online movies will become very attractive. But right now, when short movies like the ones available here take more than 10 minutes to load, it just doesn't cut it. And if you have the time to wait, you can view some interesting flicks here...some sensual, some thoughtful, some goofy.

EXCERPT:
The planet's moving picture show.

Worldwide Internet Live Music Archive

http://underground.net/Wilma/

A really wonderful music site that every serious music aficionado must bookmark! You will find details of concert venues from Ann Arbor, Michigan, to Angola and concert schedules for hundreds of artists. But the best thing about this site is the concert reviews, each one written by an average fan and not by some gun-for-hire, know-it-all snob. Really, really great stuff here.

EXCERPT:
...We've got venue listings, tour listings and other assorted live music miscellany.

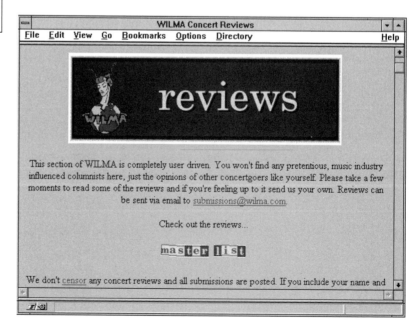

WorldWide Wellness

http://www.doubleclickd.com/wwwellness.html

Mediation, near death and reincarnation, acupuncture, progressive politics, drumming, and dozens upon dozens of other aspects to holistic health are covered here. The site also provides links to a professional directory of holistic goods and services, information on expos and events, a calendar of events, and other wellness resources.

EXCERPT:

...A comprehensive database of alternative and wholistic health information and resources....

Joseph Wu's Origami Page

http://www.cs.ubc.ca/spider/jwu/origami.html

Statistically, the most popular of the several web sites on Origami, the ancient art of paper folding. Includes tips, a photo gallery, organizations, and links to Information on Origami; Files and Diagrams; and Other Origami Home Pages. Be sure to stock up on colorful paper so you can try out the designs.

The WWW Speed Trap Registry

http://www.nashville.net/speedtrap/

Divided into sections for most of the states (with a separate section for Canada), the Speedtrap Registry lists speed traps that ensnare unwary drivers. Please send information on additional traps to the registry, and keep your money in your own pocket.

EXCERPT:

This registry was started . . . to cut down the number of speeding tickets resulting from speed traps. The "Men in Blue" of our nation have better things to do (like watch the O.J. trial)....

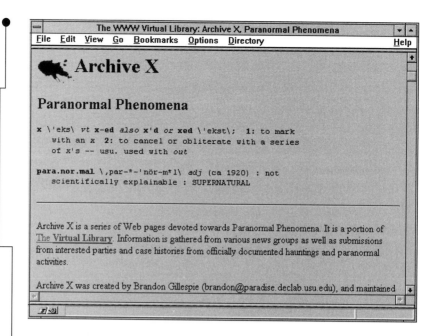

The WWW Virtual Library:
Archive X, Paranormal Phenomena

http://www.crown.net/X/

Started by Brandon Gillespie and now carried on by others, Archive X is an inexhaustible list of paranormal phenomena. Each link—such as Ghost Encounters—is a major heading for dozens and dozens of more links to personal-experience accounts of ghostly visits and meetings. There's a wealth of very mysterious, eerie, and ostensibly very real information here. The home page is very attractive and loads up with spooky speed.

EXCERPT:

Archive X is a series of web pages devoted towards Paranormal Phenomena....Information is gathered from...and case histories from officially documented hauntings and paranormal activities.

The X-Files

http://www.rutgers.edu/x-files.html

Here is just about everything you could ever desire to know about "The X-Files," a Fox TV show about two FBI agents who investigate mysterious violent crimes that often involve the paranormal. The site includes a guide to every episode of the show, addresses for the fan club, discussion groups, viewer surveys, and sound bites. This is actually one of the more comprehensive sites devoted to TV shows.

The X-Files — Trust No One

http://www.neosoft.com/sbanks/xfiles/xfiles.html

Another site about "The X-Files." This one has almost everything available at the other X-Files site—guides to episodes, discussion groups, the fan club, sound bites—but here you also get movies and more images from the show. Plus, the graphics and organization of this site are much better.

EXCERPT:

The Truth Is Here....Lets not harbor any secrets or conspiracies about this site....

X Magazine

http://michaeljones.uoregon.edu/

College kids and their Internet newspapers. This one includes Stoolz Sample—monthly reviews of games and other computer equipment—concert reviews and interviews with bands like Sugar Ray and Justin Warfield, and poetry and stories about love and relationships, written from that special college perspective. A cool place for college students to hang.

XIXIX

http://www.mindspring.com/~ism/XIXIX.html

Not much here except a nondescript set of pages, all of which are under construction, that focuses on a Savannah-based independent record label and an advertisement for a meter-maid voodoo doll. Consider it a pothole along the information superhighway.

EXCERPT:

From the safest places, come the bravest words.

Yahoo!

http://www.yahoo.com/

Everyone should bookmark this mother of all site lists. The home of "Cool Site of the Day," Yahoo has a huge search engine and web links divided into about two dozen large categories. The site tracks daily additions to the web (on some days, there are 800 or more fresh links) and provides Reuters news wire up-to-the-minute headlines from around the world. You gotta have this one.

EXCERPT:

Through use of a hierarchical index and search engine, Yahoo! helps turn

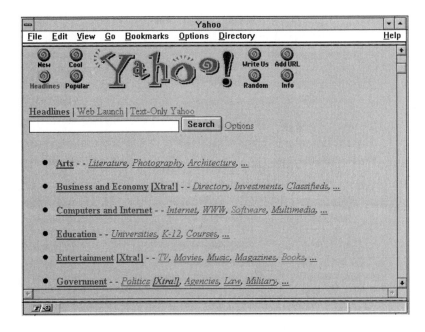

the unwieldy content of the net into something grasp-able and meaningful....

The Yak's Lair

http://yak.net/

A 'zine that's about punk, parodies of U2, computer equipment, Hungary,
and off-beat images of off-beat things. No central theme here—it's just
kind of like a closet full of stuff. The organization isn't too swift and neither is the content. Or maybe this is a site best left to the adventurists and
daredevils.

EXCERPT:

Northward, the ridge opens out in a pine pasture at 12,000 feet where a
herd of yaks, like so many black rocks, lies grouped in the cold sun....

YaZone

http://www.spectracom.com/yazone/

YaZone is one of those 'zines that makes you register before you can
browse. Its strictly for Generation Xers. Separate sections entice you to
debate timely and philosophical issues and recent news stories from a GenX
point of view and there are lots of announcements of new lingo and fads—
stay cool. Unfortunately, the graphics look like they were designed for the
pre-teen set.

EXCERPT:

A meeting place for those who are evolving and want their voice to be
heard.

Yesterland

http://www.mcs.net/~werner/yester.html

Did you know a deluxe ticket book for Disneyland cost $5 in 1966? Do you
long for the return of the Mine Train and Flying Saucers? The author of this

site waxes nostalgic over the many rides, restaurants, and other attractions that have disappeared from the Disneylandscape. There are pictures, too, and links to other Disney-related sites.

EXCERPT:

Did you ever wonder what happened to Disneyland's Mine Train, Flying Saucers, or Indian Village? These and other attractions, restaurants, and shops are now collected in Yesterland....

Your MoM

http://www.cc.columbia.edu/~emj5/yourmom/ymhome.html

A decent place for recent high school grads to hang out, this 'zine has good graphics and sophomoric humor. A recent issue included a parody of a college aptitude test and an article theorizing about what would happen "If Mexican Food Ran America."

EXCERPT:

YOUR MOM...began when two people were bored one day...they made a little newsletter and wrote Your MoM on the top of it....

Z

ZAM! The game

http://metro.turnpike.net/J/jimt/zam.html

The story of ZAM is that you live in the 21st Century and the Internet is the central machine in everyone's daily life. Everyone is free thanks to the net, but a bad guy who looks a lot like David Letterman wants to give it back to the "corporate snobs." You are the hero who can stop him. If there really is a game here, it's pretty obscure.

EXCERPT:

The year is 2031 and cyber-explorer Ziff Crandon is about to embark on a mission that will change his life, and Corbin Frethmore will try to stop him at any cost.

Zapper's Lounge

http://www.mca.com/tv/zap/

Call it survival of the fittest web-page builders. Builders of hot pages submit contest entries and then square off in a weekly contest in which everyone out in the web landscape can either vote for the site or zap you. It's web Darwinism, and it's cool.

EXCERPT:

Hello. I'm Deka, the hostess of Zapper's Lounge. I'll be bringing you the hottest sites on the web and then I'll let you pick who's the best and zap the rest into oblivion!...

More and more marketers are setting their sights on the World Wide Web (WWW). The Web's unique features—colorful graphics, interactive capabilities and hypertext links to other sites—offer an attractive alternative to traditional forms of advertising....While some home pages focus strictly on business, providing information such as press releases, newsletters and annual reports, others combine clever marketing strategy with creative designs, interesting stories and eye-catching graphics.

Brenda Kukla, in *Online Access*

Zarf's List of Interactive Games on the Web

http://www.cs.cmu.edu/afs/andrew/org/kgb/www/zarf/games.html

Wow. Computer games have come a long way since Atari. Look at all these links to tons of games you can play on the web. They range from fantasy sports teams to casinos to trivia to an interactive model railroad in Germany in which a video camera records the results of this WWW-built train.

EXCERPT:

Multi-player games, user-versus-computer games, adventure games, anything else which sounds like a game....

ZD Net

http://www.ziff.com/

ZD Net has more advertisements on display than the side of a race car. (It's maintained by Ziff-Davis, the publisher of leading computer magazines.) But once you get past the blatant commercialism, you'll find a lot of useful stuff like up-to-the minute computer news, special reports on high-profile software such as Windows95, and links to the online versions of many ZD magazines. There's also downloadable software, product reviews, online columns, and discussions.

EXCERPT:

ZD Net is the authoritative source of computing information on the World Wide Web. It's a high-value information service created by Ziff-Davis....

Zen

http://sunsite.unc.edu/zen/

Amongst all the clitter-clatter and chatter of the web, here's a chance to find yourself in poetry, essays, dialogues and more aimed at spiritual enlightenment through Zen. You can also find Buddhist texts and other Zen projects in this well-designed and well-organized site.

EXCERPT:

If you've wandered here wanting to know what Zen is, then more than likely you will come away disappointed. This is a question that is easily asked but not easily answered....

Zima.com

http://www.zima.com/

More commercialism, pure and simple, on this page that looks like an online billboard for Zima, that clear, beer-like alcohol. It lists virtually everything anyone would ever want to know about Zima, including the fact that Zima gets its name from the Russian word for "cold;" where to buy Zima stock; the caloric and sugar content of the brew, and refutes the rumor that Zima doesn't show up on breathalyser tests—it does.

EXCERPT:

At Zima Beverage Company, we want you to have a good time, however we also want you to have a responsible time. Do us all a favor the next time you have a cold Zima....keep your cool.

ZIPZAP Universe

http://zipzap.com/

Poetry and art—interviews with poets and artists—many moods and many styles. Everything in ZIPZAP is very contemporary and very similar to the stuff in hundreds of other web cultural 'zines. In this one, though, extraneous graphics delay loading of the page. So much for the creative spirit.

Zonpower

http://www.neo-tech.com/zonpower/

Finally, an online version of those late-night, get-rich-quick infomercials on TV. Someone went to great trouble to create this treatise of psychobabel that claims to hold the secret to limitless wealth and a "god-like" mind and body. Is it true? Are all the answers as close as this web site? You decide.

EXCERPT:

Zon's editor...cuts across the boundaries of physics, chemistry, astronomy, mathematics, biology, medicine, chaos, economics, politics, business, philosophy, and nonmystical religion to integrate the widest knowledge into a single whole—Zonpower.

Zoom Street

http://eden.telalink.net:80/~vagabond/

Zoom Street is a pretty entertaining hang-out enriched with good graphics. Visit the cybercantina for some chat and learn how to make a raspberry margarita. You can follow the offbeat adventures of a guy called Vagabond Jim and pick up a guide to the radical environmental organization Earth First!

EXCERPT:

Today you live in a world where technology is in danger of advancing faster than human imagination. Zoom Street is here to make sure that never happens.

category index

369

Bravo
Fortean Times on line
Internet and Comms
  Today
Pure Sheng
The Seed: U.K. Alternative Information
Skywings on the Web

Great Titles
The Bastard Operator
  From Hell
Big Black Hole of Pain
Flightless Hummingbird:
  A Pseudo-Periodical

Greeting Cards
See MailBox

Gregorian Chants
Monastery of Christ in the
  Desert

Hackers
CandyLand
GridPoint
IHTFP Hack Gallery

Hang Gliding
Hang Gliding

Hangman
See also Games
Letter R.I.P.

John Harvey
NetJohn's Gallery

Hawaii
Hawaii Home Page
Hokeo Hawaii
Internet Island
Turtle Trax—A Marine
  Turtle Page

He Shoots, He Scores!
I Am Online
National Hockey Players
  Association Web Site

Health
The Diabetes Home Page
Healthwise
The Heart Preview
  Gallery
Sumeria
WorldWide Wellness

High Finance
American Stock
  Exchange
Asia Inc. Online
Tripod

Hiking
Dirty Sole Society
University of Tennessee
  Canoe & Hiking Club

Hispanic America
Candela

History
See Those Were the Days

Hmmmm?
Ideal Order Psychic TV
Twilight Zone
The Void
The Weird Zone

Hockey
See He Shoots, He
  Scores!

Hollywood
See also Film Festivals;
  Movies
Academy of Motion Picture Arts and Sciences
Hollyweb
Internet Entertainment
  Network: Hollywood
  Online
Mr. Showbiz

Hoop Dreams
Michael Jordan Page

Horror
See Chills & Thrills

Household Hints
40 Tips to Go Green

HTML
Clay Shirkey's Home
  Page
HTML Validation Service
Nutscape

Victor Hugo
Les Miserables Home
  Page

Human Rights
Amnesty International
  USA, Berkeley, CA
  Local Group

Hypertext
FEED

**If You Thought That
Was Funny...**
Comedy Central's Totally
  Free Web Site
Comic Relief
The Doctor Fun Page
Monty Python Page
Pat Paulsen for President
Seinfeld
Why Ask Why?

Images
Collection of 3-D Pictures

India
Darpan

Infantnet
Aidan Christopher Kolar
Internet in a Baby

Intelligence
Bordeaux and Prague

Interactive Art
International Interactive
  Genetic Art

Interactive Stories
About US

Marius Watz's WWW Site

Mirsky's Worst of the Web

Netscape Server Galleria

Point — The Top Sites of the Web

Psycho-Babel

Ranjit's HTTP Playground

SpinnWebe

Starwave Corporation

Studio X

Terra IncogNeta

Uncle Bob's Kids Page

URouLette

The Virtual Town

VRTower

World of Interest

Yahoo!

Los Angeles

Buzz Online

Los Angeles Webstation

Love Is In the Air

Cupid's Cove

The Cyrano Server

Public.com.personals

The World Wide Web Dating Game

Macs

See An Apple a Day

MailBox

Build-A-Card

The Electric Postcard

Letters from Abroad

The NetGram Snailmail Postal Proxy

Maps

See Where In the World

Bob Marley

Bob Marley's 50th Birthday Celebration

Martial Arts

The Practice Hall

Dean Martin

The Rat Pack Home Page

Gabe Martin

The Borderline

Mascots

Banana Slug Home Page

Max Headroom

Network 23

MCI

Gramercy Press

Mechanics

PM Zone

Men

See Boy Toys

Messages

Automatic Talking Machine

Metalheads

Megadeth Arizona

Metalworking

The ArtMetal Project

Metaphysics

Suns'n'Roses

MGM

Species

M-I-C-K-E-Y

Spacecoast Hidden Mickeys at Walt Disney World

Middle Ages

Gargoyle Home Page

Missouri

Branson Net Home Page

Moms

Mothersongs

Monastaries

See also Gregorian Chants

Monastery of Christ in the Desert

Monty Python

See And Now For Something Completely Different

MOOs

See also Games; MUSHes & MUDs

Multimedia MOOs

Mountain Climbing

Climbing Archive

Movies

Academy of Motion Picture Arts and Sciences

Batman Forever

BRETTnews

Buena Vista Movie Plex

The Cabinet of Dr. Casey—The Horror Web Page

Cannes.On.Cyber

CineMaven Online

Enzian

The Festival

Film.com

Flicker

The Gigaplex

Godzilla

Hollyweb

Interactive Movie Reviews

Internet Entertainment Network: Hollywood Online

Internet Movie Database

MCA/Universal Cyberwalk

Oscarnet

Plan 10 From Outer Space

Pulp Fiction

Sounds from Movies

Species

Stanley Kubrick Page

Terra IncogNeta

377

Pulp Fiction
> David Siegel's Home
> Page

Puzzles
> Jumble

Quilting
> The World Wide Quilting
> Page

Quotes
> *See* "So he says...'

Racing
> SpeedNet
> Sunrayce 95

Radio Waves
> Alex Bennett's World
> The BBC Home Page
> Casey's Top 40
> The Cathouse Archives,
> LTD.
> The Eyesore Database
> Soundprint Media Center

Rants
> Big Black Hole of Pain
> Celebrity Snack Palace
> The Enhanced for
> Netscape Hall of Shame
> Pure Sheng
> Rant of the Week
> Useless Web Pages

Raves
> Hyperreal
> Transeform

Religion
> Snake Oil: Your Guide to
> Kooky Kontemporary
> Kristian Kulture

Research
> DejaNews Research Ser-
> vice
> How far is it?
> The Internet Sleuth
> loQtus

NYNEX Interactive Yel-
low Pages

Revenge
> Avenger's Front Page
> The Barney Fun Page

Rocket Science
> Starship Home Design
> Page

Romance
> *See* Love Is In the Air

Roommates
> The Spot

Russia
> St. Petersburg Press Home
> Page

Safe Sex
> Condom Country

Sailboarding
> Cyberboarder!
> Everything Extreme

Sailing
> America's Cup On-Line

San Francisco
> AIDS Walk San Francisco
> Apple/Examiner Mac-
> World San Francisco
> Home Page
> San Francisco Examiner
> Home Page
> San Francisco Free Press
> TeleCircus San Francisco

Satan
> Hell—The Online Guide
> to Satanism

Sci Fi
> Dark Planet
> The Dominion
> Future Fantasy Bookstore
> J.V. Jones
> The Magic of Xanth

Mystery Science Theater
3000 at Portnoy's Com-
plaint
Science Fiction and
Anime Page
The Troll Hole

Science
> CRS4 Animation Gallery
> Discover Magazine
> ExploraNet
> The Franklin Institute Vir-
> tual Science Museum
> Ion Science
> Mark's List of Internet
> Activity
> Nye Labs
> Project Mind Foundation
> Weird Science

Self-Improvement
> The Body Electric

SexNet
> Brian
> CakeTimes
> InterSex City/The Point of
> No Return
> Media Whore Studios
> SHOT Gallery
> WETFUN

**Shameless Self-
Promotion**
> Austin City Limits
> Batman Forever
> Betty Boop Archive
> Branson Net Home Page
> Bravo
> Buena Vista Movie Plex
> Burlingame Online
> Chicago Mosaic
> Christmas in New York
> Comstock Web Site
> Crayola
> Cyber Publishing Japan
> Cybertimes
> Dahlin Smith White
> Digital Planet
> Discovery Channel
> Online

category
index

Comedy Central's Totally Free Web Site
Comic Relief
Discovery Channel Online
The Dominion
ESPNET Sportszone
Late Show with David Letterman Home Page
Network 23
The Sofasphere II Project
Sound Bytes: The WWW TV Themes Home Page
TV Net
Universal cHaNnEL
What's Miles Watching on TV

TV Series
See also TV; Twin Peaks
Aeon Flux
Duckman
The Endless Star Trek Episode
Friends
The History of Rock 'n' Roll
Lurker's Guide to Baby-lon 5
Mystery Science Theater 3000 at Portnoy's Com-plaint
Nadia: The Secret of BlueWater
The ReBoot Home Page
Seinfeld
Smurfs
Star Trek: The Next Gen-eration
Star Trek: Voyager
Taz-Mania
Theodore Tugboat
The X-Files
The X-Files — Trust No One

Twin Peaks
Bravo
IRC Cheers Channel Gallery
The Kids in the Hall

Typefaces
FUSE '94

Unexplained Phenomena
Fortean Times on line
Magic 8-Ball
SETI Institute Home Page
Smitty's UFO Page
The WWW Virtual Library: Archive X, Paranormal Phenomena
The X-Files
The X-Files — Trust No One

United Media
The Comic Strip

U.S. Government
American Memory of the Library of Congress
AskERIC
Astro-2 Live
The Capitol Steps
CIA Home Page
The FBI's Current Ten Most Wanted Fugitives
Hubble Space Telescope's Greatest Hits 1990-1995
1990 U.S. Census LOOKUP
Reinventing Government Toolkit
Thomas Legislative Infor-mation Service on the Internet
The White House

University of Illinois at Urbana-Champaign
Darpan

Unpretentiousness
Kibo

Urban Legends
The cathouse.org Urban Legends Archive

Vampires
Vampyres Only

Vancouver
See also Oh, Canada
The Green Cart Magazine
NWHQ

Vanderbilt University
Restroom Utilization Measurement Project

Venus
The Face of Venus Home Page

Jan Vermeer
Paintings of Vermeer

Videos
Aaron A. Aardvark's Aardvark Abstract
CineMaven Online

Virtual Cities
Rocktropolis
Virtual Nashville
The Virtual Town

Virtual Reality
Open Virtual Reality Test-bed

Voting
California Election Info.
1994 California Election Home Page

Wacky Races
Future Pirates Inc.

Walkathons
AIDS Walk San Francisco

Wall Street
American Stock Exchange

Walt Disney
Spacecoast Hidden Mick-eys at Walt Disney World
Yesterland

EarthLink Network™

Earthlink's TotalAccess software package is included on CD-Rom for all *CyberHound* purchasers.

That's about $90 worth of software free.

Enjoy total access to the Internet. No censoring. No restrictions.

EarthLink's Total Access software is a high quality package that features total access to the Internet: text, graphics, E-Mail, plus all the regular Internet capabilities. Browse away at your leisure: TotalAccess does not censor the places you can visit, and files can be transferred throughout the 'Net without restrictions.

Bring a friend on board and receive one month
FREE for each new subscriber.

The TotalAccess software comes with:

- NETSCAPE NAVIGATOR™, the highest rated and preferred web browser. At least 70% of the Internet is designed to be viewed with Netscape.

- EUDORA E-MAIL, the most popular E-Mail software in the world. And there's no additional charge for E-Mail services.

- A "PLUG 'N PLAY" design that makes access to the Internet easy.

- A FREE 100K home page.

Customer Support services that were rated "A" by *The Net* **magazine. Support is via a toll-free 800 number and is available 24 hours a day, seven days a week.**

Customer Support lines are answered by live humans, not voice mail.

Get TotalAccess to the Internet with EarthLink Network

EarthLink now services over 150 U.S. cities and is growing daily. All the necessary software is enclosed in one easy to launch package. Your FREE TotalAccess software includes the latest version of Netscape (the world's most popular web browser), Eudora (the world's most popular E-Mail program), automatic dialer, auto registration, and all the regular Internet access capabilities. Look for the software on the inside of the back cover of *CyberHound*.

Internet access costs $19.95 per month for 15 hours. Each additional hour is only $1.95. EarthLink's one-time registration fee of $25.00 per hour will be waived as part of the *CyberHound* package.

Your access service includes unlimited tech support on EarthLink's toll-free number (1-800-395-8410) and a FREE 100K home page.

With this software you could be "surfing" the 'Net in five minutes. Just install, launch, and we'll see you on the 'Net!

To install and get started

Windows™:
1) From the program manager **"FILE"** menu, choose **"RUN"**
2) Enter **"INSERT DIRECTORY NAME HERE"** and click **"OK"**
3) From the TotalAccess installation dialog box, select **"INSTALL"**
4) Follow the instructions to register your new EarthLink Network TotalAccess™ account
5) If at any time you need additional help, click the **"HELP"** button

Windows 95™:
1) Double-click on the **"SETUP"** icon
2) Follow the instructions to register your new EarthLink Network TotalAccess™ account
3) If at any time you need additional help, press **F1**

Macintosh
1) Call EarthLink for Mac info

EarthLink Network Customer Support: 1-800-395-8410